SEO
MADE
EASY

Everything You Need to Know About SEO and Nothing More

Evan Bailyn

SEO Made Easy: Everything You Need to Know About SEO and Nothing More

Copyright © 2014 by Pearson Education

ISBN-10: 0-7897-5123-2

ISBN-13: 978-0-7897-5123-2

Library of Congress Control Number: 2013936602

Printed in the United States of America

First Printing: December 2013

Trademarks

Warning and Disclaimer

Special Sales

For information about buying this title in bulk quantities, or for special sales opportunities (which may include electronic versions; custom cover designs; and content particular to your business, training goals, marketing focus, or branding interests), please contact our corporate sales department at corpsales@pearsoned.com or (800) 382-3419.

For government sales inquiries, please contact governmentsales@pearsoned.com.

For questions about sales outside the U.S., please contact international@pearsoned.com.

Editor-in-Chief
Greg Wiegand

Executive Editor
Rick Kughen

Development Editor
Rick Kughen

Managing Editor
Kristy Hart

Senior Project Editor
Lori Lyons

Copy Editor
Keith Cline

Indexer
Lisa Stumpf

Proofreader
Jess DeGabriele

Publishing Coordinator
Kristen Watterson

Cover Designer
Alan Clements

Compositor
Nonie Ratcliff

CONTENTS AT A GLANCE

TABLE OF CONTENTS

10 Converting Your SEO Results into Paying Customers **183**

11 Social Search: The Intersection of Social Media and SEO **201**

About the Author

Evan Bailyn is an Internet entrepreneur and the author of *Outsmarting Google* and *Outsmarting Social Media*. He is primarily known as a search engine optimization expert, having used his ability to rank at the top of Google to build and sell five businesses, including one of the largest children's websites online.

Currently, he offers marketing services through his company, First Page Sage. Under Evan's tutelage, clients have established multimillion dollar businesses, become *New York Times* bestsellers, clinched top sports awards, and won key elections. As the founder of the Evan Bailyn Foundation, he helps to promote emotional awareness in children and adults.

Mr. Bailyn has been interviewed on ABC and Fox News and featured in *Forbes*, *New York Times*, *The Wall Street Journal*, *Advertising Age*, and *Money Magazine*. He is a frequent speaker, having keynoted numerous national conferences.

Dedication

To my wife Sasha, whose support has made me the person I am today.
To my brother and business partner Brad, who always has my back.

Acknowledgments

Peter Shankman: I will always appreciate that you sparked my professional writing career.

Rick Kughen: You have been phenomenal to work with on each of my books, and I'm grateful to have you as my Editor. Thanks for your confidence and guidance.

Tina Davison, Jessica Rippey, Corianne Burton, Lily Atherton, and the rest of the First Page Sage team: I couldn't do what I do without you guys. You have my highest gratitude.

Russell, Mom, and Dad: Thanks to each of you for your support, and for being who you are.

We Want to Hear from You!

As the reader of this book, *you* are our most important critic and commentator. We value your opinion and want to know what we're doing right, what we could do better, what areas you'd like to see us publish in, and any other words of wisdom you're willing to pass our way.

We welcome your comments. You can email or write to let us know what you did or didn't like about this book—as well as what we can do to make our books better.

Please note that we cannot help you with technical problems related to the topic of this book.

When you write, please be sure to include this book's title and author as well as your name and email address. We will carefully review your comments and share them with the author and editors who worked on the book.

Email: feedback@quepublishing.com

Mail: Que Publishing
        ATTN: Reader Feedback
        800 East 96th Street
        Indianapolis, IN 46240 USA

Reader Services

Visit our website and register this book at quepublishing.com/register for convenient access to any updates, downloads, or errata that might be available for this book.

Introduction

If you own any other books on search engine optimization, throw them out. They belong to the mass of misinformation that has been swimming around for years, keeping people from making their websites truly appealing to search engines. And no surprise, Google loves it.

What I am about to share with you are the real, gritty, tried-and-true tactics that have made my websites consistently show up at the top of Google for 9 years and have made me a millionaire. My relationship with Google is love/hate. On the one hand, I am astounded by the brilliance of a company that makes my life easier every day and continues to come out with innovative products that push the level of communication and organization in our society to new heights. On the other hand, they have done everything they can to darken the picture of how to make great websites get the exposure they deserve.

One thing I should make clear from the beginning: I don't do any black hat stuff. For those who aren't familiar with search engine jargon, that means I don't partake in unethical schemes or employ any tactics that do nothing more than fool Google into thinking my websites are more valuable than they actually are. No, what I have done is become intimately familiar with Google's rule book—the one they would do anything to hide from the public—and play by those rules *very closely*.

You see, outsmarting Google is not a matter of being a mathematical genius like many of the people they employ. It's a matter of looking at Google's intentions as a search engine, studying the accepted rules of SEO (search engine optimization), and then patiently trying every method that comports with and breaks each of those rules until you've brewed the perfect concoction. That can take years, of course, but reading this book should take only a week.

I first got started with search engines in 2004 after dropping out of law school to start my own company, a college essay counseling service. Soon enough, I learned that I had no idea how to acquire customers. Search engines were already pretty mainstream, and it was a fair guess that people were going to use them to find pretty much everything in the future—including college essay counselors. So I decided to focus on them head-on. Short on money, I spent 8 months sitting in front of the computer reading about SEO on an online forum called webworkshop. net. In researching for this book, I see that the forum is now defunct. Back in 2005, when I was on it every night from 11 p.m. to 4 a.m., it was a hive of eager amateurs mixed with some so-called experts all trying to figure out how certain sites showed up at the top of the search results and others weren't even in the first 1,000 results. The amount of ignorant nonsense that was spewed in that forum could fill the Library of Congress. But a few valuable tricks slipped in.

Instead of racking my brain trying to figure out which information was credible and which wasn't, I spent a lot of my time researching the people on the forum. I would Google their usernames and connect them to their business websites and then see whether those websites ranked for the keywords that they were obviously targeting. Most people's websites, including the moderators of the forum, were either nowhere to be found or hanging around in the top 50 search results. But a couple actually had top 10 rankings. I was on those guys like white on rice. I would go back and read every post they had ever written, trying to figure out what they knew. I looked for commonalities among them. Soon enough, I found a couple of phrases that seemed to matter like "anchor text links" and "meta title tags." And I wrote myself a little playbook filled with my best guesses of what made Google happy.

Around that time, I had about $6,000 in the bank, at the bottom of which was a ticket to go back to Long Island, live at home, and start looking for 9-to-5 jobs. Running out of money was my greatest fear. I had spent $650 buying and developing a website for my college counseling business. I had spent another $500 buying a few other websites to play around with and teach myself about the way sites relate to each other. Having studied the Google founders' original research paper, which established the idea of Google, I knew that they believed that the relationships between websites were the best way to determine the value of each individual online property. That is, if websites were people, who would be the most well liked? Is it the guy who simply knows the most people? Or the guy who has the most powerful friends? It certainly isn't the guy who just moved to town and doesn't know anybody. Soon it became clear that Larry Page and Sergey Brin, who went on to found one of the most successful companies of the last decade, thought of the Web as a big popularity contest.

My $500 bought me three crappy websites, but more than anything, it bought me an education. Apparently, gone were the days when all you had to do to get a top ranking in the search engines was write your keywords a thousand times on your home page. Search engines, especially Google, had gotten much smarter, and now all that mattered was how many times other websites linked to you and how they linked to you, and when, and why. I hadn't the foggiest idea how to make my website show up at #1 in Google yet, but I did know one thing: It had everything to do with links.

That brought on a painful 6 months of trying every way of linking from my three test websites to my college essay counseling website. By day, I handed out flyers at Penn Station trying to make up the cost of my office rent, and by night, I linked. In that stretch of life, I linked in big letters, small letters, bold letters, italic letters, invisible letters, and no letters at all. I linked from the top of the page, bottom of the page, side of the page, and not on the page at all. I linked at 9 a.m. each day and every other Tuesday. I linked in plain text, images, and Flash; on every page of the website and on only one; on the home page and in the site map; and from each website to every other website. Damn, was it boring! The worst, and most devilishly clever part of it all was, Google updated its rankings only once per week, so every little permutation of linking I tried required a week of saint-worthy patience. And yet, none of it was working. My website had never showed up in the top 100 results—and it seemed like it never would. Every day felt like walking through complete darkness, swinging my arms around in the hopes that I would hit something. I was very near giving up by the time that momentous Monday morning rolled around.

That Monday, just the same as every other day, I typed college admission essay (my keyword of choice) into the search box of Google. Thousands of times I had done this, and thousands of times Google had come up with the same search results, a tired collection of established companies and institutions of higher learning. But that day, to my shock and delight, the #1 result was *my* website.

"Oh my god! Oh my god! I did it! I cracked Google!" My neighbors in the tiny office suite poked their heads in to see what the racket was. Annoyed that it was nothing more than an overzealous 24-year-old screaming at his computer, they went about their business as I hugged my brother and business partner, Brad.

From that point on, my business got a steady stream of customers. And in the following years, armed with the power to rank at the top of the search results for any keyword, I started lots of different companies. Now, five sold businesses and lots of experience later, I still work side by side with my brother, but we apply what I discovered back then (which I've honed greatly) to other people's businesses to make them money. My reputation as a search engine guru has spread, making its way to the ear of an editor at Pearson Education. And that is how this book came to life.

Now that you know a little of my history, sit back and get ready to learn what Google is hiding.

What's In This Book

This book contains everything you need to know—no more, no less—to get your website to rank on the first page of Google's search results. The 12 chapters of *SEO Made Easy* are organized as follows:

- Chapters 1 and 2 explain the system underlying Google's algorithm, TrustRank, and the five ingredients of successful Google optimization. By themselves, these two chapters could bring a novice up to proficiency in this area.

- Chapters 3, 4, and 5 cover specific strategies to get your website to rank at the top of the results, discussing links, aging, and the ultimate ranking strategy—the Nuclear Football.

- Chapter 6 is the technical chapter. It lays the foundation for you to understand the best free traffic measurement tool in existence—Google Analytics.

- Chapters 7 and 8 are all about clarity and contain interesting information about optimizing for Google that will help clear away common myths and misunderstandings.

- Chapter 9 tells you what you need to know to rank on Yahoo! and Bing.

- Chapter 10 is a particularly important complement to search engine optimization, detailing the best ways to convert your search engine traffic into revenue for your business.

- Chapter 11 covers the role of social media in Google and the ways in which social media and search engines will soon meld together to form a new basis for discovering information, products, and services.

- Chapter 12 is a self-contained tutorial on how to use SEO to start your own business.

Who Can Use This Book?

SEO Made Easy: Everything You Need to Know About SEO and Nothing More was written for all knowledge levels, with a special emphasis on the novice marketer. More than anything, it was written for people who are seeking simple and direct information about how to get their websites to rank at the top of Google's results. I have assumed a blank slate and built a picture of the search engine's algorithm from the ground up, using simple language and analogies. I also have tried to keep the book moving along quickly, never getting too philosophical or bogged down with dense material. This book was meant to be like celery—crisp, easy to eat, and nutritious—and yet, even those who have years of experience in online marketing should find a fresh perspective in these pages. I hope you enjoy the read.

1

Trust: The Currency of Google

If we could peer into the secret room where Google keeps the computers that rank every website on the Internet, this is what I think we would see (see Figure 1.1).

Google analyzes unimaginable amounts of data from millions of websites and whittles it down to the 10 to 20 results that are most relevant for your search. As you will soon see, only a few factors ultimately determine the order of search results. But the Big G likes to have all sorts of data available so that it can return relevant web pages for highly specific searches such as why does my dog like watching baseball. *After all, most searches are specific. General searches such as* dog *make up a relatively tiny slice of the search pie.*

As a website owner or marketer, you don't need to worry about the more arcane data points that Google analyzes. You should focus instead on the two most important factors for ranking on Google:

- *Links*
- *Page title*

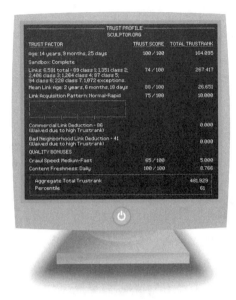

Figure 1.1 *An illustration of how I believe Google views websites.*

Understanding how to optimize these factors allows you to rank for popular search terms, which causes you to get the most visitors to your website in the shortest time, resulting in new customers. But before I show you how to do that, you need to understand how Google looks at the Web.

PageRank

When Larry Page and Sergey Brin set out to organize all the Web's information as eager, bushy-tailed grad students at Stanford, they made one concept the foundation of their entire algorithm: links. Links, they hypothesized, were the currency of a new, democratic World Wide Web, just as votes are the currency of an election. After all, a voter only casts his ballot for the candidate he believes in, and similarly, a website owner only links to another website if he finds it genuinely valuable... right?

Nope. Not in a free-market economy. The moment people figured out that Google ranked websites based on links, a new cottage industry was born. People started buying, selling, and trading links like it was their job. And for some, it was. At its peak in 2007, the link industry was worth hundreds of millions of dollars.

Even after the purity of the Google founders' system was disturbed, it was tremendously innovative for its time. In fact, that same link-based system, called

PageRank, is still the foundation of the most popular search engine in the world. But nowadays, dozens of restrictions apply to which links can count as legitimate votes.

PageRank works in very much the same way as popularity in grade school. Generally speaking, the more friends you have (and the cooler they are), the better. So if you have six friends who are sort of cool, you're pretty comfortable. If you have only three friends, but they happen to be the coolest kids in the school, you're even higher in the pecking order. But of course, the most enviable situation of all is to be the most well-liked kid in the whole school. Then you have more aggregate coolness than anyone.

Now let's turn to the way Google looks at PageRank. Technically, PageRank is a predictor of how relevant a web page will be for any given search. It is similar to popularity, which could be said to be a predictor of how much a person will be liked by any other given person. Every web page on the Internet is assigned a PageRank, which is a number from 0 to 10. The higher the PageRank, the more relevant Google considers the page to be, and the better its chance of showing up at the top of the search results. It is exponentially more difficult to achieve higher PageRanks in each successive bracket, and most websites never get past a 4 or 5. PageRanks of 6 are hard to come by, and 7s are downright rare. 8s and higher are reserved for the Apple.coms and Microsoft.coms of the world, and there are fewer than a dozen PageRank 10 websites on the entire Internet, including Facebook, the World Wide Web Consortium, and Google itself. You can see a site's PageRank by downloading the Google toolbar and enabling the PageRank bar (see Figure 1.2).

Figure 1.2   *This is what PageRank looks like on the Google toolbar. This particular PageRank is a 4 out of 10.*

As in the grade school analogy I used earlier in this chapter, PageRank is based on how many other sites like you—that is, link to you. More importantly, if the sites that link to you are very popular—that is, well linked—themselves, you get an even higher PageRank. So even if only one website links to your page, if it's a super-high PageRank site like, say, Huffingtonpost.com, your page will get a much higher PageRank than one that has 20 links but all from lesser-known sites. And of course, the best situation of all is to be that universally liked kid in school and have many websites of varying PageRanks linking to you. That gives you the highest aggregate PageRank of all. A shining example of a site that everyone seems to like is Wikipedia, which is why it has a PageRank of 9.

The analogy goes even further when you consider the special rules that Google has imposed on PageRank (see Figure 1.3).

THE RULES OF PAGERANK

- The more links – and the higher the PageRank of the pages that contain those links – the better.

- New sites incur an aging delay on receiving the benefit of their PageRank, which will last at least 2 months.

- "Bad-neighborhood" sites are not allowed to have PageRank, and can negatively affect your site if they link to it.

- PageRank flows to the pages on your site that are most well-linked. Even though the highest PageRank page is usually the home page, it needn't be.

Figure 1.3   *The rules of PageRank.*

You know how it stinks to be the new kid in school—how it takes a few months to make friends and establish a reputation? Well, it's exactly the same with new websites. Even though Google assigns a PageRank to a new site pretty quickly, they won't allow it to enjoy the value of that PageRank—that is, rank well in the search results—until the site has been around for a couple of months.

A second important rule of PageRank is this: You are who you hang out with. If you hang out with the druggies and the dropouts, you are considered one, too. Similarly, if your website has anything to do with porn, pills, or gambling, consider your site an outcast that will never rank in the regular search results. In fact, if you run any sort of adult site, you will be placed in a separate set of results that this book does not cover.

On the other side of the coin, if you keep company with the valedictorian and the salutatorian, you can expect a sterling reputation in the community; and in the same way, if your site is linked to by educational, governmental, or high-profile nonprofit websites, you can expect a generous helping of PageRank.

The third and final special rule of PageRank is that it flows unevenly throughout the pages on your site. Instead of being assigned to your website as a whole, PageRank is spread among all of your website's pages based on the number and quality of links each page has. Even though your home page is usually the page with the highest PageRank—as it is the one other websites typically link to—it is possible for another page on your site to have a higher PageRank. The most common example of an inner page that might have a higher PageRank than the home page is a blog. If your blog is the main attraction on your site but is housed within a larger website, say http://www.*yourname*.com, http://www.*yourname*.com/blog will probably have a higher PageRank.

I might be going out on a limb here to extend this analogy, but I liken this rule of unevenly spread PageRank to the kid who is popular only because of his baseball card collection, or his swimming pool, or his hot older sister. He may still be considered popular overall, but those specific aspects of his life are more popular than he himself. If you have an inner page on your website that gains a higher PageRank than your home page, you should place an ad for your product or service on that page because it is more likely to rank highly in the search results.

TrustRank

Now, I hope you don't kill me for saying this, but PageRank doesn't really matter that much anymore. Back in 2004, it was basically synonymous with high rankings. Today, it is more of an indicator, a correlation rather than a conclusion. Above all, PageRank is a pretty mirage to keep you from thinking about the real measure of a site's popularity, better known as TrustRank. TrustRank is the degree to which Google trusts that your website will be valuable to visitors if presented as a search result.

So why did I explain PageRank in the first place? Simply because it's a must-know term, probably the most commonly used of any vocabulary word associated with Google optimization. Also, it happens to be the only publicly available measure of a site's value. TrustRank is a closely guarded concept, one that Google has never officially recognized. Back in 2007, when it became clear that a high PageRank didn't necessarily guarantee a good ranking, we in the SEO industry needed a word to describe what we all thought we were talking about when we said PageRank— that is, the actual importance of a web page in Google's eyes.

So let it be known from here on out: When I talk about PageRank, I am talking about the press piñata, the public evaluation that Google gives to every page on the Internet but which has only a loose correlation with a page's actual value in

Google's eyes. When I talk about TrustRank, I am referring to the bottom line for every optimizer: Google's willingness to place your website highly in the search results and therefore deliver new business. TrustRank is earned in the same way that PageRank is: by receiving links from other sites. The age of a site and the number of +1s its pages receive can also increase its TrustRank. (You learn more about the concept of +1s in Chapter 11, "Social Search: The Intersection of Social Media and SEO.")

If every web page had a public TrustRank value the way it has a public PageRank value on the Google toolbar, the link industry would be revolutionized. There would be a gold-rush-like frenzy to acquire links on web pages that Google truly trusts. But Google would never make a search engine optimizer's life that easy.

 Note

A word about link buying: At a certain point in most people's SEO education, they realize that there are webmasters out there who sell links. The link buying process can be as simple as "Pay me X dollars, and tell me what site to link to and how you would like the link to look." If you didn't know anything about SEO, you'd think it was a pitiful form of advertising—a tiny link on the side of a site being sold for the same price as your cable bill every month. These links aren't even designed to be seen or clicked on. Their entire value is in being recognized by Google so that they can pass TrustRank from the site that is hosting them to the site that bought the link.

For years—and even today—the standard way for people to determine the value of a link in the open market was by looking at its PageRank. A web page with a PageRank of 2 usually gets around $25 per month for each link it sells, and PageRank 7 links sell for up to $2,000 per month. This system is remarkably flawed, and literally millions of dollars have been wasted on it. Why? High-PageRank links will not necessarily increase your Google ranking! To begin with, the PageRank found on the Google toolbar, on which the entire commercial link industry relies, is updated only every 2 to 3 months, so the PageRank you see today could differ significantly from the page's actual PageRank, which Google tabulates daily.

Most importantly, Google has publicly stated that it penalizes websites that buy links and websites that sell links. Google punishes sites that sell links by crippling their ability to transfer TrustRank. And Google does not inform these crippled websites that they have lost the ability to pass TrustRank to other sites. This change has made the commercial link industry into a shell of what it once was. I estimate that 90% of the links that are sold today are from penalized pages and have absolutely no value to their buyers. Determining which sites haven't been crippled, and thus truly pass TrustRank, is a difficult task. Thus, SEO today is far more about acquiring links organically from websites that have never sold links.

Clearly, the question on the lips of everyone in the SEO community right now is this: How do I know whether my web page has high TrustRank? Very few people are able to answer that question. I am one who can.

In late 2008, I developed a tool for measuring the TrustRank of a web page, which is now the engine behind my SEO company. I would tell you how it works, but that would be very boring, and I fear that I might find more than a few Google ninjas at my door. Not to fear, though; I won't leave you in a lurch.

The best way to determine a site's TrustRank, and the foundation of my proprietary tool, basically comes down to taking an educated guess. Here is the logic:

1. Google gives the most TrustRank to sites that have links from well-linked web pages. (Or, in grade school language: Google gives the most popularity to kids who have lots of popular friends.)

2. Google does not allow sites that sell links to pass trust but shows no indication of the sites that have been disallowed to pass trust. (Nature punishes the corrupt popular kids who have allowed their friendship to be bought, making them unable to confer popularity on other kids. Even though these punished kids remain popular, they cannot make anyone else popular.)

3. Therefore, a site has a high TrustRank if its links are from websites that, to the best of your knowledge, have never sold links. (If you only become friends with the kids in your grade who have never sold their friendship for money, you can be sure that you are truly popular.)

Guessing which sites are penalized versus unpenalized is easier than you would think. If a site looks professional, has been around a while, and doesn't have anything spammy written on it, it is likely to be in good standing with Google and will transfer TrustRank properly (see Figure 1.4). You should approach as many of these sites as possible and ask them if they'd be willing to place a link on their site.

Figure 1.4 shows an example of a web page that has the ability to pass TrustRank. If I had never seen this page before, I would believe it was unpenalized because it looks like a legitimate, "un-spammy" page and doesn't appear to be selling any links.

In contrast, Figure 1.5 shows a page that I believe is penalized, and I wouldn't request a link from in a million years.

Figure 1.4   *A site that appears to be unpenalized, free and clear to pass TrustRank.*

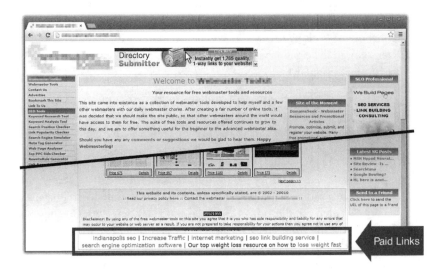

Figure 1.5   *A site that appears to be penalized, unable to pass TrustRank.*

Notice the difference between the two pages. Figure 1.4 shows a home page from a nonprofit website that appears to be professional and care about the user's experience. The layout is clean, the message is coherent, and links to other respected nonprofit websites appear at the bottom. Figure 1.5 shows a disorganized site covered in links, including many clearly paid links. I would bet money that a link on the first site would pass TrustRank and boost your site's Google rankings, but a link on the second site would do absolutely nothing for your website's rankings. The six or seven companies that purchased links on the second site do not realize this fact; otherwise, they wouldn't be wasting their money. And just in case my earlier statement about PageRank being irrelevant wasn't clear enough, note that the lower quality site has a PageRank of 4 on the Google toolbar.

You know a site is penalized when it seems to be actively selling links. When the title of the page is My Travel Diary, and it inexplicably links to websites that sell insurance, poker chips, and software programs... it's penalized. If you can plainly see the links on the site have an unnatural quality to them, Google probably can too. Through their legions of Stanford- and MIT-trained engineers, in addition to turning webmasters on each other by asking them to report sites that sell links, they have gotten very good at spotting link sellers and penalizing them. It is because of this new skill for identifying link sellers that Google is getting ever closer to their original ideal of a perfect Internet, where links are given based on merit, not money.

Google's Circus

To Google, TrustRank is a closely guarded secret. It is the very essence of its algorithm—the last remaining relic of Larry and Sergey's original vision of how the Web should be organized. That is why they want professional optimizers nowhere near it. And to make sure that search engine optimizers never gain insight into TrustRank, they have created the ultimate distraction by continuing to include a PageRank meter on the Google toolbar. That little green bar—an essential tool to most search engine optimizers—is nothing more than a mirage to keep intelligent people expending their brainpower on anything but TrustRank. Sound like a stretch to you? Consider this: If displaying a page's PageRank really helped search engine optimizers do their job better, why would Google continue to do it? After all, the feature is used only by search engine optimizers. Nobody but a search engine optimizer would even take the time to enable the PageRank meter through the toolbar's Settings menu.

In keeping with their strategy of distraction, Google appointed a spokesperson by the name of Matt Cutts in 2007. His job is to interface directly with the SEO community, encouraging webmasters to use the Internet in the same way they did before Google came along—mostly by linking to only relevant, interesting content. Matt provides his fair share of drama by describing in great detail Google's latest algorithm updates and giving them fancy names such as Big Daddy, Caffeine, and Penguin.

Not surprisingly, his presence prevents a lot of innovation in the SEO industry from occurring. A person very much like me, who has the ambition to truly learn how to cause his or her site to rank higher on Google, could easily spend months digesting the carefully worded corporate messaging that Matt imparts and never spend a moment doing real, productive work. That is not to say he doesn't offer good business advice; it just isn't good for people trying to rank high on Google. You could sum up his entire message in one sentence: Create a website that people truly get value from, and it will naturally rank well on Google over time. Again: completely true statement, just not helpful to most businesses.

The first time I visited Matt Cutts's blog, I was struck by the fact that he is not a member of the search relevance department; instead, he is the lead spam engineer. This was the moment I realized that Google considers search engine optimizers to be spammers, and I knew not to trust anything they put forth specifically for search engine optimizers.

What Google has done with releasing the PageRank meter is similar to Coca-Cola releasing one of the most irrelevant ingredients of its secret formula. Although it seems obvious that Coke could reap no benefits from doing so, nobody seems to notice. Instead, they fixate on it as if it were accidentally leaked information and try to discover what makes Coke taste the way it does. Meanwhile, the company continues to avoid telling people that the ingredient plays no real role in the soda's taste despite existing in small traces. Rival soda companies take the bait and spend years analyzing this ingredient. Coke then goes a step further and appoints their head of anti-competition to be their official liaison from the company. He is a nice guy, and his message usually goes something like this: Develop a delicious soft drink, and people will buy it. Yet none of the rivals see anything wrong with this picture, instead choosing to believe that Coke is really going to help them re-create its formula.

When we understand that Google's strategy for protecting its algorithm is to create a circus to divert people's attention from the real measure of a site's value—TrustRank—we can get back to the job at hand, which is to figure out how to make our website rank higher on Google.

How to Mine TrustRank

So now that we know not to believe what Google tells us about SEO, how do we clear the fog and figure out which sites have real TrustRank and therefore would be good targets for us to approach about selling or trading links? I've already covered the "is it spammy looking?" intuitive test. But there is an even simpler way to determine a site's TrustRank. In fact, it's so simple that it might have already crossed your mind: Just look at where a site ranks in the search results. For instance, if you sell apple peelers, type `apple peeler` into Google. The top 40 results definitely have TrustRank. The top 10 results definitely have a lot of TrustRank.

When using this method to determine a site's TrustRank, remember to search only for competitive terms. If you enter an uncommon search term (if you own an apple peeler site, an uncommon term would be something like `top rated metal apple peelers`), even your first five results might not have a lot of TrustRank, as Google will probably be scraping the bottom of the barrel to find you results that are relevant to your search.

To solidify your understanding of this method of mining TrustRank, let's review a hypothetical situation. Suppose, for example, that you just opened an online surfing supply store. Naturally, you want to receive as many high-TrustRank links as possible to beef up your own TrustRank. You should start by typing `surfing` into Google (as shown in Figure 1.6).

Figure 1.6   *A Google search for the term* `surfing` *is a good place to start.*

Note

You will see in Chapter 7, "Google Optimization Myths," that I am one of the few people who doesn't think the links you acquire always need to be relevant to your website; however, relevant sites are a convenient place to start looking for links.

As you scan the top 10 results, you should be looking for organizations, resources, conference pages, and any other established site that might be willing to link to your website merely because you are a member of the industry. Those kinds of pages are the low-hanging fruit for which you would typically be looking. Apart from industry sites, seek out any site from which you have a reason to request a link. Let's dive in and see what we find. In Figure 1.7, I have searched for `surfing supply`.

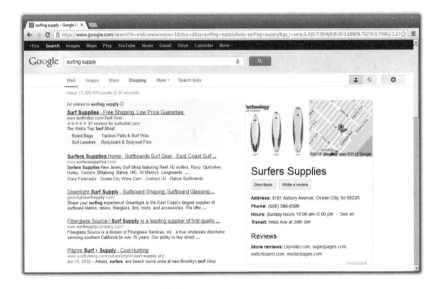

Figure 1.7 *A Google search on the term* `surfing supply`.

Because `surfing` is a high-volume search and these are the top 10 results for it, we can immediately feel certain that each of the 10 results has a good amount of TrustRank. Therefore, any of them would be good targets to approach about acquiring a link on their sites. Because two of them—*Surfer Magazine* and Wikipedia—are editorial in nature, you can immediately assume that there is no way they will link to your business on their sites (although, if they did, your site would get a big shot of TrustRank). So that leaves the others. Examining them, I see that a few are informational sites about surfing, which are perfect places to put your link, providing you can convince them that your website is worthy of inclusion. (I address the many ways to secure links in Chapter 3, "How to Reel In Links.")

If you could get a link on even four of the sites on this first page, you'd be well on your way to the top of the results for most surfing-related keywords.

Next, let's try a slightly less-common search (see Figure 1.7): `surfing supply`.

Here we find 10 results that we can still feel pretty good about, TrustRank-wise. `Surfing supply` is a common enough phrase, and looking above the results I see that companies are buying ads alongside the search results. When you see a lot of ads come up around a search, it usually means that the search seemed worthy enough to other businesses that they were willing to invest money in it. That's a sign that the search is competitive and the top 10 results probably had to earn their spots on the first page with a healthy amount of TrustRank.

So once again, I'd feel good about getting a link from any of these sites, but notice that the two major editorial sites, Wikipedia's "Surfing" page and *Surfer Magazine*, aren't on this page. I also don't see any other surfing names I've heard of (I have a bit of familiarity with surfing), so I would definitely say that this group of sites is a notch below the surfing search in terms of TrustRank levels.

Finally, Figure 1.8 shows a search for a much less-competitive phrase: `premium surfing supply`.

Before even seeing the results, we can infer that because the search is obviously not an especially common one, we are not going to be able to feel confident that any of these sites have enough TrustRank to spend our energy approaching them about links.

When we actually inspect these results, we observe that a number of them are not actually surfing supply stores but rather individual product pages about random items like surfboard leashes. In fact, a Google Books result for the original version of this book, *Outsmarting Google*, shows up as well. This indicates that the Big G was straining to find relevant sites and so had to dig deeper into its repository. If this were a clear product-oriented search like `buy surfboards`, I would expect plenty of product pages, but because `premium surfing supply` is more of a store search, it's clear that Google was unable to return good results. Now is the time when the intuitive test I described earlier kicks in. Clicking the sites on this page, I see that almost all of them are pages from e-commerce sites. There is very little chance that an e-commerce site would link to another website because it would distract buyers from making purchases. Some of these websites, however, are worth considering based on the fact that they have links right on the landing pages, such as Surfline.com. This site appears to be a high-quality resource for surfers and has a section on its footer called "network," where links to related surf sites are displayed. If you are in the surfing supply business, you probably want to reach out to that website asking for a link.

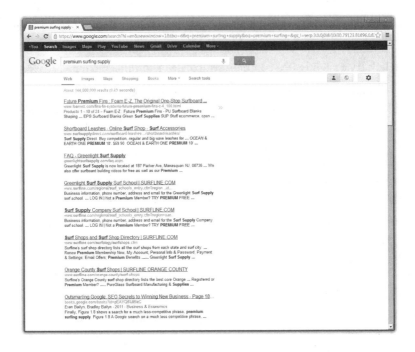

Figure 1.8 *A Google search on a much-less-competitive phrase:* premium surfing supply.

 Note

You might also notice that all of these search result pages are personalized. Because I live in San Francisco, I get a different set of results than someone who lives in another city. In fact, even two people who live in the same city could get different results because Google also factors in your search history. For this reason, an online surfing supply store would want to try variations of search terms such as surfing supply new york and surfing san diego when seeking out link targets.

Now that you have an easy way to see which web pages are most trusted, you can quickly compile a list of websites that you should be approaching to ask whether they might link to your site. If your site were to receive a link from every website that shows up in the top 40 or 50 results for your most competitive search terms, I guarantee that it would soon become the #1 spot on Google and you would be flooded with business. In reality though, you would never get all those webmasters—many of which are competitors—to agree to give your site a link, so we need to come up with some more creative ways of gaining high-TrustRank links for your business.

A Final Word on TrustRank

In the SEO game, you should now be at the point where you understand what the playing field looks like from a high level. If you haven't been paying attention, it basically comes down to this:

- Try to get a lot of websites to link to your website that
  - Have many inbound links
  - Have never sold links

This will give your site TrustRank and cause Google to send it traffic.

The next few chapters explain how TrustRank interacts with other factors to determine your website's Google rankings and how to use SEO to get the most targeted visitors to your site.

2

The Five Ingredients of Google Optimization

You now understand a bit better how Google ranks the millions of sites on the Web. As a business owner or marketer, you are on a constant quest to gain Google's trust. And on your quest, you need to keep exactly five factors in mind. I call them the five ingredients of successful SEO. You already know the most important one: links (the very currency of trust in Google's eyes). The others are keyword selection, meta page titles, URL structure, and time. Even if those terms sound like jabberwocky to you right now, I promise they'll be second nature by the time you finish this chapter.

Before we get started, I want to make sure you understand a few basic vocabulary terms that will make your reading of this chapter much easier:

- **Keywords**—Keywords, or search terms (these expressions are interchangeable), are the words that are typed into search engines such as Google.

- **Inbound links**—As Google is analyzing its vast database of websites, trying to determine which ones to select as the final, first-page contestants, it puts a high price tag on what's known in the industry as inbound links. Inbound links are links from other websites that point to your website, which you hope result in your site gaining Google TrustRank.

- **TrustRank**—We know from the preceding chapter that the more links your site receives from other trusted websites, the higher its TrustRank will be, and therefore the higher its likelihood of showing up at the top of the search results. TrustRank is one of the two main factors Google uses to determine which results to show on the first page for a search.

- **Meta page title**—A meta page title, the other main factor used by Google to determine which results to show on the first page for a search, basically is a short description of what your web page is about, which people who program websites put into a special area of the website code. It is like the headline of a newspaper. There is a different meta page title for every page on your site, and Google pays special attention to it.

- **URL**—A uniform resource locator (URL) is the same thing as a domain name, or a web address. It's the http://www.example.com that you type in when you want to visit a website.

Ingredient One: Keyword Selection

Now that you understand some of the basic terminology and concepts behind ranking, let's get down to the nitty-gritty of keyword selection. Selecting your search terms (or keywords) is not difficult. All you do is think about what you would like people to type into Google to make your website pop up. For example, I would like it if my personal website, http://www.evanbailyn.com, were the first result when someone typed in who is the handsomest man on earth. This would cause people to believe that I am considered the most handsome man on earth. Why? Because Google says so! People put a lot of trust in Google's rankings.

If I managed the website for a personal injury law firm in New York, I would want that website to show up when someone types in personal injury lawyer new york. How did I choose that search phrase? I just thought about it for 2 seconds and decided that people would probably type it in if they were looking for a personal injury lawyer in New York.

Those phrases—who is the handsomest man on earth and personal injury lawyer new york—are keyword phrases. I chose them because they seemed like the best searches to bring new visitors to the two websites in question for their respective purposes.

Of course, there are more scientific methods for choosing keywords in addition to the "think about it for 2 seconds" method. Here they are.

Take an Informal Survey

Ask your friends what they would type into Google if they were looking for the product or service your company sells. If you own a website that sells shampoo for people with dry hair, ask people around you: What would you type into Google if you want to find a new moisturizing shampoo? Their answers might be as general as buy shampoo, or they might specifically search for dry hair shampoo, or they might start with some research and type what are the best shampoos for dry hair. These are three very different keyword phrases, and it is invaluable to know which of them most people would type so that you can set your strategy.

Use the Google AdWords Keyword Planner

This free tool is the de facto standard for keyword selection in the SEO world (see Figure 2.1). It shows statistics of how many people are searching for the keywords you enter, along with a list of related terms and their search volumes. You can access the tool directly using this link: https://adwords.google.com/ko/KeywordPlanner/Home. Without a doubt, bookmark this tool for future use.

Capitalize on Competitors' Work

Your competitors have probably already spent a lot of time and energy doing research on the keywords that make them the most money. Why not take a few seconds and avail yourself of all that work? To do so, simply type into Google what you believe to be your main keyword, and look at the blue underlined heading of each of the 10 results that subsequently appear (see Figure 2.2). The keywords you find in those headings are probably the ones that your competitors have determined make the biggest difference to their bottom lines. Why do I say that? Well, first of all, to have gotten into the top 10 results for your main keyword, your competitors are definitely doing something right, SEO-wise, so it's reasonable to assume they know a thing or two about keyword selection. Second, one of the oldest rules in SEO is that you put your main keywords into your meta page title, which Google ports directly into your site's blue underlined heading whenever your site appears as a search result.

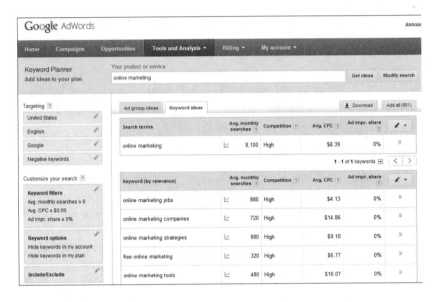

Figure 2.1   *The Google AdWords Keyword Planner.*

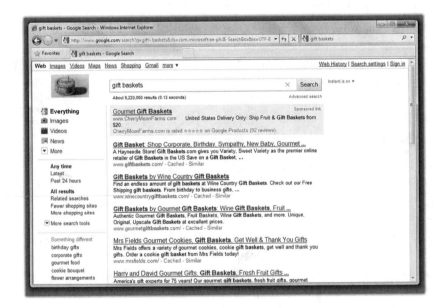

Figure 2.2   *Don't overlook what you can learn about the keywords your competitors deem important.*

So let's say I sell gift baskets. Is the right keyword for me gift baskets? Perhaps it's gift basket as a singular. Or perhaps it's order gift baskets online. I'm not sure, but I'm going to see what my competitors think by typing gift baskets into Google (see Figure 2.2).

After a quick glance at the headings of these results, I can immediately see that my competitors believe the keyword gourmet gift baskets is a lucrative one. Two out of the top four websites have the keyword gourmet in their headings or descriptions. So I will now add it to the list of keywords I plan to optimize for my gift baskets company. It also seems that my competitors like birthday gift baskets, food gift baskets, and wine gift baskets. All three of these keyword phrases will be considered because I know from looking at these websites that they have put a lot of work into their companies, so they probably have a good sense of which keywords deliver the most new sales.

Another somewhat sneakier and more awesome way of capitalizing on your competitors' hard work is using free traffic measurement services to spy on the keywords for which your competitors are already ranking. I used to think that this kind of tool couldn't possibly exist because only I have access to my internal traffic logs and therefore know which search keywords bring my site the most traffic, but then I tried running a tool against my own site and found that it was about 75% accurate.

The best free keyword-spying tool is Alexa. Go to http://www.alexa.com, type in a competitor's website, click the Get Details button, and then scroll down to the section that says "Where do example.com's visitors come from?" On the right side, you see Top Keywords from Search Engines (see Figure 2.3). Keep in mind that Alexa's estimates get more accurate the more popular a website is. I tend to trust Alexa's search analytics data for the top 10,000 websites on the Internet, but once I get outside the top 100,000, I put little stock in it.

Using Alexa or other free keyword-spying tools is one surefire way to know which keywords are actually delivering traffic to your competitors. The keywords from which they receive traffic might be the best keywords for you; however, keep in mind that just because a keyword delivers traffic to a site doesn't mean it delivers *new sales* to a site. If there were a New Sales Spying Tool out there, it would be quite popular. However, the next best thing to a New Sales Spying Tool is a pay-per-click campaign.

Figure 2.3 *Alexa.com's Search Analytics report for etsy.com, showing the top keywords delivering traffic to the site.*

Spend a Few Bucks on a Pay-per-Click Campaign

There is no better way to understand the effect of your website showing up on the first page for a particular keyword than instantly getting it to the first page and seeing how many sales you make from it. This is essentially what you can do with a Google AdWords campaign (http://www.google.com/ads/adwords/). For a few hundred dollars, you can get your website to show up above the regular (organic) search results, in the shaded Sponsored Results area. While the sponsored results are less trusted by the average searcher than the organic results, there are definite advantages to spearheading an SEO effort with a brief Google AdWords campaign.

The most significant benefit of running a paid campaign on Google is that you can quickly learn which keywords produce the most sales for you. In the keyword selection process, this knowledge is invaluable. Not only can you try out the couple of keywords you think would bring the most benefit to your business, you can try out hundreds of keywords at once and not pay unless someone clicks your ad. In doing so, you might stumble upon the fact that the plural of your main keyword performs much better than the singular; one of your three most obvious keywords outperforms the other two by a wide margin; or some random keyword you never would have thought of is a sleeper, producing numerous sales.

When you gain a better understanding of your best-performing keywords, you can gradually wean yourself off the expensive Google AdWords system and focus on SEO (although there is nothing wrong with keeping a pay-per-click campaign running at the same time as doing SEO, as long as you are carefully watching the campaign to make sure that you are making more money than you are spending). Google AdWords can be an effective tool for targeting the keywords that your site is unlikely to rank for in the near future. It is also useful for testing out new product niches because it gives you an instant verdict on whether a niche is viable for you—the equivalent of having a focus group at your fingertips. I have some clients that use paid search to try out new keywords; when they determine that a keyword produces new sales, they begin the process of optimizing their website to rank for it organically.

Ingredient Two: The Meta Page Title

Do not skip this section, even if it sounds boring. I promise I won't hammer you with techie-talk. The meta page title is the second most important factor in all of SEO.

When your website was first created, whoever was programming it had to fill in a section of the coding called the meta page title. If your web designer knows a thing or two about SEO, he or she will have paid special attention to this seemingly random bit of code that is a part of every website.

The reason this primitive bit of information matters so much is because search engines have, for a while now, considered the meta page title to be the one true description of a web page. The meta page title is like the headline of a newspaper story or the front cover of a book. It encapsulates a web page in about 15 words or fewer.

Google's decision to make it such a huge factor in ranking websites is pretty arbitrary. They could have made the meta description tag, the meta keywords, or any other section of the website code the defining attributes of a website. But because they decided that this area matters so much, we are compelled to pay attention to it too.

First off, let's get this out of the way. Figure 2.4 shows what the meta page title actually looks like inside your website's Hypertext Markup Language (HTML) code. I use the code from my website as an example.

Feel free to forget that image if it seems complicated. What that code turns into on your website is the words at the very top of your Internet browser, above the address bar (see Figure 2.5).

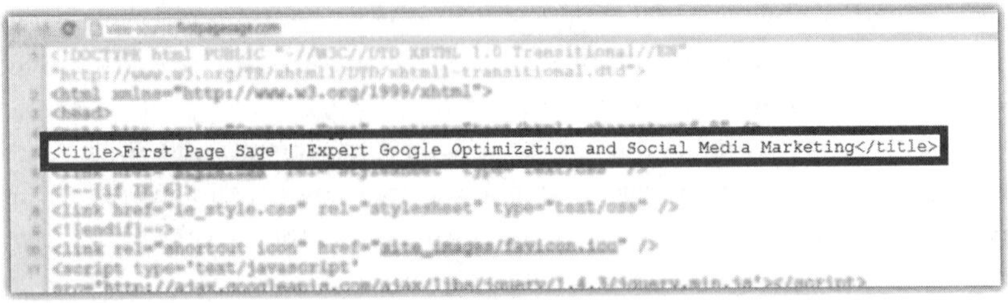

Figure 2.4 *An example of how the meta page title appears in a web page's HTML code.*

Figure 2.5 *The meta page text is what appears at the very top of the user's web browser.*

The only other place you will encounter meta page titles as a normal Internet user is when you are looking at search engine results. Those blue underlined headings on the first line of every Google result are simply a direct copy of each site's meta page title, as shown in Figure 2.6.

It is your job to decide what your page title should be before asking your web designer or tech person to put it into your site's code. But not to fear—when creating a meta page title, you need to know only the following three things:

- It needs to summarize what a web page is about in a simple way for the sake of visitors but also contain keywords so that Google knows which terms your website should rank for.

- Keep it to a maximum of 100 characters, although Google will show only 65 or so.

- After you've finished formulating it, send it to your web designer (or anyone who does your web work) and say, "Please make these words the meta page title of my site's home page."

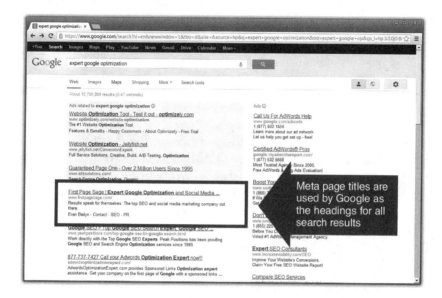

Figure 2.6 *Google also uses a site's meta page title as the heading for its search results.*

Now that you see this meta page title thing is quite doable, let's go into how you can maximize its impact.

Maximizing the Effectiveness of Your Meta Page Titles

The key to a really effective meta page title is including all your most valuable keywords in a human-friendly *and* Google-friendly way. To demonstrate this idea, consider this example of a long-time client of mine, a criminal lawyer in Los Angeles. He wants his website to show up at the top of Google whenever someone is looking for a criminal lawyer in Los Angeles. After doing his research, he realized that all his keyword phrases contain the words `lawyer`, `attorney`, `los angeles`, `criminal`, and `defense`. In other words, if you combine these words in different ways, you will end up with the various keywords that people type in when they are looking for a criminal lawyer in Los Angeles (for example, `criminal defense lawyer los angeles`). He also wants his website to rank high for searches related to criminal law representation in three areas outside of

Los Angeles: Glendale, Pasadena, and Burbank. Add those three city names to the list of words that a potential client might enter into Google to find him, and he's looking at more than 20 different keywords. That's a lot of keywords to stuff into a 100-character title. How will he do it? Well, back in 2004 or 2005, it would have been common for webmasters to simply list their keywords, in order of importance, in the meta page title tag like this:

```
Los angeles criminal lawyer, los angeles criminal attorney, los
angeles criminal defense attorney, los angeles criminal defense
lawyer, los angeles criminal defense, los angeles lawyer, lawyer
in burbank, glendale, pasadena
```

That type of meta page title is not only unfriendly to visitors, but would also get your site labeled as spam and dropped to the bottom of the results. The main thing that this meta page title lacks—other than adherence to the character limit—is the fact that Google can read words in any order as long as they are written one time. So if your three keywords are `red delicious apples`, `delicious apples`, and `apples`, you could simply make your page title "Red Delicious Apples for Sale." That would cover all three keywords just fine. With that rule in mind, here is a perfect meta page title for my client, the Los Angeles criminal lawyer:

```
Los Angeles Criminal Lawyer | Defense Attorney in Burbank,
Glendale, and Pasadena
```

This meta page title incorporates all the words that my client wants to rank for, and because Google doesn't care about word order, my client is getting credit for every permutation of those words. This means that if someone types into Google `pasadena defense lawyer`, Google will consider my client's website an ideal match. Same with `criminal defense attorney los angeles` or any other permutation of the words in his site's meta page title. We've covered them all in a short, human-friendly way.

So far, I've been focusing on just your home page meta page title. But nowadays, especially with Google's newest algorithm updates, it is important to get many pages of your site, not just your home page, to rank. This means you should be specifically concerned with the meta page titles on all the pages of your website, not just your home page. My client, for instance, did not need to construct a meta page title for his home page that covers every important keyword. He could have a specific page that focuses just on criminal defense in Burbank, and the meta page title of that page could be `Burbank Criminal Defense Lawyer | Attorney in Burbank, California`. Creating separate pages, all with unique meta page titles for every keyword, is a good idea because it gives visitors a page that specifically suits their search, whatever it may be. It also gives Google lots of opportunities to rank your website's pages for niche keywords. Ultimately, it is the sites that have hundreds, or even thousands, of pages on niche topics that receive the most over-all traffic from Google. I discuss this strategy further in Chapter 5, "The Nuclear Football."

If you totally understand how to craft the perfect meta page title now, skip ahead to the "Ingredient Three: Links" section of this chapter. For those who really want this idea hammered home, I have included two case studies.

Case Study One: The Baby Store

A client of mine has an online store that sells clothing for babies and toddlers. Using the Google AdWords Keyword Planner, she found that her potential customers type in the obvious—baby clothing—but also use the word clothes in place of clothing and add the descriptors girls and boys in their searches. So already she was looking at the following list of keywords:

```
baby clothing

baby clothes

girls baby clothing

girls baby clothes

boys baby clothing

boys baby clothes
```

On top of that, potential customers with older kids were also typing in toddler clothing and kids clothing. So there were at least a dozen more permutations of keywords she wanted her site to rank for. After much thought, here is the page title we came up with:

```
The Baby Store | Baby and Toddler Clothing | Kids Clothes
for Girls and Boys
```

As you can see, all the words that make up the keywords she wanted to rank for are represented in this innocent-looking page title. It just took a few minutes to arrange the words in a way that seemed natural but was also rich with keywords. As you can see, I'm a fan of the "pipe," the long vertical line that is above the Enter key on most keywords, because it separates bits of the page title neatly.

Case Study Two: Games

A client of mine who owns a games website wanted to rank for the keywords: free online games, fun games, and best games. Let's say his site name was Floofy.com.

(I just made that up because it's fun to say.) A good page title for him would be this:

```
Floofy.com | The Best Fun, Free Online Games
```

As with the previous two examples, this page title incorporates all the words that make up his three keywords and therefore would be called forth by Google when someone types in fun games, free online games, or best games. Because this is a relatively short page title, he could include some other keywords as well. Or he might want to keep it that way because people do make the decision of which site to click on in the search results based on that blue underlined heading, which, once again, is a direct copy of the meta page title.

Ingredient Three: Links

You should now understand the meta page title. You might be wondering, though, how it fits within Google's algorithm. Well, if I were an oversimplifying kind of person, I would tell you the following:

> When someone does a search on Google, the first thing Google does is locate every site whose meta page title contains the words in that search. It then looks at how many trustworthy links each web page in that result set has and puts the ones with the most trustworthy links on the first page and the ones with the least trustworthy links at the very end.

So, after you've got the right page title, it's all about links.

It amazes me how much I still hear that SEO is about the things that are on your website. In fact, the main service many so-called SEO companies sell is one where they work on your website to cause it to attract search engine traffic. This boggles my mind because, other than the meta page titles, what's on your website barely even matters to Google! It's all about links.

Links are to Google what grades and SAT scores are to a college admission officer. Does the admission officer care what you look like on your interview? Sure. But he wouldn't have invited you for the interview in the first place if you didn't have high enough grades and SAT scores. Similarly, does Google care about how user friendly your website is, what's written on it, and how fast it loads? Absolutely. But they won't even give it the opportunity to rank if it doesn't have the right quality and quantity of links.

That said, if you have great links but maintain a poorly coded, slow website with nonsense copy written on it, you won't have much luck ranking on Google (just as you wouldn't have much luck getting into college if you have perfect grades and SATs but show up late to your interview wearing sloppy clothes and making wise-cracks at your admissions officer).

The point I'm trying to make is this: Links matter much more than any other factor. And if you get the link component and the meta page title component right, you've got 85% of the job done right there.

In Chapter 1, "Trust: The Currency Of Google," you learned how to determine a high-TrustRank link versus a low-TrustRank link. In Chapter 3, "How to Reel In Links," you will learn how to acquire links. So for now, let me just explain a bit more clearly what a link is and what makes it valuable so that you know exactly what you're hunting for.

For the purposes of this book, a *link* is anything on a website that, when clicked, brings you to another web page. The granddaddy of links, the one that was there in 1994 when the Internet was still something only nerds cared about, is the *text link* (or, as I like to call it, the blue underlined link). Figure 2.7 shows a snippet from the Announcements section on evanbailyn.com that contains four text links.

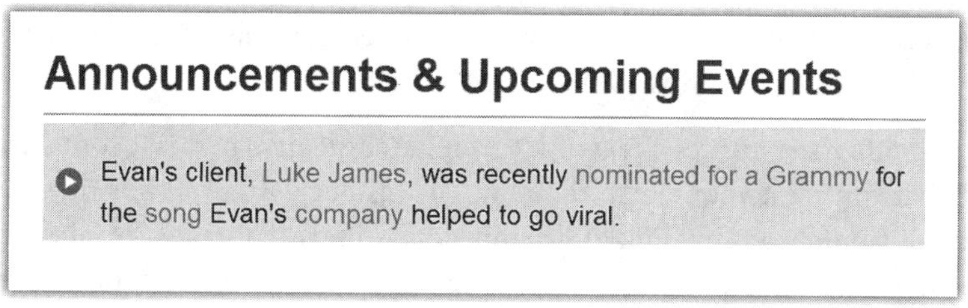

Announcements & Upcoming Events

⊙ Evan's client, Luke James, was recently nominated for a Grammy for the song Evan's company helped to go viral.

Figure 2.7   *An example of the way links are used inside text: They guide visitors to other web pages to supplement the information on the current page.*

I had my web designer add these four text links into the announcement so that people could learn more about our accomplishment with a few clicks. That is generally the purpose of links: to allow people to discover new content or web pages quickly.

Text links are usually blue and underlined, but there are exceptions. Sometimes you'll catch webmasters being creative with their text links. Also the color of a text link usually changes when you click it; this is to remind you that you've already visited the site that the link references. A clicked-on link is usually purple, but again, that is up to the web designer. No matter what color it is or what it looks like, if it takes you to another page, it's a link.

The other type of link is the *image link*. As the name implies, this kind of link is in the form of an image but functions exactly like any other link in that it brings you to another web page when you click it. We've all seen plenty of image links; every display advertisement you see on a website is an image link.

You know by now that Google gives your website credit every time another website links to your website. However, certain types of links are more valuable than others. Text links are the most valuable types of links because Google can easily read the words in and around the text link to get a sense of what the link is referring to. An image link has the same magnitude of value as a text link, but without all the description. In other words, an image link is like an overall vote for a political candidate, one that says "I like this candidate." A text link is like a detailed vote for a political candidate, the equivalent of "I like this candidate because of his stance on health care." Text links are valuable because they tell Google what a site is about. This information allows Google to decide which specific keywords to rank that website for.

As explained in Chapter 1, the reason links are so important is because they pass TrustRank. Text links pass highly detailed TrustRank. Image links pass general TrustRank. When asking other websites for links, you really want a text link, but if you can't get one (for instance, if text links don't fit into the site's aesthetic), you can settle for an image link. Ultimately, your site will rank higher with a mix of both, because Google's engineers have determined that most sites would attract both types of links in a world without SEO.

When another site creates a text link to your website, it is best if it contains a keyword that you want your site to rank for. For instance, if I print business cards for a living, I would want my link to be embedded in text that reads "business cards," preferably within the context of a sentence or paragraph. While your SEO goals will be best served by a text link that contains only your keywords as the linked text (for example, `business cards`), Google considers dead-on text links like these to be suspicious, so you want very few, if any, of them. Instead, it is better if the text surrounding your keyword is also linked, or if your keyword is near the linked text, but not linked itself. Alternatively, it is fine if your site is simply linked through its URL or an image; this will not pass TrustRank to your site in the optimal way, but links like these are necessary if Google is to believe that your website's linking patterns are natural.

So, to be clear, you want your link to appear on other websites in one of the following ways:

Tip

> These examples are in descending order of SEO value, but you need a mixture of all five types if Google is to trust that your site earned its links fair and square.

- Nowadays, there are many ways to send people your contact details. But you can never underestimate the convenience of old-fashioned paper business cards.
- When I am looking to get anything printed, I turn to Jim's Cards, the best business card printer in the industry.
- Personally, I like Jim's cards, which provides better business printing services than I've found elsewhere.
- http://www.jimscards.com
- Business Cards

You do not want your links to appear on other websites in one of the following ways:

- Business cards
- Business cards, stationery, printing

If you can manage to get text-based links on other websites with your keywords *inside* or *near* them, you will quickly notice an uptick in your Google rankings for those keywords.

The Psychology of Link Building

Now that I have presented a simplified explanation of how other sites should link to your website, allow me to add some nuance. All websites are operated by people, and trying to control how they link to your website is akin to trying to control those people—a fruitless effort. The skill involved in getting others to link exactly the way you want them to is the stuff of conmen and pick-up artists. That is why paid links, directories, and comment spamming is so tempting; it gives us the illusion of control over our SEO. But alas, in links as in life, we must take what we are given.

What you will get, as a humble suitor of another website, is whatever suits its webmaster best. Most of the time, *no link* will suit them best. However, every now and then, you'll find yourself with a perfect link. Link acquisition is indeed an art, an exercise in stamina and skill to which I have dedicated the entire next chapter.

Having studied Google's algorithm since 2003, I have seen many changes in the way it deals with links, and I can honestly say that it has not altered its core algorithm. Instead, it has imposed filter after filter onto its ranking rules, making it ever more difficult to penetrate the spider web of restrictions around which links count, which links don't, and *how much* each link is worth.

For the vast majority of Google's existence, simple text links with keywords inside them were the greatest weapon in a search engine optimizer's arsenal. In mid-2009, Google slammed the SEO world with a link filter that caught sites with too many same-keyword text links pointing to them. In other words, if I had been telling webmasters for years to only link to me with the stand-alone text links "business cards," my site would have dropped way down in the rankings. In 2012, Google imposed a slew of updates to its "unnatural link" filter, naming it Penguin and striking fear in the hearts of webmasters worldwide. (Ironic, because penguins are cute.)

This was the point when many bloggers declared that "SEO is dead." For many, it was, because Easy Street was closed—and not just blocked off, but being taken apart by wrecking balls and cranes. What was left—the SEO of today—is one in which Google can easily tell a natural link from a negotiated link. You have to earn links by creating clever enough content that other webmasters *want* to link to. In effect, PR companies have become more valuable than ever, because they've been doing precisely that all along.

Although I've experimented with all forms of link building, I always came home to a conservative link-acquisition philosophy, one that focuses on requesting links from sites that have clear value because of their intrinsic, long-term dedication to quality (for example, Huffington Post, Forbes, Slate). I like to think of myself as the Warren Buffet of link investing.

Because you won't have the luxury of deciding how other websites link to you, you should not focus on any particular formula for it. However, keep in mind that text links are better than image links, so bloggers and journalists are usually good targets. By creatively and consistently pitching people who may have an interest in covering what you do for a living, you will end up with all the links you need.

DUMMY LINKS

Before moving on to the next ingredient, I must warn you about a certain type of link that passes no TrustRank at all and that you must avoid at all costs. I call these links *dummy links* because they look just like real links but contain none of the substance that helps your website to rank. Keep dummy links in mind because there is nothing worse than finding out that some of the links you have worked hard to earn are not actually passing any TrustRank. Here are the two types of dummy links:

Redirect Links

If a webmaster is trying to prevent TrustRank from being passed via the links on his site, he can have them coded in such a way that when someone clicks on a link to an outside site, that person is first sent to a page on his own site before arriving at his final destination website. This is called a *redirect*. In other words, visitors hit an intermediate page before they get to the page they intended to visit. Visitors are usually on the intermediate page just for a split second, so they never even notice they visited an intermediate page. This is a sneaky way of withholding the site's vote—that is, their TrustRank—from ever being cast. Google gives all the TrustRank they would have given to the outside site to the intermediate page, which is just some random page on the originating site. You can identify this kind of dummy link by hovering your mouse over any link on another site that seems to be going to your site and then looking at the bottom left corner of your screen where the URL that the link is pointing to is displayed. As long as it reads http://www.yoursite.com, you're good. If it reads something like http://www.othersite.com/redirect.php?url=www.yoursite.com, it is a dummy link.

No-Follow Links

The most sinister type of dummy link is the no-follow link, simply because you can't tell that it isn't passing TrustRank without looking at the HTML code of the web page. No-follow links are normal links that have been intentionally crippled via a short bit of code whose purpose is to prevent TrustRank from leaving a web page. They are an invention of Google, created to give webmasters a way to indicate when the links on their website are not necessarily endorsements of the sites that are being linked to. For instance, a webmaster might use a no-follow tag on a link to an advertiser, or on links within the comment section of a blog. For a couple of years, the no-follow link has been a subject of debate in the SEO world. Google holds that they are merely trying to figure out which links are true editorial mentions and which are paid mentions. (Google only wants to give ranking credibility to the former.) Many webmasters think that they should not have to change the way they link to advertisers just to please an outside company, even one as important as Google. Naturally, advertisers don't like being labeled with a no-follow tag because TrustRank is one of the chief things that they are paying for.

When another site links to your site as part of an arrangement you made, check to see whether it has a no-follow tag on it. If you catch a site linking to you with a no-follow tag, you have license to be upset with them. The only good use of a no-follow tag, in my opinion, is in the comments of a blog because there are so many spammers who leave comments with links in them just to steal TrustRank from your site. Many sites, including the *New York Times* website, place a no-follow tag on all comments. If you'd like to check a link yourself for a no-follow tag, find the View Source button on your web browser's menu (you can usually access this option by right-clicking the page) and do a search for your site's URL. If you see "rel=nofollow" next to your link, you know that the webmaster is withholding TrustRank from being passed to your site. Many sites also use a "cover-all" no-follow tag at the top of the HTML code to indicate that all links on the page should be marked with a no-follow tag.

In the past few years, no-follow and redirect links have become more and more common on social networks—a sign not just of Google's influence, but of many websites' efforts to combat aggressive SEO tactics. As a result, any links you place on Twitter, Facebook, LinkedIn, Pinterest, Tumblr, and most of the other big social media websites will not pass any TrustRank.

Ingredient Four: URL Structure

Sometimes Google is so easy to read that people miss what it's trying to tell them. The role of the URL in SEO is one of those times. Simply put, the keywords you would like each page to rank for should be in the URL of that page. For example, if you own a video-sharing site and your keyword is funny videos, there should be a page on your site called http://www.yoursite.com/funnyvideos. If you have many keywords, as most webmasters do, make sure that every keyword has its own landing page with the keyword somewhere in the URL. The most standard way to format keyword-specific URLs is as follows:

http://www.yoursite.com/keyword1.html

http://www.yoursite.com/keyword2.html

http://www.yoursite.com/keyword3.html

When I speak about this topic, I get lots of questions about the best way to include your keywords in your URL. So let me break it down for you. Start with the most fundamental part of your URL: your domain name. It's possible that Google has some dusty tablets lying around that define the relative credibility of the top-level domains (or TLDs, such as .com, .net, and .org), but ultimately, the difference between them seems negligible from an SEO perspective.

Of course, when choosing a domain name, try to get the .com version of the domain you're seeking, if only because of how established that TLD is in people's minds. As far as branded domains versus keyword-based domains (JennysLaserWorld.com vs. Lasertag.com), Google does give *some* extra ranking weight to domains with keywords inside them, but they give much less than they used to. You don't need to fixate on having a keyword-based domain name.

If you can't get the .com you're looking for—which is probably the case since domain squatters own most of the brandable .com names out there—try another TLD such as .net, .org, .biz, or .me. Google basically gives the same weight to all of them, although some might sound better in combination with your company name than others. For instance, if you owned a self-help site called Discover, then a .me TLD would be fitting: discover.me.

In summary, while the branding of your website is certainly an important consideration in domain name selection, remember not to pay a premium for SEO purposes; what you do *after* you buy the domain is much more important than the name itself.

Let's shift our focus away from domain names and toward the entire URL of a page. As mentioned earlier, it is always best to have keywords in your URLs as opposed to having numbers, letters, or other characters that do not improve a person's experience with your site:

> Good: http://yoursite.com/balloons

> Bad: http://yoursite.com/products/cat1.php?prodid=1234&sort=date

When including a keyword *phrase*, as opposed to a single-word keyword, in your URL, you have a choice of separating the words with underscores, dashes, or not at all. Never use underscores. Between the other two methods, it is fine to have no spaces between the words (for example, http://yoursite.com/redballoons) for Google's purposes; however, because your URL is visible to people within Google's search results, I recommend the method that is more pleasing to the eye: using dashes. For example, http://yoursite.com/red-balloons.

Note that if your site uses a content management system (CMS), such as WordPress, it is likely that your URLs will be formatted with dashes automatically.

At the start of this section, you read that it is wise to have a separate web page for every keyword that matters to you. These keywords would correspond to items on your website's menu, services it offers, or products it sells. For instance, if you were a business consultant, some of the URLs on your site might look like this:

http://www.yoursite.com/business-consulting

http://www.yoursite.com/executive-coaching

http://www.yoursite.com/ceo-training

Keep in mind, though, that although this describes a best practice, if it doesn't feel natural to create a separate landing page for every keyword you care about, you do not need to do so just for the sake of SEO. After all, when it comes to on-page SEO, the URL is much less important than the meta page title. The same business consultant would do almost as well with a single page that targets all three of the listed keywords (business consulting, executive coaching, and ceo training) that has the URL:

http://www.yoursite.com/services

and the page title:

```
John Smith | Business Consultant Specializing in Executive
Coaching and CEO Training
```

This page would lose a few points with Google for its generic URL, but it would gain many more points for clearly identifying its keywords in the meta page title. On balance, it would be a clear win for that page.

If, instead of a business consultant's website, we were looking at a sporting goods website with a catalogue of 200 products, it would be optimal to have a separate page for each product with the main keywords in both the URL *and* the page title.

Although most websites created in the past few years do use a CMS that creates SEO-friendly URLs automatically, some CMSs still create dynamic URLs. Dynamic URLs are more complicated URLs that are meant to track a website visitor activity. They look sort of like this:

http://www.example.com/article/bin/answer.foo?language=en&answer=
3&sid=98971298178906&query=URL

As you now know, these types of pages—although readable by Google—are not as helpful to your site's rankings as simple URLs like the ones listed previously. When executed correctly, a page on your website designed to attract searches for a particular keyword should look like the site in Figure 2.8.

Figure 2.8   *A recommended URL structure when the keyword being targeted is* keynote speaker fees.

This page is targeting the keyword phrase keynote speaker fees, and so its URL is correctly formatted with that phrase in the URL. And, of course, the phrase is also included in the meta page title.

After you have your keywords together, links to your website, proper meta page titles, and the correct URL structure, you've done an excellent job impressing Google. Like a well-prepared prom date, you have shown up to meet your date's parents looking your best, armed with compliments, polite manners, and diplomatic answers. And you've succeeded: The parents like you! But you haven't earned their full trust yet.

Ingredient Five: Time

Like the prom-goer who has impressed his date's parents on the first meeting, you will be in great initial shape to rank high on Google if you've implemented the first four ingredients correctly. Now it's up to you to continue this good behavior over time. Bring her home at 4 a.m. on prom night and you're *out*, buddy. Bring her home before midnight and keep exhibiting good manners in the coming weeks and months, and you're building a real relationship. Google is just as unforgiving as a pair of protective parents; they can handle imperfections and a few awkward missteps, but cross a line that violates their trust, and you will not be welcome inside Google's house again for a long time.

In a website's first few weeks, it cannot rank for any competitive keyword. I've heard about websites that were just released and immediately hit the top of Google, but I've never seen one; and the times I *have* seen sites that claim this meteoric rise, they were ranking for wholly uncompetitive keyword phrases such as turkish cotton substitute.

Google intentionally imposes a ranking delay on new websites. This tradition traces back to the early 2000s, when Google was still combating spam sites, which were threatening to take over their index. These spam sites, most of them automatically generated blogs made up of paragraphs of senseless content to fool Google into thinking they were legitimate websites, had found a way to rank on Google for hundreds of thousands of keywords. By late 2003, the situation had gotten so bad that it was threatening the relevance of Google's results. I remember this period well; although the search experience on Google was not awful, for most searches you typed in you had about a 10% chance of clicking a site that seemed to be written by a lunatic. The new ranking delay stopped the spammers cold in their tracks. No longer could they throw a website up, get it to rank in a week, make a few bucks from ads or identity-theft schemes, and then disappear. Now they had to stick around and prove their worth for a while, a task few of them seemed eager to take. From 2003 to 2006, the period in which I started studying SEO, Google required new websites to wait over a year to rank for any significant keywords.

From 2007 to 2009, this ranking delay, known to the industry as the *sandbox*, shortened. I remember seeing websites ranking for competitive keywords on Google in just 6 to 12 months, sometimes as few as 3.

In the post-2009 world of SEO, Google seems to have regained their confidence that they can return spam-free search results without resorting to the draconian measures of the past. New, high-quality websites are now ranking almost as quickly as their TrustRank levels warrant.

What this means for you is that you should keep your expectations low for the first few months of your website's life. If you're doing everything I recommend in this book, then within a couple of months you will see your site beginning to rank for lots of organic search terms. After 6 months, you should be getting a substantial number of visitors per month from your SEO efforts, resulting in new leads and sales. When I start a new website, I expect its success to depend on how interesting the content is to my potential customers. If I've done a bang-up job, I expect to have a real business going within 6 months. By a year and a half, I am usually dominating my website's niche.

You should not expect the exact same results as me, of course. It can take some time for all of this information to become second-nature. But the good news is that today you can at least reap the rewards of the work you've put into your website.

Time is not just a friend of your website; it is a friend of your website's *links*, as well. In the same way that Google takes a little while to trust a new website, it also takes a little while to trust a new link pointing to a website. As you begin the all-important process of attracting links, keep in mind that the links you secure today will impact your website's TrustRank—and hence, its rankings—several weeks later.

Final Thoughts

Congratulations on having made it through this chapter. It is, by itself, a record of everything that causes a website to rank on the first page of Google.

If you feel like you understood most of the information discussed, you officially know more about Google optimization than the vast majority of Internet business owners. Now it's time to deepen that knowledge.

3

How to Reel In Links

At this point, I am confident that you understand how important links are to your website's rankings. Now it's time to show you how to actually acquire them. The easiest way to get a link on another website is to ask the owner—by email, phone, smoke signal, or whatever. They will probably know how to do it; but if not, they can always ask whoever handles their web development. It should take about 2 minutes for them to decide whether it would suit them to link to your website.

Now, when I say that the easiest way to get a link is to ask the owner of the website for one, I am oversimplifying it a little bit; most webmasters are protective about links on their sites, thinking of them as Google does—as editorial votes that only merit passing out to highly worthy web pages. So for the most part, when you are trying to attain links, especially high-TrustRank ones, you have to be quite clever.

The art of convincing webmasters to link to your site is very similar to the art of publicity. It requires creativity, people skills, and the ability to "pitch." If you own a website, you've probably received emails from SEO companies asking you in one form or another to link to one of their clients' websites.

That kind of approach is what I *won't* be teaching you in this chapter. Instead, I focus on how to convey a kind of online charisma that makes the person receiving your email understand that there is real value in adding your link to their site.

Avoiding Bad Neighborhoods

Before learning the many exciting ways to acquire links, it is crucial that you understand which links are worth having. As mentioned in Chapter 1, "Trust: The Currency of Google," you do not want links from any website that promotes spam or adult content. Whereas for years the SEO community believed that links from other websites could not negatively affect a site's rankings (The reasoning went like this: "After all, how can you control who links to your site?"), by 2012, Google admitted that they, in fact, do. If we can set aside the implications of that admission—that "Google bowling," or competitors buying spammy links and pointing them to your website to lower your rankings, is possible—then Google's statement can simply be taken at face value. Generally speaking, if you can steer your website clear of bad associations, it'll stay in Google's good graces.

I doubt many readers of this book are involved in spam or adult content (if you are, oops—this book is about "white hat" SEO only). I emphasize this point only because, in the process of attracting links, you will undoubtedly come across emails from various SEO companies promising you "expert link building" or something of the sort, which usually means placement on hundreds of already penalized spam websites. Although joining up with spam networks such as these is often an innocent decision, to Google it's about as innocent as joining a devil-worshipping cult under the pretense that you were just trying to make new friends. Your "new friends" will surely ruin your reputation.

Far more common than enrolling oneself in a spam network is working with a third-party SEO vendor who engages in "gray-area" SEO practices. I might even go as far as to say that the majority of my company's clients came to us after having a scarring experience with a supposedly reputable SEO company. The reason this situation is so common is that Google's spam rules tightened dramatically between 2009 and 2013, and most companies that were around before then are still using their old practices. If you're thinking of using an SEO company for link building, let it be known that the following old-school practices no longer have any value:

- Buying links
- Trading links
- Getting links from directories

- Arranging paid blog posts
- Submitting to article banks
- Building websites solely for the purpose of linking

Although these practices are a step above linking your site to pornography or gambling websites, they have a very similar net effect. Whereas there has been a penalty for associating with a bad neighborhood in the early days of the search engine, Google covered the rest of their bases in 2012 with their Penguin update. Today, there is only one effective link-building method left: obtaining links in a natural way.

The good news for all of us trying to get our websites to rank highly on Google is that there is a huge amount of latitude in natural link building. There are as many ways to build links as there are ways to communicate the value of your business. And mastering this method will equip you with a business skill that is useful well beyond the field of SEO.

Link Building 101

By this point, you probably understand which sites you should *not* seek links on and which sites you *should* seek links on. It is probably worth reemphasizing that, when scouting out links, you should look to sites that already rank high on Google. Sites that don't rank high for the keywords that define their site probably have very low TrustRank and will not confer much ranking value on your website. With that in mind, here is a list of the places you should look for links first—the low-hanging fruit:

- **Websites belonging to family and friends**—Because any link on a "good neighborhood" site is a good link, why not start in the obvious place: your network of family and friends (see Figure 3.1)? Does your Uncle Dave have a blog? Does your cousin Suzie have a website for her start-up? Maybe your bro from college knows a guy who has a *Jersey Shore* fan site and would totally link to your business website if you asked him nicely. Work all those avenues!

- **Complementary websites in your industry**—Every business dwells in its own small universe, with many stars and planets circling around it or nearby. If you own a stapler company, you're in the same universe as staple remover companies, paper companies, paper clip companies, binder clip companies, and so on. These are perfect folks to ask for a link. Of course, you're also in the same universe as other stapler companies, but they'd like to crash their spaceships into your planet, so they're probably not the best candidates to approach.

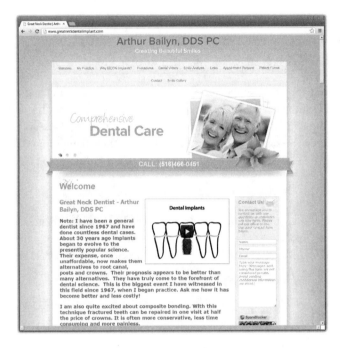

Figure 3.1 *My dad's dental website. It doesn't have that much TrustRank, but it's an easy link. I'll take it!*

 Tip

There *is* actually a way to get links from your competitors. While some will always ignore you, others may feel a kinship with you if you ask in the right way. Try something like: "I know we vie for the same customers, but working together is a lot more productive than pretending the other one doesn't exist. If we help each other to succeed, we can both take more of the pie as a result, and who knows, maybe we can even make the pie larger for all of us."

- **Guest posts**—If you consider yourself a true expert in your niche, you have the opportunity to use your knowledge to obtain links. Guest posts are a fairly common tactic in the link-building world, but they are still as valuable as ever. The way it works is simple: Approach the owners of high-TrustRank blogs and tell them you have been in the industry for *x* number of years and have an interesting point of view that you'd like to share with their audience. Say that you would be happy to publish a guest post on their blog free of charge. Common guest post etiquette is to place a small (sometimes even just one line) credit box after the post that links back to the guest blogger's website. Like with all content, the key to a successful guest posting strategy is quality. If you cough up an article just for the sake of the link, the blogger who owns the site will probably not accept it; and even if they do, your post is a public reflection of your expertise, so you'd be squandering your opportunity to entice new business from the blog's readers— not to mention depriving yourself of an excellent example guest post to show other bloggers when you approach them. Figure 3.2 shows a guest post that I wrote.

Figure 3.2 *A guest post I did for a social media blog. I worked hard to write a great post, not just for the link, but for the positive exposure to this blog's audience.*

At this point, I anticipate that some of you are teeming with ideas about how to get links for your site. Others, however, are probably thinking, "It's all well and good to tell us these strategies, but I'm not sure I'll be able to implement them." Indeed, link building is a skill that takes a certain personality, patience, and dedication. The ideal link builder, in my mind, is part creative, part salesperson, and part soldier— not an easy combination to find. However, it's important to realize that you don't need to be perfect at it to succeed. In fact, you don't even need to do it yourself if you can afford to hire someone to be specifically dedicated to it.

Most of link building comes down to knowing how to write an effective email. What you are essentially doing is relating to another person. When we relate to other people, we don't just talk; we listen. The most interesting person in the world is not going to make any meaningful connections if he doesn't acknowledge the needs and wants of the people around him. Writing about this subject reminds me of the countless conversations I've had with guy friends who have failed at online dating.

Many guys who are new to online dating write to women and tell them all about themselves. Perhaps they'll relate to one thing on the woman's profile, but by and large, their message will be a self-presentation. This type of approach doesn't get responses; I'd call it the main reason why so many guys complain about not getting replies when they reach out to women online. The better way to craft a message is to seize upon an important detail in the woman's profile and make your message about *her*. For instance, "I see your favorite book is _____. If you like that book, I know you would absolutely love _____ by _____. It takes the main conclusion and sheds a new light on it."

You might continue with an emotional insight: "It seems from your profile that you are a really practical person, but with a streak of idealism that maybe you keep hidden a lot of the time." Again, keeping the conversation about her. Afterward, you would want to include one thing about yourself. Say, "I find I'm the same way; I've always wanted to be a screenwriter, but I've also enjoyed my career as a paramedic." It is not necessary to say much more about yourself on the first communication; the goal is simply to receive a response. Once you do, you are far freer to open up and make the conversation about both of you.

Now let's move back to link building. The most common type of email I see when someone is seeking a link goes something like this:

Subject: Link Offer

Dear Webmaster:

I am working on behalf of bobslawfirm.com. We are seeking a high-quality link exchange that will benefit both of our websites. Would you be interested? If not, I would be willing to pay for a small text-based advertisement on your site.

Thanks,

Shubi J.
Linkpartners.org

Most people would be about as eager to reply to this kind of email as they would to an email telling them they've just won the Nigerian lottery. Putting aside the fact that Shubi here is suggesting two ideas that could easily result in a penalty from Google, his main offense is that he didn't take the person on the other side of the email into account. Just using the word *webmaster* doomed his chances from the start. Personally, whenever I receive an email that starts with "Dear Webmaster," I delete it without reading further.

The better approach is to do research on the person you're emailing (noting, of course, that it's a person, not a website, you're writing to) before you even type the first word. What does she publish on her website? What does she seem to care about most? Do you know anything personal about her from a bio that may be present on the site, or perhaps elsewhere on the Internet?

Following is an example of an email that has all the elements of success in securing a link. The person reaching out is from a recycling company and the website being targeted is an environmental blog.

> Subject: A Compliment and an Idea
>
> Hi Teri,
>
> My name is John Smith. I found your blog recently through a Google search and I've genuinely enjoyed reading your articles. My favorites were "A Green Masterpiece" and "Aluminum Can-Can." I sense that you and I share a common goal of making the world a better place.
>
> Myself, I run Recyclezone.com, a site that is dedicated to making people aware of their local recycling centers. I just put up a new article on clever ways to recycle your old phones that I think fits well into the ethos of your site. I'm wondering if you'd consider covering it in an upcoming blog post? Thanks in advance either way, and keep up the great writing.
>
> Best,
>
> John Smith
> Recyclezone.com

Similar to what we saw in the dating scenario, John's focus was on Teri's website—rather than his own website—from the start. He also struck an emotional chord when he talked about a potential common purpose at the end of the first paragraph. In my experience, an email like would receive a response one in five times. Why only one in five? Simply because it's hard to get a response to a "cold" email no matter what you say. In contrast, the email from Shubi would get a response about 1 in 100 times.

Another approach that I have found effective is writing a short, to-the-point, informal email. People are somewhat used to receiving link requests as "pitches"; imagine if they got an email like shown here:

Subject: Hey Teri

Teri, hope all is well. Just put up an article you will love; it's called "Tin Towers." Let me know what you think, and if you'd like to cover it on your blog.

John Smith
Recyclezone.com

Ultimately, those who can relate best to others and think of the most creative ways to request a link will come out ahead. In a few pages, I reveal every way I can imagine to acquire links. But while we're still talking Links 101, I'd like to make sure that you can justify the presence of your link to reluctant webmasters.

While performing link outreach, many people receive replies that go something like this: "I think your site is interesting, but I'm not sure where I'd put a link since I don't usually write about other websites."

This is a good position to be in, as long as you can provide a good reason to host your link. The right response is this: "Thanks for your email. I have a couple of ideas about where you could mention my website in a way that adds value for your visitors."

From there, you can suggest one of the following locations:

- **The home page**—Google tends to give more TrustRank to links from home pages because placement on the cover of a website signals value. However, asking for a link on someone's home page can feel over-reaching unless there is a clear place for it. Most blogs have a blog roll, a listing of favorite websites, right on their home page. This is an ideal place for a link to your website if the website owner is willing to add it. Sometimes you can find the equivalent of a blog roll in a Friends, Partners, or Favorite Websites area (see Figure 3.3). While getting a link on a site's home page is quite valuable, you wouldn't want the majority of your links to be on home pages because it would look suspicious to Google. After all, the majority of links on the web are on inside pages—pages other than your home page.

- **A Resources page**—Many websites have a page that links out to other websites that they find useful (see Figure 3.4). Usually, this is called a Resources page. If you ever get turned down by a webmaster who says there is no room for your link, you might politely suggest adding a Resources page to his site and including your link on it.

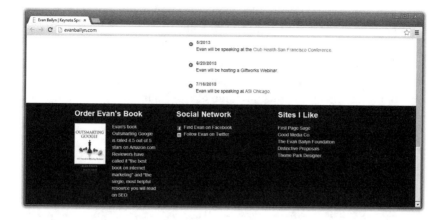

Figure 3.3 *A list of links on the bottom of my professional site under the heading "Sites I Like." This list of links does not interfere with my site's aesthetic or draw much traffic, but each link passes TrustRank to the website it points to.*

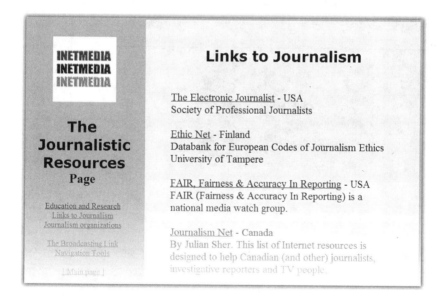

Figure 3.4 *A Resources page: a great place to host links when there is no other convenient spot on a website.*

- **Within a blog post or article**—Probably the most common place to obtain a link is within a regularly updated blog. If any page of your website (including an article on your own blog) relates to a topic that another blog typically covers, you have a clear opening. For instance, if you sell city guides and you come across a travel blog, it makes sense to ask the owner if they would mention your guides in one of their upcoming blogs. Keep in mind, once again, that you will be much more successful getting a link if you make a thoughtful, personal appeal to the person you're writing to. Perhaps the blogger once complained about the limitations of a particular travel guide he used. In your initial email, you might remind him of his frustration with the other guide and explain how yours excels in the areas the other one lacks. Hook him on the uniqueness of your guide, and he may just decide to feature your company—and link to your site—in an upcoming post (see Figure 3.5).

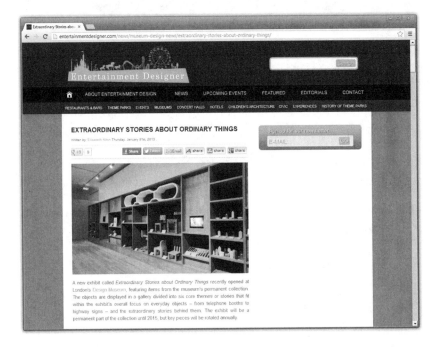

Figure 3.5 *A blog post linking to a museum's website. This is the kind of link that could have resulted from the museum reaching out to the blog, citing its past coverage of museum design. This particular blog would be a good potential target for the museum's marketing department.*

With this basic tutorial, you should now have a way to get started on your link-building journey. Just utilizing these tactics alone, you could build 50+ links inside of a year and reach the first page of Google for a medium-competitive keyword (assuming you have proper meta page titles and URL structure, of course). But this first push will not be enough to rank on the first page for highly competitive keywords. Are you ready for the big guns?

The Bible of Link Acquisition

In the coming sections, I include every tactic for gaining links that I can think of. Most of them fall into one of two broad categories:

- Systematic emailing involves doing a lot of repetitive work to gain links, and I recommend getting an employee or intern to do these tasks after you've mastered them yourself.
- Link bait, or creating something so interesting or useful that people really want to link to it, is a highly creative—and sometimes quite ambitious—endeavor.

Systematic Emailing

The surest way to get a large volume of links is through good old-fashioned cold emailing. Find a list of webmasters in a specific niche, put their names, websites, and email addresses into a table, and then go down the list, writing a personalized email requesting a link to each person. This method has garnered me many links. Earlier in this chapter, I gave an example of a simple customizable email you might send to a website from which you are seeking a link. The more you personalize your emails, the higher your response rate will be.

Systematic emailing should be a crucial part of all your link-building efforts. No matter which of the following link bait techniques you use, you need to tell people about your content; otherwise, they won't know about it. Even the most viral videos on the Internet didn't become popular until a few key websites shared them.

Link Bait

Fishermen know this: You're not going to catch the fish without the bait. In the case of online marketing, the bait is content so interesting, funny, or useful that people can't help but to share it with others. Link bait can be in the form of an article, video, chart, graph, image, cartoon, infographic, slide show, or any other type of content you can think of. Basically, if it will get webmasters to share it with their audience, it is effective link bait. I've seen link bait succeed in the form of a downloadable scientific research paper, and I've seen it succeed in the form of a picture of a golden retriever in a tutu.

Of course, you want your content to be targeted—that is, of interest to the people who buy whatever it is you sell. And rest assured, no matter what niche your business lies in, there is a way to come up with content that will grab the attention of your potential customers.

Following are some forms of link bait that have worked well for me.

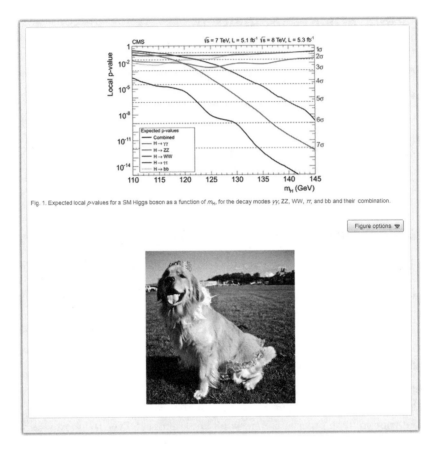

Figure 3.6 *Successful link bait comes in many different forms.*

Create Funny or Ridiculous Content

Got a penchant for humor? An eye for the outlandish? Even if your site is completely serious, there is always room for an offbeat-yet-tasteful section, and it doesn't even need to be linked from a place where your everyday visitors will see it (that is, your home page). Many sites will link to your website if the people behind it find your content genuinely entertaining, and those links will count toward your site's overall link popularity.

So what kind of crazy stuff could you create? Well, it depends on your industry. I have had the good fortune of running an online paper doll site for girls, which gave me the opportunity to create dress-up dolls of characters that weren't just for kids. For instance, during the 2008 primaries, I created dress-up dolls of then-candidates Barack Obama, Rudy Giuliani, and Hillary Clinton. I made sure to look up all I could about their personal lives first so that I could add all kinds of gimmicks—from campaigning props to college sweatshirts—that political junkies would get a kick out of. My goal was to attract at least 10 links from political sites and maybe even the online versions of newspapers because I knew those sites carried a lot of TrustRank. With that goal in mind, I emailed about 50 political writers whose names and email addresses I got from a site that rounds up articles by various pundits. I told them merely that I had created these dress-up dolls, that they could find them at a particular URL on my website, and that I hoped they would have some fun with them. Figure 3.7 shows one of the dress-up dolls I sent them.

Figure 3.7 *A dress-up doll of Barack Obama I created in 2008 to "bait" political websites to link to my kids' paper doll site.*

The dress-up dolls were a hit. They attracted links from 34 different websites, most of them blogs. The writers apparently found the dolls wacky enough that they just *had* to share them. And the jewel of the whole effort was the fact that the *New York Times* blog picked it up as well, delivering my site a gloriously high TrustRank link.

When trying to procure funny material, it helps a great deal to use people or subjects that already matter a lot to people. Politics is an especially fertile ground for humor because people take it so seriously. And if you satirize a political figure, you stand to benefit from the many people who dislike that figure, or at least find him or her too stuck up for his own good.

During the time of the Eliot Spitzer scandal, for instance, we had a moment when a man whom many people disliked was publicly embarrassed. I guarantee that if you had taken action the moment the news broke, writing a mock public apology from the desk of Eliot Spitzer or a song that made fun of his perceived hypocrisies, people would have loved it. Whatever site you hosted this content on would have gotten links aplenty. The same with Tiger Woods. If you do a Google search for `tiger woods humor` or `tiger woods funny`, you will see dozens of joke pieces that people created to capitalize on his 2009 cheating scandal. And so, while I'm not necessarily telling you to use people's tragedies for your own benefit, I am telling you to use topics of mass public interest to attract links because many people already find them fascinating.

But be careful not to be too general. Lots of things are universally funny, such as tripping and falling, but the Internet is built around niche interest groups. So if your site can attract the attention of political junkies, or car lovers, or lawyers, or equestrians, it will quickly spread around to the many websites in that contingent's circle and garner you a payload of links.

To give you another example of a successful piece of link bait catering to a niche group, a few years ago I created a humorous website on a domain I owned, www.irony.com. Because I wasn't doing anything with this great domain name, I figured I would try to create a highly linkable website and see what happened. I hired an artist to draw cartoons that satirized different issues of importance to many people, targeting a number of different interest groups. One of these groups was Internet geeks. Figure 3.8 shows a cartoon I came up with, called *If the World Wide Web Were a City*.

Figure 3.8 *A cartoon called* If the World Wide Web Were a City, *which I created to attract links to my website from Internet tech websites.*

This cartoon drew the attention of about 15 blogs and computer interest sites after it was featured on the home page of a particularly popular blog.

Just be careful; people can be sensitive. Use your judgment to make wise decisions based on the comfort level of your intended audience.

Create Interesting Content

Although humor is a particularly popular content category, it falls within a larger category that matters much more: things that are interesting. If you can make something that someone will look at and say "Hmm!" you've just created an excellent piece of link bait.

Of course, many things could be considered interesting, but the Internet makes it much easier for us to know what people like. If you want to know which videos people find the most interesting, for instance, look on YouTube's Popular on YouTube channel. If you want to know which news stories people find the most interesting, look at the front page of Google News or Yahoo! News. If you want to know which topics people are talking about the most, look at Google Trends or the Trending Topics area of Twitter. These are all excellent ways to draw inspiration for your very own piece of interesting content.

Another thing I like to do is Google `most shared Facebook stories 2014` (you can insert any recent year). This gives a clear idea of what people were fascinated with in a particular year. As a creator of link bait, I am more interested in the approach the article's writer took rather than the content itself. Specifically, I look for the following things:

- **Topic**—Was the article on a massively popular topic such as health, celebrities, or holidays? Or did the writer find success with a more niche topic like archaeology?

- **Title**—Was it a superlative title such as "The Best Brownie Recipe of All Time" or a title that challenged people's common perceptions such as "Sunscreen Is Bad For You"? Perhaps it simply covered an amazing event: "Man Falls Into Grand Canyon, Lives."

- **Layout**—Was the article a straight news story with paragraphs and one or two pictures? Or maybe a slide show with long captions? Some popular stories are short and sweet but have a viral video embedded into them.

- **Writing style**—Did the writer take a high-minded journalistic approach or a cutesy second person stance using lots of "You's" and "Your's"? Maybe the piece read like a campfire story.

You can learn a lot by studying what's already worked. In fact, that's probably the best way to learn almost anything. Because articles are the most common form of interesting content, I have spent years studying viral articles to increase my odds of creating more of them myself. I found that certain themes tend to be particularly interesting to people (see Figure 3.9).

POPULAR ARTICLE THEMES

Best and Worst
"Cheese declared best in world auctioned for $8400"
Uncomfortable Situations
"The day I came out to my 10-year-old daughter"
Scandal
"Angry Birds impostor strikes Android users"
Precious Things
"Governor asks Fed to stop horse slaughterhouse"
Money
"The world's least affordable cities"
Overcoming the odds
"Grandpa wins a billion dollars in 20-year patent dispute"

Figure 3.9 *Some of the most popular themes for articles.*

You don't have to report breaking news or publish a brilliant piece of journalism to make good link bait. You can simply give your outlook on a news story in an original way, or even just find some cool pictures and put them in an unusual context. For example, one piece of content my company created for a client's website was called "15 Incredible Animal Emotions" (see Figure 3.10). It was just a series of pictures of animals that seemed to correspond to different human emotions—a dog looking sad, a cat looking mad, a squirrel looking curious—but presenting them as an exposé on animal emotions got the site more than 100 links!

Top 10 Lists

I could have discussed top 10 lists in the preceding section, but they're so important that they require their own heading. People love lists. David Letterman has proved this over many years of reading a top 10 list every night. There's something very appealing about the existence of an official list where only 10 items have "made" it and only *one* item resides at #1. I might even go as far as to say that top 10 lists are the quickest, easiest form of link bait.

Imagine, like Dr Doolittle, we could talk to the animals. We would no longer have to try and figure out what they were thinking or feeling; we'd be able to get the information first-hand. But then do animals really feel emotion, or is it pure anthropomorphism on our part - a wish to see human behavior and characteristics where they don't necessarily exist?

Yet, when you see the helplessness in abused animals, the intense sadness of a mother gorilla that has recently lost her baby or the abandoned joy of a dog simply running after a stick – how can we say animals don't feel? It would be

Figure 3.10   *A picture essay on animal emotions my company created for a client's blog.*

Another great thing about top 10 lists is that they can be written for almost any kind of website. If you're in an industry where you can unbutton your top shirt button, you can write a top 10 list for your website. To prove my point, here are some examples spanning vastly different fields, beginning with the starchiest:

- **Accounting**—Top 10 Most Annoying Things About QuickBooks
- **Real estate**—Top 10 Most Expensive Homes Sold in This Decade
- **Law**—Top 10 Most Impactful Decisions in the Modern Era
- **Jewelry**—Top 10 Gaudiest Engagement Rings
- **Dog training**—Top 10 Must-Knows for the Advanced Show Dog
- **Pest control**—Top 10 Scariest Insects Ever to Invade a Home
- **Music**—Top 10 Greatest Rockers of the Twentieth Century

Top 10 lists give us license to be superlative. What is the best, the greatest, the most essential of your field? That kind of information interests people—and will earn you links.

Compendiums

If this chapter were online, it would probably get a lot of links. Why? Because it's a compendium: a definitive, organized set of information. I intentionally named this section something cool sounding, "The Bible of Link Acquisition," so that it would get psychological credit for being a comprehensive resource. Even if I have missed a link-acquisition technique in this chapter, its name is confident enough to cause people to link to it. You can do the same in your industry, no matter what it is. And, as with top 10 lists, your creativity is key. I'll brainstorm through a number of examples, and my doing so should spark an idea or two for you.

My first example has nothing to do with any website I can picture a reader of this book having, but I think a list and description of every candy ever made would be awesome. I guarantee that if you created *The Ultimate Candy Encyclopedia*, it would get a ton of links because so many people would like to get the official background on their favorite childhood candies. If that has anything to do with your business, please do it. Next time I'm in the mood for something sweet (probably in about an hour), I'll thank you for it.

Here are compendium ideas across a few different industries:

- **Sports**—A glossary of sports terms (*strike, let, balk, nutmeg, shuttlecock*—there's plenty of great material there).

- **Environmental**—A Green People directory. It might not be the first compendium that comes to mind for the environmental industry, but there are already so many green dictionaries. I would think it would be cool to compile a list of the people who are most influential in the green world. I haven't seen that done before, and I believe that if you wrote up bios of even the green industry folks who don't have Wikipedia pages it would attract links for being an original and interesting compendium.

- **Horticulture**—A list of endangered plants. Compendiums of natural wonders are particularly fascinating to people of all ages. Add a sense of limitedness (hence the *endangered, rare* adjectives), and you have a very link-worthy list.

- **Fashion**—A timeline of fashion throughout the past century. Although this sort of idea has been done before, I believe it would be interesting to many people, especially if categorized by social class so as to capture the full spectrum of fashion in each decade.

- **City culture**—A guide to bathrooms in the city. Bathrooms are a part of every restaurant and nightclub, and everyone has a personal experience with them, but few people publicly comment on them. So I think it would make an engaging list. Even if you start with just one tiny area of the city and try to evaluate every bathroom, I can guarantee you that anyone who sees your list will be intrigued by it. That means links.

When you're thinking about making a compendium—be it a dictionary, glossary, encyclopedia, or plain old list—here are a few things to keep in mind:

- Try to limit your time expenditure on this project to a certain number of hours, days, or weeks. After all, a compendium is meant to be link bait and not a direct route to sales. So although it justifies a real time commitment, it should not distract you from focusing on your core business responsibilities.

- It doesn't have to be exhaustive; it just has to have enough information that it can pass as exhaustive.

- You can get almost all the information from the Internet. That means it won't be hard to collect. Just try to get your info from credible sources. People appreciate that.

- You need to tell people about it or else your awesome compendium might never be seen. If it's cool enough, sending a personalized email to 25 blogs that are somewhat related to your compendium should do the trick; after all, it takes just one or two good mentions to make a piece of content go viral.

Contests

Self-servingly, contests usually give something away so as to attract attention. Attention can easily equal links, especially if your contest is interesting or offers a good prize. Take a treasure hunt, for instance. I hadn't thought about clue-driven quests for a while until I saw a link for a modern-day treasure hunt on a blog. While checking the links for the website that was holding this treasure hunt, I saw that dozens of other sites also found this concept cool enough to link to, including several online newspapers. (To learn how to see all the links pointing to a website, check out "Link Reverse Engineering" later in this chapter. I expand on this subject even further in Chapter 6, "Tracking Your Progress with Google Analytics and Other Helpful Tools.") With the same money and creative resources, this treasure hunt site could have built a compendium or interesting online tool. But instead, they buried some gold coins probably worth a few thousand dollars, wrote 10 clues, and emailed some blogs to tell them about it. The cool nature of their contest took care of the rest, earning their website a ton of TrustRank.

A tried-and-true method to draw links to your contest is to involve the followers of your brand. The classic case study is a cutest pet contest. People love their animals and take any opportunity to get them featured as the cutest or the best at anything. If your site has any lifestyle component to it and already has at least a few thousand visitors per month, try holding a cutest pet contest. After you have a few hundred entries, put a picture of each pet on its own unique page, and then tell everyone that the one with the most online votes will win a year's supply of pet food and supreme recognition on your website. People's reactions will be to immediately send out emails, publish blog entries, and post all over their social media sites "Vote for my dog on this website!" Every blog entry from a contest entrant is a potential link for your site, and some of the social media pages may be as well.

This concept can be applied to many things that people become passionate about. Cutest baby, best nature photograph, and coolest car are three photo-related contests that jump to mind. Videos are great, too, because most computers and many phones have simple video-creation functionality. I think that best singer, best dancer, most talented pet, and funniest baby are good subjects for video contests. If you want to keep it simple, you can hold a community member of the month contest or most inspiring teacher contest asking for a few sentences about why a person in one of your readers' communities should be recognized on your site. Even if you just get 10 good entries, your contest page will still get a lot of links as people spread the word about their favorite entry.

Press

Press is exposure, and in today's Internet-driven society, that equals links. Investing in a good publicist was one of the best decisions I ever made. Having worked with two different publicists in the past 5 years, I have found that if you can find someone affordable, publicity can be a real boon for your business. It can provide credibility, new business connections, better customer conversion on your website, and links all at once.

There are generally two types of press hits:

- **National**—The most obvious type is a big national hit, where you get that dream phone call from your publicist: "I'm calling to tell you that I have just secured a feature on your company in the *New York Times*." Even a less-substantial outlet like a radio show or cable TV station can get your business's phone ringing. This is the best type of press hit in terms of overall potential.

- **Blogs and Internet publications**—The more common type of press hit in the media world of today takes place on a website. For link-acquisition purposes, it is better to get published on a small blog than in the print version of the *Wall Street Journal* (although, of course, the effects of such a prestigious hit could be far more valuable for your business overall), which is why many publicists are more concerned about their relationships with top bloggers than with traditional journalists. Naturally, there are tiers within the category of blogs. Depending on your industry, there are the A-level blogs—TechCrunch and Mashable for tech, Engadget and Gizmodo for gadgets, Perez Hilton and TMZ for Celebrity gossip, and so on—the B-levels, and all the way down to the newcomers that nobody has heard of.

If you do hire a publicist, make sure that from the beginning you clearly articulate your expectations for the campaign. Your goals should be greater exposure for your business, new links, and new sales. By those standards, one hit on a small unknown blog would not be an acceptable outcome for a month's work. Several hits on small blogs would be great for your TrustRank, however, so that might be a good use of your money. (Figure 3.11 shows a press hit from a small blog.)

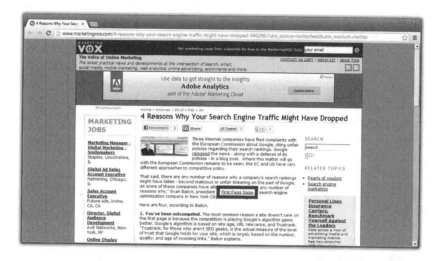

Figure 3.11   *A typical press hit from a small blog containing a link to my website.*

Even just one hit on a specialized industry blog that hundreds of potential customers read would be an excellent outcome. You should evaluate your publicist's success according to the following rules:

- Hits on small blogs that few people read are only valuable for their links, so you would need several of them per month to make a successful outcome.

- Hits on niche industry sites can be valuable for exposure, new customers, and new links; one per month in addition to a few other less-significant hits would be a good outcome.

- Hits on large, popular blogs are exceptionally valuable because of their high TrustRank levels and can also yield exposure, customers, and business development opportunities; one every few months would be an excellent result.

- Online and local radio shows, regional TV spots, and hometown newspapers tend not to be particularly valuable hits; they usually do not produce links and, apart from the potential for phone calls from friends who heard your interview and think you're cool, don't lead to much business.

Widgets

A widget is a small online application that helps people do something simple, such as editing a photo, creating an icon, or looking up the meaning of a name. You can easily place a widget on any web page, and almost all widgets contain a link to the site that created it. A widget is an excellent way to attract links to your website.

The key to making this strategy work is to create a widget that is so interesting or useful that lots of webmasters want to place it on their sites. Facebook, for example, has done an excellent job making widgets that people genuinely want to put on their sites. One of Facebook's widgets displays your brand page's latest status updates and number of "likes" (see Figure 3.12). Because people often want to show off their Facebook page on their company website, this widget is widely used and amounts to tens of thousands of links back to Facebook.

Figure 3.12   *The Facebook fan page widget, which I display on my personal website.*

Another exceptionally popular widget—and, in fact, one of the best examples of link bait I have ever seen—is the statcounter.com widget. This tiny box goes at the bottom of your website and simply displays how many times your website has been visited in the past 30 days (see Figure 3.13). If you click it, it brings you to that site's web statistics page on statcounter.com. Because thousands of people like the idea of publicly displaying their visitor count, statcounter.com has become a Goliath of link popularity and ranks exceptionally high on Google. It even has a PageRank of 9. Offering this widget for free was a brilliant move by statcounter.com and has been the key to the wide exposure the company has received.

Figure 3.13   *One of statcounter.com's simple, free widgets that measure website hits. You can place this at the bottom of your website if you want to show visitors your site traffic.*

A widget I also like a great deal was conceived by a site called 1800Recycling.com. They offer a free little search box that tells you the location of your nearest recycling center (see Figure 3.14). A simple idea, this widget appears on many high-TrustRank websites, conferring tremendous SEO value on their website.

Figure 3.14   *The Recycling Location Finder widget created by 1800Recycling.com.*

This should give you an idea about what widgets are and how their simplicity makes them so appealing. Creating one, however, is not always easy. It requires an experienced programmer who has made widgets before. Depending on the complexity of programming behind the widget, it can become costly to produce. To give you a relative scale, a widget that converts users' text into a shareable online badge would probably be on the lower end of the price scale, costing about as much as a new computer. A widget that reports the rock density of a given land mass by latitudinal and longitudinal points, however, could have expensive technology behind it and cost as much as a car.

Social Media and Social Bookmarking Sites

Creating a page on a social media site and listing your website on it seems like a great way to get a valuable website to link to you. But as we know by now, all the big social media sites place no-follow tags on their outbound links, preventing TrustRank from passing to other websites. However, hundreds of smaller social media sites offer you the opportunity to create a free profile, on which you can place your link. Many of them do not use a no-follow tag on their links.

 Note

Want to see a thorough listing of most of the social media sites out there? Check out http://traffikd.com/social-media-websites/.

Social bookmarking sites—websites where users post links to interesting content and discover new websites—are another way to get backlinks. However, many of the popular social bookmarking sites use no-follow tags. Others employ the rather clever system of no-follow-tagging all new content but automatically removing those tags when the content reaches a certain level of popularity within the community. This kind of policy points to a more general rule that you should keep in mind if you plan to make social media and social bookmarking sites a part of your link-building strategy: You will succeed if, and only if, you produce great content. Even putting aside the fact that many social sites simply don't pass TrustRank, the greatest reward for submitting content to these kinds of sites is the potential for your content to become popular and get picked up by other websites, resulting in a payload of new links. And so once again, I implore you to focus on creating excellent content.

Awards

If you think your site has any prominence within your industry (oh hell, even if it doesn't!), come up with an award to give out to certain websites. These sites can be within your industry or in a related industry. The key to this kind of link bait is that your "award" is a graphic that the winning sites place on their home or about page, which links back to your website.

When creating an award, focus on quality. Have an excellent graphic designer make the award so that sites will want to feature it. Think carefully about the recipients of the award: Do they truly deserve this award, and would other people feel the same way? Even more important, does this award recognize a characteristic that they value highly and would be beneficial for them to display on their websites? For instance, because of the value of recruiting good employees, many companies would be thrilled to receive a Best Places to Work award. This would attract

job applicants. Another example: Best Web Design. Any site that has clearly done
something original with its design would love to receive recognition for it. But be
sure not to give the Best Web Design award to a company that doesn't take pride
in their design; it will just be wasted. Your recipient should feel they worked hard
for, and highly deserve, your award.

When thinking about awards as link bait, it is important to address the psychology
behind the act. If your award is simply a ruse to acquire links, it probably will not
succeed. For people to care about this award, it needs to be conceived genuinely.
It's okay to have an eye on marketing, but authenticity always goes a long way.
So think about an award you feel qualified to give—in an area in which you're an
expert—and prepare yourself to truly get behind the effort.

When informing site owners that they have won an award, be sure to word
your messaging carefully. The voice of your email should be warm yet serious.
Something like this:

> Subject: Excellence in Customer Service Award
>
> Dear Recipient.com:
>
> I am writing to say congratulations on behalf of ABCstaffing.com.
> We've chosen your site as a winner of this year's Excellence in
> Customer Service Award. As a staffing agency that has been in the
> business of placing qualified candidates in jobs for over a decade, we
> know good customer service when we see it. Recipient.com is a leader
> in this category, and we are proud to have selected it from among 500
> candidates to receive this award. To see all the winners, please visit our
> awards page.
>
> The attached graphic may be added to your site's home page or about
> page simply by copying the attached code into the HTML of the page.
> If you have any questions, please feel free to contact Bob Smith at
> 212-XXX-XXXX.
>
> Keep up the great work!
>
> Sally Anne Jones, CEO
> ABCstaffing.com
> www.yoursite.com
> 212-555-2364

Take special note of the mention of "the attached code" in this email. Any web
designer can provide you with code that adds a graphic to a website. The purpose
of giving the award recipients a code is ostensibly so that it will be easier for them

to place it on their websites, but it is also to ensure that the graphic links back to your site. And if they choose to add the graphic without the link (which some companies might do), make sure the name of your company is at the bottom of the award. It won't help your site's TrustRank, but it might send over some visitors.

Here are some other nice touches for your award:

- Mail a physical copy of the email to the recipients on your company stationary to give it that old-fashioned, take-me-seriously feel.
- Establish a yearly tradition of giving out the award so that you can refer to the award's history each successive year when you give out the award (Our Third Annual Best Marketing Award).
- Do some press—or at least some press releases—around the award so that when recipients Google it there is something for them to look at.

Guest Posts

Most blogs, including the prominent ones, are always looking for material. A guest post is a welcome suggestion to the owners of these blogs, providing that the post is well written, on topic, interesting, and not too self-serving. Reaching out to blogs to secure a guest post is the kind of job that a publicist usually handles for you, but you can easily do it yourself. The goal of a guest post (in addition to the visibility it may get you) is the link to your website that is typically included in your accompanying bio.

To score a guest post on a popular blog, you need to be good at "pitching," but in all truth, this is not so hard for anyone with good people skills and writing ability. Just compose an earnest, mildly flattering email suggesting that you contribute a blog post and include some reasons why you are qualified to write such a post. Spin that bio of yours as best you can; work those accomplishments! This is the time when they need to shine.

If you are not confident in your ability to sell your guest post to the owner or editor of the blog, hire a writer to do the pitch and—if successful—the blog post for you. A tip on hiring writers: There are many great ones out there who are just getting started and don't charge much. You do not need anyone beyond a bright recent college grad, and you do not need to pay a lot of money for this task.

To guide you in the right direction, here is an email I sent to the owner of a popular Facebook blog requesting a guest post.

Hey Guys,

I am a daily reader of Facebookblog.com. It has replaced TechCrunch as my #1 read. I would love to do a guest post explaining how to get tens of thousands of fans for your personal brand. I have 57,000 fans all gained within the past 8 months. There are very few non-celebrities besides me with that level of fans.

If this idea is interesting for you, I can write up a draft for you today.

Thanks for taking the time to read my email.

Best,

Evan Bailyn

If you are concerned that you don't have a standout accomplishment to mention in your email like my number of Facebook fans, don't sweat it. You just need to prove your expertise in the area that the blog covers, and often people will be impressed if *you* believe your accomplishments are impressive. Even if the best recognition you've received is a science award in high school, you can still call yourself "award-winning"; you don't need to get into how your science teacher printed the award on his home computer and made a copy for each of the 20 students in your class. The other route is to state that you have done extensive research on the topic and would like to report your findings. Ah, and what better transition into our next link-acquisition strategy?

Research Results

One of the awesome things about the Internet is that anyone can become a journalist or researcher. If I take a survey of 500 people of varying demographic characteristics and then write up a well thought-out analysis of my findings and it gets published on a high traffic blog, it will probably reach more people than research conducted at significant expense that is published in a trade journal. Granted, it might be trusted less, but that's not the point here; the point is that research is a respected form of content that *you* can create—and it can be a great way to get a link from another website.

The trick here, as in many other link-acquisition techniques, is to make the research results interesting and relevant to the site you are pitching it to and to write the email in a genuine but excitement-inducing way. Let me bring you through an example. Suppose, for instance, that I want to get a link on a big social media blog. I begin by identifying what the blog cares about. A social media blog exists for the purpose of observing the phenomenon of people being social on the

Internet. In a larger sense, this kind of blog probably sees itself as a beacon of the progress of the Internet in our society. This is just my hunch. So I would think that a survey which finds that people have deeper relationships with friends they meet online than friends they meet in person would be very interesting to them; it would signal a major societal change.

Now, obviously, I am not going to submit this information unless it's true and I have a reasonable way of taking the survey. So I am going to test it. The only cost-efficient way for me to do this is by polling the members of my website. After I get at least a few hundred, or (fingers crossed) even a thousand responses, I will make my conclusion. It is essential, however, that I do not rely on the results of my poll alone. I must analyze these results and publish my analysis on a page of my website that is well designed and includes cool charts and graphs. After the information has been neatly packaged, it is ready to be pitched. If you make the subject of your email a few-word summary of the results, your email is likely to be read.

One site that I love to read is called rjmetrics.com. It is one of the better procurers of research that I've seen. Granted, it is a research company, not a business that is looking to publish some interesting research results to get a link. But its authors write analytical blog entries so well, coming up with original findings on topics that range from Twitter to sports feats. In one blog entry, the company researched the likelihood that a minor league baseball player would break the league's all-time hitting streak (see Figure 3.15).

A website that covers minor league baseball would very likely be intrigued by this study and link to rjmetrics.com's blog. The presentation of information in this blog post is well executed. There is a simple-looking graph of the probability of this player breaking the record, followed by a chart of probabilities of him achieving certain hitting milestones. Any similarly competent explanation of a study—no matter how carefully the study was conducted—would attract links from blogs.

"Link-Only" Photos

Not a photographer? Wait, don't skip this section yet! One of the cleverest ways I've seen people attract links to their sites is by having a page of their own interesting photos on their website. Every webmaster knows the difficulty of obtaining photos for his or her site. Most companies pay a stock photo site for images; however, the same stock images are usually found on multiple websites, shattering the illusion that those professional-looking folks actually work at your office. The other option—getting professional photos—is expensive. There is a third option that is becoming increasingly common, and that is taking photos that are licensed under the "attribution" condition of Creative Commons. If you've never heard of Creative Commons, it is a set of standards for the ways artists' work can be used on the Internet. The "attribution" condition basically states that you can use certain artists' photos on the Web as long as you link back to their owners' website. For the owners of the photographs, this can create a gold mine of links. Of course, this form of link bait only works if your photos are both interesting and applicable to the various needs of webmasters.

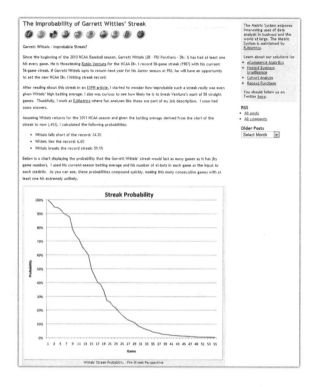

Figure 3.15   *A blog that presents homegrown research very neatly, tempting other websites to link to it.*

Here is the link to the Creative Commons search engine so that you can browse the tens of thousands of images that can be licensed in this way:

http://search.creativecommons.org

If you're thinking that this link-acquisition strategy is not for you, keep in mind that you don't need to be a professional photographer to gather interesting images. With most of today's phones capable of taking high-quality photos, anyone can snap a masterpiece. It could be fun to try your hand at taking useful or striking photos; or, failing that, perhaps you could hire an amateur photographer to take some photos for you. Amateur photographers, like writers, are often not going to charge a lot for their work.

Link Reverse Engineering

With a bit of simple know-how, anyone can see the links pointing to a given website. I will give you that simple know-how: http://ahrefs.com. This is the URL of the only reliable tool I've found for showing all the links a website has accumulated. Although a paid tool, I've found it to pay off in spades when it comes to measuring your own link progress and peeking at your competitors'. No doubt there are free tools that list links, but I haven't found one that is both comprehensive and supported by a reputable company. It seems most of them are created by SEO companies as a form of link bait and are rarely updated because they don't bring in any revenue directly.

To see all the links pointing to a given website, just go to ahrefs.com and in the search box type in any website. That will bring you to the Overview page. Click the External tab. Next to the number of results is a One Link per Domain check box. Make sure that box is checked, because Google assigns TrustRank based on the number and quality of unique domains linking to a website rather than on the number of web pages (see Figure 3.16). (It wouldn't make sense to credit every link on an individual web page because one website could link from thousands of web pages.)

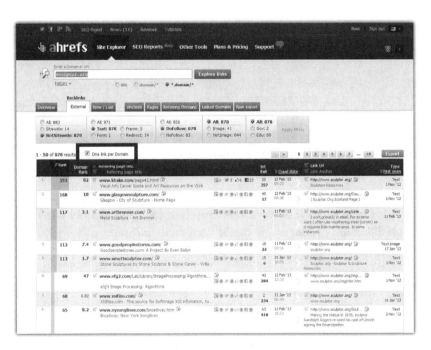

Figure 3.16 *Ahrefs.com, an excellent online tool that shows you all the links pointing to any given website. Always check the One Link per Domain check box to see only the number of unique domains linking to a website.*

As mentioned earlier, one of the best uses of a link tool is spying on competitors' progress. To help you understand how to use the tool in that way, here is an example of an internal dialogue I might have if I were the owner of a website that competes with dog.com and I were browsing that site's links on ahrefs.com.

> Hmm, they have a link from garden.com. What the heck is that? Wonder if these people own a bunch of one-word .com domains and they interlink from all their sites. Maybe I should do that too? Nah, too expensive.

> Ah, a link from American Kennel Club. Let me check out what kind of page the link is on and see whether this is just a free list of dog sites or if they're paying to advertise on this site. If the AKC is just including them as a resource, I should reach out to them to get my site on that page, too.

> Lots of blog links. Looks like they are getting some links just for having such a good domain name. Hmm, can't do much about that.

> Actually, upon further inspection, it looks like their images are getting linked a lot. I can't believe I didn't think of that sooner! If we create a bank of images of all different kinds of dogs—a compendium of sorts— we would probably pick up lots of natural links over time just like they did. And better yet, if I can get some pictures of lesser-known, rare dog breeds, the links would probably start coming in even quicker.

> A link from horse.com? Okay, these people definitely own a ton of one-word .com domains. Getting links from all the sites in their portfolio must help their search engine rankings a lot.

As you can see, a huge amount can be learned in just a few minutes about any other site's linking strategy purely by using a link tool.

Google also offers two free link tools, but one is unhelpful and the other is limited. The first is a simple search operator—a command you can type into Google's search box to see information about a website. Type `link:yourdomain.com` into Google and you will see a list of links. Many people have been fooled by this result set, which is indeed a list of web pages that link to your website, but one that is so random and abridged as to be utterly meaningless. The other link tool Google offers is within their Webmaster Tools control panel, a resource Google introduced in 2006 to give webmasters a view into what Google knows about their websites. This list is fairly comprehensive and a wonderful, free alternative to ahrefs.com. However, its limitation is that it sometimes includes domains that attach no-follow tags to their links.

Now that you know how to see your links, let me reinforce the reason for doing so: If you're going to invest the time and effort it takes to build links, it's important to measure your progress. Whether you choose to use a paid tool like ahrefs.com or a free tool, make sure to carefully watch the correlation between links, rankings, and new customers.

4

Using Time to Gain Trust

No matter how many links and pages your new website has, it will not be able to rank on the first page for any competitive keyword for a couple of months. This core principle of Google optimization nearly put me out of business at one time. It just didn't make sense. I had great content and lots of links; why wasn't my website even in the top 100 results? The answer: because in the world of Google, you just have to wait. I picture an old farmer sitting on the back of a truck, chewing on a piece of grass, saying, "Life ain't fair, kid." It's just one of those rules.

The Sandbox

A mandatory ranking delay for new sites is the kind of SEO principle that doesn't make sense for most websites but benefits the entire ecosystem. Google instituted the sandbox, or the waiting period that all new websites must incur before they can rank properly, to keep fly-by-night spammers out of the index. As mentioned in Chapter 2, "The Five Ingredients of Google Optimization," if you were doing a lot of Googling in the early 2000s, you might have noticed many spammy sites in the search results. These sites were set up for the purpose of making money quickly and unethically, and then shuttering their online doors after just a few weeks. Using link farms (vast, interconnected networks of low-quality links), these sites were able to rise to the first page quickly due to Google's then-weaker algorithm. Many of them took a lot of money from people before Google discovered and banned them.

Because of this group of scammers, we all have to suffer. As I was saying, the sandbox nearly broke me when I was first learning about SEO. It took a full year for my college consulting website to finally see the light of Page 1. If another three months had gone by without reward for my work, I would have run out of money. Thankfully for all of us, Google has found other ways to identify spammers, and today the sandbox is a shadow of what it once was.

In addition to the number and quality of links pointing to your website, the age of those links is also important in determining your site's TrustRank. On the day a link to your website is published, Google awards your site only a portion of the total TrustRank that link possesses. The rest of its TrustRank is earned later on, as the link settles in as a permanent part of the website hosting it.

With all the waiting webmasters have to do, I thought it would be helpful to offer an outline of the typical journey a well-managed site takes before it is able to rank for the most difficult keywords.

Prepublishing Period

What you do in the time period before publishing your site to the Web is crucial. The moment Google learns there's a new kid in town, it starts sizing him up. One of the biggest distinctions Google will make on Day 1 is whether your website is a resource or a commercial site. If you are purely publishing a blog, Google gives your site special favor; if a commercial site, it starts at the bottom like everybody else's, rising up as it earns TrustRank.

I learned of this distinction in early 2011, while creating a community for a client of mine. This particular client wasn't concerned with commercial gain at the start of our campaign; he just wanted to amass an audience interested in the general theme of his company's services. So, we built and designed a beautiful blog on the

WordPress platform for him, publishing great articles each day. We were thrilled to see the community grow steadily right from the start, reaching about 35,000 visitors per month by the second month of the campaign. This was unusually generous of Google; they were allowing thousands of keywords to rain traffic on a site that had barely been around 60 days. Well, the client was thrilled—so thrilled that he decided it was time to start offering his company's services on the site. We minimized the blog on the home page, making room for information about his services. On the same day that we compromised the purity of the blog by adding a commercial element, the traffic took a nosedive. Fifteen days later, it had halved (see Figure 4.1).

Figure 4.1   *A chart showing the traffic of a site that was originally built as a noncommercial blog, which was then converted to a more commercial site around March.*

At first we were confused, but then I started noticing similar trends in other clients for whom we had created blogs simply for branding or exposure. The interesting thing is that Google did not make the reason for the demotion immediately clear. Rather, it slowly reduced the number of keywords the site showed up for over time, even allowing a big spike in the midst of the decline. This is typical Google. If they made their algorithms too clear, more people would be able to decipher them.

0–1 Months: The Period of Nothingness

Whether your site is classified on Day 1 as a resource or a commercial entity—and the vast majority are considered commercial, including nonprofit websites seeking donations—your first month is unlikely to be a high-traffic one. Google is waiting to see what will happen with it, stealthily collecting data to understand your site's content production and link-acquisition trajectories. Make no mistake that, although few people may arrive at your website from organic search, your actions during this period will affect your site's future traffic. This is exactly the time when you need to get busy building links. If you do not build links in the first few months, your site will continue to be stagnant until you do build links.

2–4 Months: Behold, a Brave New World

After your site has been around for a couple of months, it has the opportunity to rank for some fairly competitive keywords. The number and competitiveness of keywords depends on the TrustRank you've built thus far. In my company's own campaigns, we usually see an up-and-to-the-right traffic trend begin to form in the first few months, with several hundred different keywords sending traffic by the third or fourth month. This is not time period where you should expect to rank for your most difficult keywords unless you've built a *lot* of great links (think 40 to 50) and you've got a very niche business.

4–6 Months: The Winds of Trust

If you were building links in a casual, nonaggressive way for the past few months, your site will now be able to rank for a number of valuable keywords. It could even rank for some competitive ones. If you've been an animal about link building (50 to 100 links), you could already be on Page 1 for some of your most valuable terms. However, you will almost definitely not be dominating your industry. Yet.

6–12 Months: Dropping Anchor

For the average, hardworking webmaster, this will be a time of great prosperity, where your consistent hard work building links, crafting meta page titles, and optimizing your website for conversion pays off. At this point in a site's life, it very well may have built enough TrustRank to prove out the viability of SEO for your business. Although your site still won't rank for huge terms like `mesothelioma` or `airline tickets`, it could rank for slightly longer tail terms such as `jewelry store los angeles`, `personalized china`, and the like.

1–2 Years: Welcome to the Land of Trust

If you've followed the advice in this book, this stretch will be an exciting one for your business. Your traffic graph has seen its biggest lurches upward, and is now moving up in a slower, more steady fashion each month (taking seasonality into account, of course). Google's door is now 100% open to you, and as long as you keep all of your methods above board, your site has the opportunity to rank for pretty much any keyword. Google now views your site the way society views a young, roguishly handsome businessperson—as impressive and capable of great feats but not as well respected as he will be later on in his career.

2–4 Years: A Seasoned Citizen

By now, your site should have a number of old, trusted links and be a shining member of its community. Not only is it ranking well for uncompetitive and competitive keywords alike, but your site is also a highly sought-after influencer—a site from which any other site would feel privileged to gain a link. These are the good times. With a history of building links in a natural way and continuing to attract links on a regular basis, your site may rise in search results as you please. Your site joins the ranks of those "unbeatable" websites that are always on the first page for the most competitive keywords in an industry.

May this list keep you oriented on the sometimes-dizzying road to top rankings. After publishing *Outsmarting Google*, I got emails from a number of people who experienced a trajectory very similar to the one in this list. I hope you do, too.

How to Estimate the Value of a Link Based on Aging Factors

Given how equipped you are to gain new links by this point, it's a good time to show you how to use aging factors to analyze the value of each link you obtain. Chapter 1, "Trust: The Currency of Google," provided a cheat sheet for determining the TrustRank of a website: Simply Google the keywords in the home page's meta page title and see whether the site ranks anywhere on the first few pages of results. Because the meta page title tells you which keywords a site wants to rank for, finding out whether it does in fact rank for those terms gives you an indication of its TrustRank. This test does require some judgment, though. If the keywords in the home page's meta page title are extremely competitive, it might still have a lot of TrustRank even if it shows up on Page 10. For instance, a site that ranks on Page 10 for the keyword online degree probably has a ton of TrustRank. However, if a site is attempting to rank for online veterinary degree (I truly hope such a thing doesn't exist), and it shows up on Page 10 for that keyword, it probably has very little TrustRank.

Determining the age of a website is another way to guess at a site's TrustRank, and hence the value of a link from one of its pages. Generally speaking, links from older websites are more valuable. The huge caveat to that statement is that, if the website hasn't attracted any inbound (coming in from other websites) links over its long life, its outbound links (going out to other websites) will have no value to your website. However, it is easy enough to look at the links pointing to a website and see whether many of the web pages hosting those links look old (see Figure 4.2).

So how do you determine the age of a website in the first place? You can use the InterNIC whois lookup, located at http://www.internic.net/whois.html, to see when a domain was established.

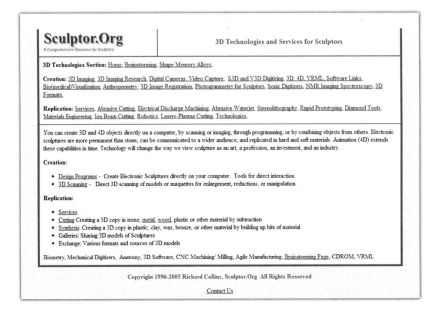

Figure 4.2 *A website with a dated look. It is a good bet that the links on this page are many years old.*

Although it might seem that the most valuable sites are the oldest ones according to the whois database, keep in mind that it is not the age of the domain that confers TrustRank, but the age of the website that sits on top of the domain. So if you see that a domain was registered in 1997, don't drop everything to gain a link on that site, because it is possible that the domain was parked for 10 years before a website was built. Even if a website was built right from the start, if the website was later taken down and the domain was parked for any substantial period of time, Google will have perceived that the domain was transferred to a new owner and reset whatever TrustRank it earned in the past. So before giving a site credit for being well aged, you should ask, "Has a website been continuously running on this domain since it was registered?" And note that if a website has in fact been running, uninterrupted, for many years, it retains its TrustRank no matter how many redesigns of the site occurred; Google expects that. Google resets the TrustRank of a website only if the domain has been parked.

If you really want to be thorough in investigating a website's potential value as a linker, you can attempt to determine the age of that website's own inbound links.

Just to reorient you, when we go down this road we are dealing with three different sites. The first is your own website. The second is the website you want to obtain a link from. And the third is one of the websites that links to the website you want to obtain a link from. You are looking into the age of that third website's links to estimate how much TrustRank that second website has, to see if you'd like it to link to the first website—your own (see Figure 4.3).

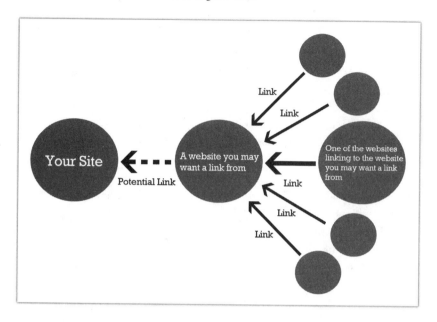

Figure 4.3 *A visualization of the three sites you need to keep in mind when you are trying to estimate the TrustRank of a link from another website.*

To evaluate the TrustRank of another website, you need to find the links pointing to it. There are two main ways to do that:

- **Google its URL**—Googling the URL of a web page enables you to see what other pages reference it. Assume you are interested in the age of the links to http://www.sculptor.org/Children/. Googling this URL brings up the page http://42explore.com/sculpture.htm. This page (as of the time this book went to press) features sculptor.org and contains a link to http://www.sculptor.org/Children/. At the bottom it states, "Updated, 04/01." So we can assume this link is 10 years old. Are we certain this link was not added later? Of course not. But based on the statement at the bottom of the page and the lack of any evidence to the contrary, it would be a reasonable guess. If other pages that reference http://www.sculptor.org/Children/ display similar clues, we could guess that at least some of those links really are quite old. Based on this fact alone, we can conclude that a link from http://www.sculptor.org/Children/ would be valuable.

- **Use a link-checking tool**—You can use any good link-checking tool such as ahrefs.com or Google Webmaster Tools to locate the web pages that link to the website you're evaluating. Let's assume we're interested in investigating the home page of cartoondollemporium.com as a potential link partner. Plugging that URL into ahrefs.com shows thousands of pages that link to the site. One of those pages is the following: http://www.allthingsprincess.com/PrincessInternetTools.html.

Looking at this page, I easily spot the link to Cartoon Doll Emporium under "Princesses Clipart and Graphics." This page contains a note at the bottom that says "Copyright 2007-2009." It also has some broken graphics on it, indicating that it probably *hasn't* been updated since 2009. Therefore, it can reasonably be assumed that this link is several years old. As with Googling a URL, there is no guarantee that a date published on a website is accurate, but all things considered, it makes for good evidence that cartoondollemporium.com has at least one well-aged link.

Determining the age of a web page's links is similar to determining the age of an antique. Most of the time you will not know for certain, but you can search for various clues that will each increase the chances that the link is from a certain date. We already saw two: a notation about the last time a page was updated, and a copyright date at the bottom of a page. Here are some other clues about a link's age:

- The link is within the text of an article that has a date somewhere in the URL. For example, http://www.10weablog.com/?m=200801 is a page that was likely created in January 2008.

- The link is in a blog or article that lists the date of publication somewhere on the page.

- The link is on a page that allows comments with dates on them.

- The page containing the link has a PageRank of 4 or higher on the Google toolbar. (A page usually will have been around for a while before it receives a high Google PageRank.)

- There are dates anywhere on the page containing the link. You might find, for example, a contest that states that entries may be submitted no later than January 5, 2014.

- There are references on the page containing the link to events that can be traced back to a certain point in time. For example, a reference to Donald Trump running for president probably indicates that the page was created in 2010 or 2011, the period in which he was discussing a run. (Let's hope there are no other such periods.)

If none of those methods work for you, it is also possible, although tedious, to use archive.org to determine when a site added the link in question. There you can look through archives of almost any website to pinpoint the general stretch of time when a new link appeared on a particular page.

If you're just looking for the quickest way to determine whether a site has a good number of old links but you don't want to spend a lot of time on it, simply look at the number of *unique domains* linking to it using a link checking tool that allows that function. If you see links from at least, say, 50 different domains listed (ignore spam and social media pages), the site probably has good link history and thus a good TrustRank.

Link Aging and Link Churning

Whether you've built a website from scratch or are working on one that someone else created, it is important to make sure that you not only build new links but also maintain the old ones. When forging a relationship with a potential linker, always try to lay the foundation for a long-term relationship. People and websites change, and if a reason arises for your link to be removed, you'll want to find a friend in the site's webmaster rather than an indifferent businessperson.

As mentioned earlier in this chapter, Google trusts links that have been around awhile more than it trusts brand new links. Once a link has been around for some time—say, 6 months—it earns its full linking power, counting maximally toward your site's overall TrustRank. After that point, it is in your best interest if the page it is hosted on remains exactly the same as it was when it was published. Google does have some tolerance for sites either archiving or removing very old links. In fact, I've been surprised to find that once a link has earned its full linking power, removing it sometimes does not affect the overall TrustRank of the site it links to. I believe this rule comes from Google's understanding that links naturally tend to get pushed back into a website's archives after a while, especially in the case of blogs. These links may not be easily findable anymore on their hosting site, but they were earned just the same. The main problems concerning link removal come in two forms:

- **When links are removed or changed within the initial trust-earning period (that is, the 6 months)**—Google's attitude toward the permanence of links is what I imagine a construction company's attitude toward drying cement would be. As long as the cement is given time to dry and harden, you can do whatever you want to it for years afterward. But if you tamper with it before it's dry, they have to break it up and redo it from scratch. (Okay, we know that construction companies are a lot less diligent about this kind of thing than Google, but let's go with it for the sake of the analogy!) Google's least favorite action within that initial "drying" period is changing the text in a text link, because this usually indicates paid linking behavior.

- **When links are mass removed**—Although Google doesn't diminish your site's TrustRank if an old link here or there is removed, it does take notice if a boatload of old links are taken down all at once. This is seen as an indication of foul play, likely the expiration of paid links or links that have been otherwise arranged in some unnatural way.

If your site does gain and lose links quickly for whatever reason, that is called link churning, and it's a bad thing. Because I've met so many companies who have had the misfortune of working with an "SEO expert" who engage in shady practices that result in link churning, perhaps this is a good time to address Google's many levels of *dis*trust.

Levels of Distrust

Google has several levels of distrust that it can apply to websites: sandboxing, a penalty, de-indexing, and blacklisting (see Table 4.1). Except for sandboxing, you can avoid all these acts of distrust by being discerning about the sites from which you receive links and the manner in which you acquire them. In the hierarchy of Google distrust, penalty status is less severe than deindexing and *much* less severe than blacklisting.

 Note

In Table 4.1, I refer often to Google Webmaster Tools, a free website provided by Google to track the way Google looks at your site. I mentioned it in Chapter 3, "How to Reel in Links," in the context of measuring links. You can find it at http://www.google.com/webmasters/tools.

Table 4.1   The Guide to Google Distrust

Act of Google Distrust	Cause	Effect	Road to Recovery
Sandboxing	A site is new or has never built links before.	Google will not allow your site to rank in its top 100 results for any competitive keyword until the site has built some inbound links and at least 2 months have passed from the start of the link building.	Build links. Wait.

Act of Google Distrust	Cause	Effect	Road to Recovery
Link Penalty (The Penguin Penalty)	Building unnatural-looking links (for example, links that all say "converter cables" in their link text) or having a substantial percentage of your links removed at one time.	Google moves your website off the first few pages, sometimes even out of the top 100, for your main keywords.	Remove the offending situation if there is one, and wait. Google may inform you that your site is being penalized in your Webmaster Tools panel. Once you make your linking pattern more natural, it will take a few months for your rankings to return. If you have paid or otherwise unnatural links pointing to your site, you can also use the Disavow Links tool, also located in your Webmaster Tools panel, to divorce your site from those links.
Content Penalty (The Panda Penalty)	Your site contains poor-quality content (content that is meant to siphon traffic from Google more than to serve visitors).	Google levels your site's TrustRank score, lowering your site's rankings across the board; pages on your site containing poor quality content may also be excluded from Google's index.	Remove all low-quality content and wait. Building high-quality links also helps your site to heal from a Panda penalty.
De-Indexing	Your site contains links to "bad neighborhoods" such as gambling, pills, or adult websites; or your site engages in offensive SEO tricks such as link farming or keyword stuffing.	Your site does not appear in the search results for any searches. It does not even show up when you type your domain name into Google. If your site is de-indexed, you might be notified by Google in your Google Webmaster Tools panel.	Visit your Google Webmaster Tools panel and fill out the form that allows you to submit your site for reconsideration. Giving a good reason, such as your site having been hacked or your being the hapless victim of a sketchy SEO firm, may result in reinstatement.
Blacklisting	Your site has engaged in black hat SEO tactics such as writing code that shows search engines different content than your site's visitors see; or your site is considered spammy or scammy.	Your site does not appear in the search results for any searches. You might be notified by Google in your Webmaster Tools panel.	You can try submitting your site for reconsideration in the Webmaster Tools panel, but Google probably will not allow your site back into the index. It is best to buy a new domain name and disassociate with the offending practices if you care about receiving traffic from Google.

Of course, I hope that Table 4.1 serves as a casual point of reference rather than a necessity. Cutting corners with links and content is a short-term fix, but leads to a long-term problem. And while there's nothing more effective at raising your rankings than a systematic link-outreach campaign, there is one way to bypass a lot of that work: buying an old website. I recommend this approach because I have personally experienced the benefits of owning a site to which someone has already attracted links and which has already aged. However, buying sites is an art and should not be undertaken until you have read the next section.

How to Find an Old Website Worth Buying

Unlike death and taxes, there is one way to avoid the sandbox, and that is by buying another website that has already earned it's TrustRank. If you have never bought a website before, please do not be intimidated by the process. It's easy. You do not need to purchase an actual web business to get an old website; you just need to buy the website itself. Therefore, you don't have to worry about doing extensive due diligence. But let's hold off on that for a moment. First of all, what is the real goal of purchasing a website for SEO purposes?

People with SEO knowledge buy websites not just to avoid a few months of sandboxing but rather to avoid years of link building. The only websites you want to consider are ones that are many years old and have lots of links, and are therefore enjoying their golden years of trust. It's kind of like marrying into a rich family— instant power! If you know precisely what you are looking for and engage in a systematic process of inquiring about the availability of websites, you will eventually find one that fits your criteria nearly perfectly. Although it does require time and effort to find a suitable website, that time and effort is a fraction of what you would have to undergo to build up a similar quality site from scratch.

So, how do you start? First, go to Google and type, in quotes, `this website is for sale`. That search query should bring up a few hundred sites whose owners have listed them for sale. You will quickly eliminate most of them because they fall into one of five "don't buy" categories:

- **Parked websites**—A parked website has no functioning website on it and exists solely to make money through low-quality ads (see Figure 4.4). Usually it will have stock pictures on it, text ads plastered over the middle of the page, and an invitation to purchase the website on the side or bottom. These domains are essentially spam and cannot be obtained for any reasonable price anyway. Skip them.

- **Irrelevant websites**—If you find a website for sale that has nothing to do with your business whatsoever, it cannot be used as your main business website. It probably can't even be used as a sister website to get visitors interested in your main site because Google will already have it classified as being about a particular subject matter and will not allow it to rank for keywords of another subject matter. For example, if you own a pet store and you find a website called customtissueboxes.net that has been selling monogrammed silver tissue boxes for the past 4 years, you do not want to buy the site. Although it would be excellent for someone who has a tissue business, home accessories business, or silver knick-knacks business, it is too different from a pet store to have any use to you. The same principle applies to sites that contain your keywords but in a different context. For example, a site about salsa dancing is not a good home for your fresh-made salsa business.

Figure 4.4   *A typical parked domain. When looking for websites to purchase, skip these low-quality pages.*

- **Relatively new websites**—People put sites up for sale shortly after registering them, often because they think they have a good domain name. Of course, a website that is less than a year old with few links is precisely what you are not looking for because it will not have high TrustRank. Again, to find out a site's age, use the public whois lookup at http://www.internic.net/whois.html. (Just search for the words *creation date* on the Internic domain page, and you will see the date the website was registered.)

- **Linkless websites**—Even if a site is 10 years old, if it has not accumulated links in that time, it's as dead to Google as a completely new website. Before purchasing any website, look up its links on ahrefs.com or another link measurement tool.

- **Websites with poor-quality links**—Probably the most deceiving type of website you'll encounter in your search is the one that is on topic, is a few years old, and has a number of links. Seems perfect, right? Well, the only issue is that those links are not of a good quality. I've assisted many prospective purchasers and this comes up a lot. You should be able to look through the links to a website and feel confident that each link was earned based on merit, not purchased or arranged.

If a site is relevant to your business, has had a functioning website running continuously for at least 2 years, and has at least 20 high-quality links, it is worth purchasing at the right price.

A second, and often better, approach to purchasing websites is to sort through websites that already rank for your keywords. Let's say you sell t-shirts. Type t-shirts into Google and look through the top 100 results. This method eliminates any chance of the site being classified in the wrong category and thus being unable to rank for your keywords—it already does rank for your main keyword. It also makes looking up the site's links fairly irrelevant because whatever number of links it has was clearly enough to earn it a decent ranking for your main keyword. In short, these 100 sites are all worth buying if you can get them for reasonable prices.

From this pool of prospects—such as the "this website is for sale" pool mentioned earlier—a few traits should turn you away immediately:

- **The domain name doesn't make sense for your business, or you don't like it**—If a site has a domain name you just can't live with, it's a no-go. As badly as you want to get a site that already has ranking power for your main keyword (and, if you don't already have a high ranking website, you should really want one of these sites), you can't ignore branding. For example, if you sell car parts and you stumble across a site for sale that is on the first page of Google for car parts but its name happens to be kidstoycarparts.com, you'll have to throw it back. Everyone will be confused by your name.

- **The ranking web page is part of a larger website**—You will undoubtedly find many search results that are web pages on a larger website that does something more general. For example, I wouldn't be surprised if a page on eBay were one of the results for a search of car parts. Obviously, you can't buy eBay. (Bill Gates, if you are reading this book, that doesn't apply to you.)

- **The website is clearly an active business**—Let's not forget that, in this scenario, you are looking to buy a website for SEO purposes. Many website owners will be confused by this, saying, "Why do you want to buy the website I spent the last 8 years building?" Answering this question correctly can sometimes land you a fantastic new website. But there are far more times when attempting to purchase a site owned by an active business will be a waste of your time. Try to minimize these kinds of encounters by avoiding websites that are clearly being used for business. If you find that a site is well maintained and the copyright at the bottom is up-to-date, skip it. The real opportunity is in looking for sites that say "copyright 2008" at the bottom or something similar, indicating that they are being ignored. A website that hasn't been updated in years is a gem because it means there is a chance you'll find a tired, busy webmaster at the other end of your email who is willing to part with his now-ignored web property (see Figure 4.5).

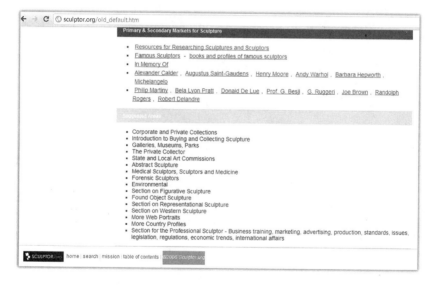

Figure 4.5 *A website that ranks in the top 100 for the keyword* `sculpture`. *This is a good prospect to buy because it looks like it hasn't been updated in a while, judging from the years-old copyright at the bottom.*

Ultimately, most of the 100 sites you look through will not be for sale for a reasonable price. However, buying websites is a game that is won with ingenuity and the power of the nudge. After you have a short list of websites that would be valuable vehicles for your business, think about each site and try to get a sense of the personality of the human being who owns it.

Let's suppose you sell watches. Say that you're doing a search for buy watches and you notice an old site that hasn't been updated in a while that is dedicated to the joy of collecting antique watches. Before reaching out, you should be having this kind of thought process:

1. The guy who owns this site is probably passionate about watches.

2. He might have a collection of his own, passed down from his relatives.

3. Maybe he discovered some old watches in his grandfather's attic when he was a kid, and the fascination began.

4. Either way, this guy created a site about watches without actually putting anything up for sale, so he's got to be a devoted hobbyist.

5. If I tell him I want to buy his personal project so that I can get a higher search engine ranking and sell my wares, he'll probably be turned off.

6. Instead, I should think about whatever interest I have in antique watches and communicate that interest to him, telling him I'd like to buy the site partly to continue what he started.

7. If he asks whether I will be selling watches, I'll tell him that I will, but that I'll keep a special section of the site in honor of his work that contains everything he's created and some of my own contributions. Everyone is happy.

As you can see, quite a bit of projecting and creative thinking was involved in determining the best way to obtain the website. If you are not prepared to think in this way, you'll have to think with your wallet. Of course, for some people, money is the only factor, and in cases like those, you should pay only what you can reasonably afford. Overpaying for a website is rarely a good idea because starting a site from scratch is still a viable option. In fact, it can be a valuable exercise in creating great content and building links, which you will need regardless of whether you buy an already-trusted site.

In the end, if you can get an old website for a livable price, go for it; but if you can't, it'll probably force you to adopt some better marketing habits anyway.

How the Buying Process Works

When you and a webmaster have agreed on a price, it is time to get the purchase process underway. I've purchased many websites and have seen the process completed in as little as two days; however, the average length of time from initial email to domain transfer is probably 2 to 3 weeks. Here is how the process generally works:

1. **Informal agreement**—Whether by email, telephone, or in-person meeting, you need to establish a "meeting of the minds," which is a casual agreement where both parties understand each other's responsibilities in the transaction. Most likely, your main responsibility is paying money. The seller's main responsibility is transferring the domain, website, and rights to the content. This agreement generally occurs after both parties have had a conversation or two and gotten comfortable not just with each other, but with the idea that the other party will follow through on his or her promises.

2. **Letter of intent**—Sometimes a letter of intent (LOI) follows an informal agreement. An LOI is an agreement to agree; it's a statement of the major terms of the final agreement that seems to say this: "Here is what we're agreeing on, generally speaking. Once we determine that we're on the same page, we'll draft up something fancy and official." People use LOIs so that they don't waste time and money drafting formal agreements only to find that the major terms of the agreement are in dispute. In place of an LOI, I prefer to just shoot over an email with the basic terms, but some people prefer to do things the old-fashioned way.

3. **Contract of sale**—When it's clear that you and the seller are both cool on the main points of the transaction, it's time to make it formal. You may want to search Google for a contract for sale of a website. I usually use a contract template that I originally found online and have since modified. If the contract contains any elements you aren't familiar with, Google some of the language to learn more about it. Aside from the main points about transferring ownership of the domain and content, most of the agreement is boilerplate that is meant to protect both parties from unlikely (but possible) occurrences. If in doubt, it is never a bad idea to seek legal counsel to ensure that the sale is handled properly.

4. **Due diligence**—After the agreement has been signed by both parties, you're almost there. Now the buyer just has to make sure that the seller hasn't been hiding or neglecting to mention anything important about the website. This is what due diligence is for. Due diligence, in this context, is the process whereby the buyer (and sometimes the seller as well) looks into the website in a more detailed fashion, often accessing domain records, financial statements, and outstanding advertising, business development, and service contracts. If you were to find, for example, that there is an advertising contract in existence that contains a clause prohibiting the sale of the website to a new entity (that is, you), that would be a deal-breaker. The sale of a website for SEO purposes does not usually involve extensive due diligence, and the transaction proceeds without too many speed bumps.

5. **Escrow/money transfer**—Ah, the most important part. Either at the same moment as, or just before, the domain and the web content residing on that domain are transferred to you, you must pay the seller. Typically, a seller requests a wire to his or her bank account because that method of money transfer is nonreversible and occurs within hours. PayPal and credit cards, on the other hand, are disputable, and checks take a few days to clear. But if you can pay by check, that's slightly safer from your perspective because, in the unlikely scenario that you are sold snake oil instead of a website, you can stop your check.

6. **Domain transfer**—The final part of the website buying process is receiving the domain. You need to have an account at the registrar with which the website you're buying is currently registered. As soon as the seller executes a domain transfer, you should see the domain listed under your domains when you visit your account page with that registrar. That event signifies that the transaction is complete with only one caveat, which is that the pages on the website are exactly the way they were before the transfer, and the domain is not parked or empty at the time of purchase. It is important that the seller acknowledge that, in addition to the domain, you are buying all the pages of content on the site in the exact structure in which you first saw them (that is, pages haven't been deleted or renamed). Part of what you are purchasing is Google's trust in the pages on the website that have been in the same place for months or years. You are also purchasing the peace of mind that the links pointing to the website will not disappear anytime soon, which is why many buyers include a clause in their contract stating that the seller has no reason to believe that any inbound links will be taken down after the purchase. If all is in working order, your purchase is complete, and you can start using your "new" Google-trusted website.

Common Pitfalls

Purchasing an old website is not without its perils, of course. Before forking over the cash for what appears to be an instant ticket to the first page of Google, you should beware of a few situations.

Beware When Shopping the Online Marketplace

One of these pitfalls concerns buying sites on an online marketplace. A few big marketplaces are known for selling websites, and a number of forums have active site marketplaces. Type `buy website` into Google, and you'll find most of them.

As you're flipping through the listings, tantalized by the high PageRanks, age, and cool domain names advertised, keep in mind that many people sell their websites for one specific reason: There's something wrong with them. This is not to say "be paranoid," but rather "be cautious."

I've come across many burnt buyers who innocently purchased old websites with great content and domain names only to find out that the websites didn't show up in any Google searches. The sites had been de-indexed or blacklisted, which is why the sellers were so anxious to sell them.

Sites That Have Nothing to Do with Your Business

Another common error new website purchasers make is buying websites that have all the right characteristics but have nothing to do with the product or service they sell. Even if you get an old website with old links, if you try to take down the previously operating website and replace it with something completely different, Google is going to get the idea that the website was recently repurposed and thus will do the only sensible thing from their point of view: reset its TrustRank. To them, the site might have been trusted in the past, but that was another life.

A complete change in content often signifies a rebirth. You can get away with changing your Christmas website to a Hanukkah website, for instance, but not with changing your Christmas website to a life insurance site.

Avoiding Expired Domains

My last warning is to avoid expired domains. These are exactly what they sound like: domains that go back into the great big ocean of available domain names because their owners have either decided to abandon them or forgot to renew them.

Mostly, the companies that specialize in expired domains are trying to profit off people's forgetfulness. I won't get into the details of this shady business, but suffice it to say that it's not a good way to acquire an old website, because the moment the domain expires, it becomes parked, and that means its TrustRank goes bye-bye.

The Nuclear Football

Within my company, a certain strategy has been bantered about for years, usually in secret. We regard it as the ultimate way to dominate the search results. It was only recently that we started publicly offering this service to our clients; before that, it was considered a trade secret. This concept never had a name until one day when I was having a conversation with a colleague and he called it our nuclear football. And right then and there, I knew I had to borrow that name, for it was only fitting for the greatest concept in Google optimization.

Before I go into the nuclear football, I should address a question that every good, skeptical marketer or CEO should have: Why am I sharing this? The reason, reader, is that it's time. No secret can live forever, and this one has treated me well. It has built numerous businesses for me, and continues to build them for me today. But in the past few years, others have discovered it, too. Not many, but some; and my feeling is, if some can know it, anyone smart enough to buy my book should know it, too.

lear Football Defined

ernment, the nuclear football is the briefcase the president keeps near him
ll times that contains the nuclear codes, allowing him to authorize the ultimate
etaliation during a crisis (see Figure 5.1).

Figure 5.1   *The seriousness of the nuclear football in government reflects the grave
damage this SEO technique can inflict on the competition. It's downright unfair.*

Similarly, this tactic is the most impactful one that you can undertake in your
SEO journey. Unlike a nuke, it is a long-term solution that unfolds over a matter of years, but it does have in common with its atomic namesake a combination
of ingredients that brings together the best research and experimentation on the
subject. The nuclear football is about links. It's about age. It's about page titles. It's
about URL structure. It's about keywords. And it's very much about content.

Simply put, the nuclear football is a strategy in which you publish content on
your website every day, meticulously creating meta page titles for each page, while
simultaneously sharing that content as widely as possible on other websites to earn
TrustRank.

How to Execute the Nuclear Football

The overall goal of the nuclear football is to attract as much Google traffic as possible from long-tail keyword searches, resulting in targeted visitors who make
purchases. To achieve that, you need a lot of content and a lot of links. I have

a favorite analogy for explaining the role of content and links in optimizing for Google: the magnet. Your site is like a magnet trying to attract traffic from search engines. When your site is new, it is more like an unmagnetic hunk of dull metal; nothing comes to it. As you add pages to the site, however, each page increases the size of that magnet, making it more likely to bring in new traffic.   .

But still, without magnetism, even the largest piece of metal out there can't attract anything. That is where links come into play. Links are the magnetism. The more TrustRank your site acquires through new links pointing to it, the more attractive your site becomes, and suddenly new traffic begins to arrive from Google. The best situation, of course, is to have a huge magnet with tons of magnetism. Lots of content and lots of links. This will ensure that your site pulls in as much traffic as Google can give.

All the popular websites I've built have been big, highly attractive magnets. And every site that gets a ton of traffic from Google is too. It's the only real way to do it; you need to get traffic from lots of keywords to build a big site organically. No single keyword is so enormous that it alone can fill a site with traffic. In the fast-moving world of the Web, keywords go in and out of vogue, websites shift positions in the rankings, and people type a wide variety of searches. So even being at the top of Google for a monster keyword such as games will not a behemoth make. I know because I've done it.

Getting my kids' website, cartoondollemporium.com, to #5 for games brought it plenty of traffic, yes, but nowhere near as much as all of the long-tail keywords combined. Organic search traffic brought Cartoon Doll Emporium more than 6.7 million visitors in 1 year (see Figure 5.2). That year, games alone made up 5% of that organic search traffic. Substantial, yes, but that other 95%—6.3 million visitors—came from about 400,000 other keywords. That's a nuclear football, baby!

 Note

Today, Google encrypts the vast majority of searches, effectively hiding the true number of keywords that send traffic to your site. But back in 2009, you were able to see all those keywords in Google Analytics.

Although it is important to keep in mind that people keep coming back to a site because they like it—not because of a search engine tactic—the reason they know about the site in the first place is because of techniques like this one.

A broader question to address here is how important organic search engine traffic is to your overall customer-acquisition strategy. In other words, how much of your marketing budget should you devote to the nuclear football? I will say this: If search engine traffic delivers high-quality leads to your business, it is very important. But it should be considered alongside other types of traffic, such as word-of-mouth leads and website referrals. I know a law practice, for instance, that spends a third of its budget on SEO and the other two-thirds on a local legal site that regularly sends it relevant potential clients. It is important to look at your approach to marketing objectively: What brings in the most money for your company? And if you find that your business, like many others, derives valuable leads from organic search engine traffic, you want to start working on your own nuclear football.

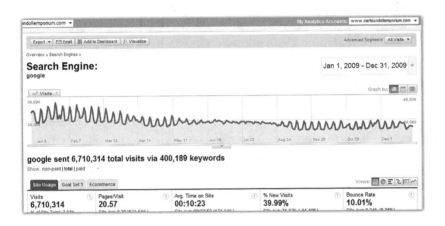

Figure 5.2   *The nuclear football in action: Cartoon Doll Emporium received 6.7 million visitors from 400,000 keywords in 2009.*

The best way to begin carrying out a nuclear football strategy is by installing blogging software on your website. This will allow you to publish regular content, which can be used to attract links.

 Note

The term *blogging software* is synonymous with content management system, or CMS. A CMS allows you to publish new content—usually, that means articles—on a site without having to program HTML code or pay a web developer to do it for you. WordPress is the most popular CMS, and the one I refer to often throughout this book. Although there are several other popular systems, such as Drupal and Joomla, I have found WordPress to be the most user-friendly and SEO-compatible among them.

With blogging software installed, you are now ready to publish targeted content. Once you've got content, you will need to use it to attract links organically. And once you have content and links, you'll have lots of qualified traffic coming to your site, and therefore will need to work on converting that traffic into sales. That, in a nutshell, is the nuclear football. Now let's go through it in greater detail.

The First Pillar of the Nuclear Football: Excellent, Targeted Content

The idea of having a blog on your website is about as original as the idea of having a bowl of mixed nuts in a bar. The key is in the quality of the content you put out. I am flabbergasted when I hear an "SEO expert" extol the value of blogging without talking about the huge range of effectiveness that blogging can fall into. If you're just pushing out a 500-word article once per week, your time would be better spent sleeping. At least then your brain might be sharper for some actual effective work. What you're really after is a blog post that is inspired, written by somebody who really enjoyed writing that post. When we start a nuclear football campaign for a client, our first step is to recruit a new writer. We never use in-house writers because we want to find people who are experts in the specific industry that our client occupies. If we sign up a new client who is a private investigator, we're looking for a former PI who is now retired and looking to do some work from home. If our client sells fresh fruit, I want a fruit farmer or an agriculturist with a side interest in writing. In addition to finding subject matter experts, we also seek out writers who can give their full creative attention to our clients' projects. We avoid the armies of professional writers who take on multiple writing projects simultaneously.

Whether you are writing content for your website or you're hiring someone to do it, I'm confident that what I've just told you will ensure that your articles are well written and high quality. But how can you be certain that your articles have that element X that makes them interesting? This is a very difficult question to answer, but I'm going to attempt to do it anyway. After all, my writers often poke fun at me for giving feedback on an article that goes something like "It didn't change my day" or "I wouldn't share it with my friends on Facebook." To them, and to you, I owe some explanation of what exactly makes an article interesting.

Niche Subject Matter

People love to learn. And when they're learning, they like specifics. No matter what the subject, it will be much more interesting if you explore its nooks and crannies rather than describe what you see right when you walk in. If I'm interested in poker, I don't want to learn how to play the game; I want to find out what to do if I've been dealt queens and my opponent raises me all-in pre-flop. If I'm interested in the Beatles, I don't want to know the name of their albums. I want to read an interview with the producer from Decca Records who rejected the group in 1961, saying "The Beatles have no future in show business." The deeper you dig, the richer the reward.

An Emotional Connection

As a person who reads dozens of writer applications each week, I am constantly finding people who would be excellent at writing an encyclopedia entry but fail to arouse any interest in me on a personal level. The key to nuclear football articles is *readability*, precisely because it equates to *linkability*. Consider the following sentence:

> *Toxicodendron radicans*, or poison ivy, is a plant that produces uru-shiol, a clear liquid compound that causes irritation and rashes.

Okay. I might have learned something new there, but I'm definitely not engaged. I feel like I'm reading a textbook. Now consider this sentence about the same subject:

> "Did you know she was allergic to poison ivy?" the ER doctor asked me, clutching my daughter's chart to her chest.

By bringing real people and emotions into the picture, I have created a first line that would probably spur a reader to continue reading. That's more than I can say for the first sentence. By writing in the first person and choosing a point of view that is personal, I have created a greater likelihood of making an emotional connection with the reader. This story could change my day. Other ways of communing with your audience include describing feelings within your articles, developing your articles' "characters" in a nuanced way, and generally making sure that your subject matter is eminently "human."

A Strong Editorial Voice

Every popular blog can attest to the power of a strong editorial voice. In blogging, as in life, confidence invites trust and respect. For many writers, it can take a while to learn how to *own* the subject they are writing about rather than simply cover it. Often, you need to fake it to make it. For instance, an article could contain the following paragraph:

> I've always felt that grapes taste better when frozen. I don't like it when people leave them out because then they lose their firmness. I even prefer frozen grapes to refrigerated grapes.

That's a fine paragraph, but it kind of leaves you with the notion "so what?" Now consider the same idea with a stronger voice:

> Grapes are better frozen. Leave a bowl of grapes out and they become soft in no time, acquiring bruises and brown spots in a matter of days. Refrigerated grapes are good, but simply don't compare to the fresh, cool burst of a frozen grape.

The latter paragraph translates opinion to fact. That's okay because everyone knows that an opinion is being given; they're just getting that opinion asserted to them rather than merely suggested. The reason this style is so much more effective is that it invites discussion. There will be some who strongly agree, feeling that their never-articulated love of frozen grapes has finally been given airtime, and others who strongly disagree, taking special offense at the cavalier way that the writer has just dismissed room temperature and refrigerated grapes. That will make them want to comment, maybe even take to their own blog to write a rebuttal. And that kind of energy... that is the stuff of links.

Openness and Vulnerability

Similar to the idea of making an emotional connection with your reader, approaching an article with openness and vulnerability is a powerful tool. Maybe the most powerful. In our society, pride runs high, and it is rare to see someone willingly show weakness. Yet, weakness exists in all of us, which is what makes it so refreshing to see. If you've had your heart broken, been down and out, had a bout of jealousy, been punished, embarrassed, or failed at anything, it would be a very brave—and effective—move to put it into writing.

Digestible Data

As anyone who produces Internet content knows, today's audiences have short attention spans. So if you're trying to hook someone in, you need to do it quickly. Those who use data in their content have the added challenge of presenting something that most people find boring (at least in large doses). That is how the concept of the infographic was born. With infographics—or graphical representations of data—numbers become fun again (see Figure 5.3).

As popular as infographics are, there are many other ways to visualize data. In fact, the original infographics were simple charts and graphs, which, when done right, are just as interesting today as ever. In the following examples, I show how data can be presented in digestible, linkable ways.

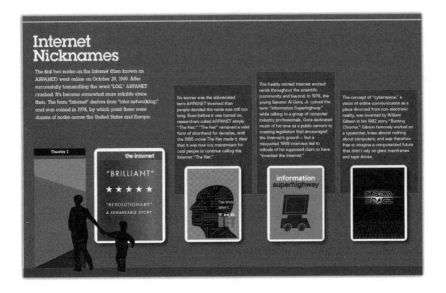

Figure 5.3 *An infographic by designer Josh White. This one is a timeline of the differ-ent names we've called the Internet, from "The Net" to "Cyberspace" to "The World Wide Web" and beyond. The infographic continues to the right but was too long to print in this book.*

Let's suppose I am a high school guidance counselor trying to illustrate what kind of SAT score you need to get into Harvard. I have SAT scores and admissions results from the past 10 years. One option is for me to present the data in written form, like the following:

> Of the 18 students from our high school that have gotten into Harvard in the last 10 years, 11 scored in the 99th percentile on their SAT; 3 scored in the 96th–98th percentile; 2 scored in the 93rd–95th percen-tile; and 2 scored in the 90th–92nd percentile.

Or, I could present the chart shown in Figure 5.4.

The bar chart shown in Figure 5.4 allows casual readers to quickly grasp the con-clusion that scoring in the 99th percentile on your SATs greatly increases your chances of getting into Harvard.

Now let's say you are an activist trying to prove that auto accidents aren't linked to marijuana usage. You could go into paragraph after paragraph of statistics, which might take the reader a few minutes and risk losing their attention. Or, you could show them the chart shown in Figure 5.5.

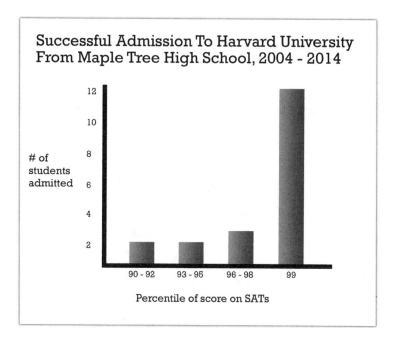

Figure 5.4   *A chart illustrates my point in a way that a text description cannot do.*

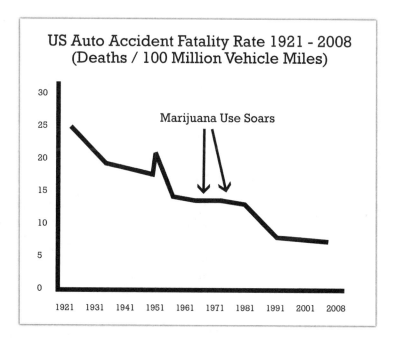

Figure 5.5   *A chart delivers information quickly and keeps the reader engaged.*

Finally, let's say you are trying to make a point about Apple's decision to come out with a white iPhone. You could opine in a full-length article, or just publish the pie chart shown in Figure 5.6.

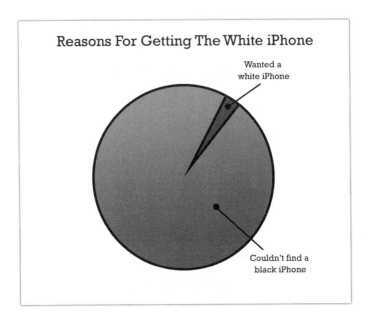

Figure 5.6 *A chart shows in seconds what it could take several paragraphs to describe in text.*

As you can see, data is way more interesting in visual form. In fact, it has long been known to marketers that elaborate infographics are one of the best forms of linkbait around. Although they often require a good deal of time, creativity, and money to create, they can be worth a ton of TrustRank.

Large, Clear Images (Usually Involving People)

The truth of the old cliché "a picture is worth a thousand words" should be especially evident to you by now, given our highly visual plugged-in world. But there are some specific points worth noting about images. The first is that finding a *fitting* image for your content is very different from finding an *interesting* image for your content. Most people forget the latter, and settle for the former. Consider the article shown in Figure 5.7, which was found on the blog of a successful small business.

This a very common kind of blog with the best of intentions. It has an appropriate picture, a reasonable title, and is filled with good information. The only problem with this article is that it is totally uninteresting in every way. As much as I would love to go into the soporificness of the content, I will hold my tongue because this section is about images. The main image for the content is a stock photo, and not even an interesting one at that. It may as well be invisible, because it adds nothing in the way of visual appeal.

Figure 5.7   *An uninteresting photo with equally uninteresting text results in informa-tion not many visitors will actually read.*

Because there is so much content online, if you don't have a good title and main image (also known as the *cover image* or *thumbnail image*), you stand little chance of getting your content read. So, for this particular article, which is essentially about making more money in a services-related business, a better image might be something like the one shown in Figure 5.8.

I like this image for this particular article because it in unposed and journalistic (like something you'd see in a newspaper), shows people with their guards down, and clearly illustrates people contemplating their business. Considering that the article covers service businesses specifically, it also does a good job of highlighting the human element.

Figure 5.8 *An unposed photo like this one delivers much more punch.*

Ideally, the cover image should be far from the only picture in the article. It's rarely a problem that there are too many pictures in a piece of content; much more often, the opposite is the case. Some of the most successful viral articles on the Internet only contain text to supplement the incredible images contained within. As a rule, in our attention-fragmented online world, people prefer to *see* things rather than read them whenever possible.

Before we move on from this all-important point, I want to take a moment to describe exactly what kinds of images work best in most articles. The key to a good non-infographic image (also known as a *regular picture* to most people) is emotion. To demonstrate this point, let's start at the extremes. A picture of a soldier scream-ing out in agony as he stands over his comrade's grave is enough to move almost any person. In another direction, a picture of a newborn baby, just a few seconds old, being presented to his weary but proud mother, is very affecting as well. In yet another direction, a picture of Angelina Jolie wearing a slinky backless dress would also give most people pause (or palpitations).

Now let's go down a notch in emotion: to pictures that have less *magnitude* of emotion but may even linger longer than some of the extreme examples discussed. (Images with a more subtle emotional resonance are often better for business use anyway.) Picture this: An image of an older woman sitting at her desk, her head in her hands, her computer in the background showing a shopping website, and a pile of credit cards and bills scattered across her desk. Even though I wrote it, it still made me sad to imagine that. Next, picture a well-groomed man, late 40s, dressed in a shirt and tie inside a professional office, absolutely beaming as he hugs another man dressed similarly. In the foreground is a contract opened to the signature page with two freshly inked signatures on it. Did this man just sell his business? Close a big deal? We don't know, but we can feel his joy, sense that he's put in years of hard work to experience this moment.

Without continuing down the ladder of emotions, I hope you get the idea. When selecting images for your content, you should be thinking of the way you want customers to feel when interacting with this single touchpoint of your brand. Maybe you want people who come across your content to sense how happy they'll be if they become customers; or, maybe you want to relate to the pain or inconvenience people in your target audience must be feeling not having become your customers yet. You have the power to affect people's moods as long as your images feel original, high quality, and emotional.

Now that you know what interesting content entails, I'd like to go through a case study that involves my favorite nuclear football client of all time. I like this client so much that I can honestly say that I am in love with her. Okay fine, it's my wife.

All kidding aside, my wife's site, entertainmentdesigner.com, was the first official nuclear football I ever created. I had been using the nuclear football strategy since I cracked the Google code in 2005, but didn't formalize it into the three-pillar format that it is today until much later on. Today, the nuclear football is the only SEO service my company provides, and I have my wife, in large part, to thank for it.

When she and I were discussing her aspirations to become a theme park designer a few years back, it seemed like an insurmountable goal. It's a unique profession, and she's not a technician of the sort that typically succeeds in the theme park industry (that is, an artist, engineer, or craftsman). So, we had to get the industry's attention indirectly. Using my SEO experience as my guide, I knew we had to create a website that had excellent potential to get links—something authoritative, timely, and of course, interesting. We came up with the idea of creating the ultimate news source for the themed entertainment (or "entertainment design") industry. We registered a good if slightly over-long URL, designed an attractive site, and hired a writer to publish a blog post every day. As the site grew, my wife thought it would be a good idea to interview some of the greats of the industry, the people who had designed the best theme park rides in existence. She sent out emails inviting them to do an interview for what was now a small but quickly growing daily news site. Because many of the top theme park designers aren't interviewed that often, they were happy to participate. With each interview, we gained exclusive and highly link-worthy content. The site eventually grew to become the largest site about theme park designers online. And guess what my wife does for a living? Yes, she designs theme parks around the world. After getting to know many of the top designers, she asked to do some work for them to prove her creative abilities, and impressed them. Now she's busy with projects all the time, ranging in scope from local themed restaurants to multinational theme parks. It took under 2 years to accomplish her goal, and it was the nuclear football that started it all.

But the site actually had a bit of a rocky start. The first writer we hired billed himself as an "SEO expert," working for multiple clients. As such, the articles he wrote were more or less churned out, and resembled encyclopedia entries much more than thoughtful, inspired editorial pieces (see Figure 5.9). This was a mistake we quickly corrected.

Figure 5.9 *An article prepared by writer with a self-described "SEO background" who works for multiple clients. It is well-written but is neither interesting nor link-worthy.*

The new writer we hired was a genuine theme park enthusiast, and thankfully had barely any idea what SEO was. Her articles always contained opinions, and covered breaking news that affected the industry. We also encouraged her to create top 10 lists in interesting areas, such as tallest water slides, fastest roller coasters, and most exotic themed hotels (see Figure 5.10).

ZIP-LINING WAITERS SERVE GUESTS AT THE DINING POD, THAILAND

Written by: Staff Friday, March 23rd, 2012 .

Some of our favorite projects are the ones that draw on the simple pleasures of childhood for inspiration. One of these pleasures is without a doubt the tree house. Even though we don't spend as much time in tree houses as we'd like to these days, we love to see them incorporated into entertaining experiences: and today's featured project does exactly that. Among the many dining options at Soneva Kiri Resort in Thailand, one is set high up in the branches of the resort's lush forest.

Figure 5.10   *An article prepared by a writer with a real passion for the industry she is writing about. The article is timely and the writer includes her own opinions, resulting in an interesting and readable piece.*

Without a doubt, the high-quality content on entertainmentdesigner.com was fundamental to its success. I continue the entertainmentdesigner.com case study later in this book. But, before we move on to the way the nuclear football strategy deals with links, I want to address one final important point about content: targeting.

As obvious as it may seem to write about things that relate to your industry, it can be tempting to create link bait that has at best a tenuous connection to what your business sells. While it's not a bad idea to write tangential content once in a while if you really think it's going to bring in links, you always want to keep your content focused. That way, you won't attract an overly broad audience that doesn't buy anything. When writing content, keep the following rule in mind: *The title of every article should contain a keyword phrase that would be searched by a potential customer.*

For example, if you are a financial planner, a targeted title would be "The 5 Qualities Your Wealth Manager Should Possess." Of all the titles you could choose for that particular subject matter, this one works well because it contains the valuable keyword phrase `wealth manager`. That term is also somewhat specific to this industry, meaning it would be searched by people with some level of sophistication. Most importantly, searchers who use that term are likely to be more well-off, as *wealth manager* usually refers to a financial planner who manages large amounts of money.

However, an article called "Making Cents: How to Use Couponing to Save Lots of Money" would not be helpful to your business, because the title contains keywords having to do with saving money and couponing. Both of those topics are more likely to attract searches from people who probably wouldn't be in a position to hire a financial planner. Note that `couponing` and `save money` are both popular search terms, and the article *could* attract links; but because it would bring in the wrong type of audience, it's not worth publishing.

If you can manage to include targeted keywords in your titles, you're doing things correctly from a technical point of view. But always keep in mind that your titles must also be charismatic (or human-friendly, as I like to say). It is only by appealing to people that your articles will be able to attract that all-important arbiter of TrustRank: links.

The Second Pillar of the Nuclear Football: Authentic, Personalized Outreach

After you have a plan in place for creating lots of pages of good content, it's time to focus on links. Your plans for getting links in the context of the nuclear football do not need to be any different from your normal link-building plans. Obtain lots of links in a natural way—that is, through doing great work and telling people about it (and the links will come). So, how do you tell people about what you're doing in a way that is both socially acceptable and effective for SEO? In Chapter 3, "How to Reel In Links," I gave an example of the type of warm, personal email you might send to another webmaster to procure a link back to your site. It's the same idea here. The only thing that makes the emails one sends within the context of the nuclear football different from the emails one sends within an everyday link building campaign is the presence of tons of content that can be used as link bait.

In our client campaigns, we always make sure that our writer is in close communication with our outreach specialist—that is, the person sending out emails on behalf of the client. The two positions are naturally connected. If we just published a fascinating article for a client who is a rare coins dealer about a new discovery of gold doubloons, we're going to mention that article to at least a dozen webmasters that day. We hand pick these webmasters based on their interest in rare coins, specifically gold doubloons. And we find people interested in those items by searching on Google. For example, an outreach specialist for my company might start looking for link targets by Googling `gold doubloons` and narrowing the search to only news or blog websites. Anyone who recently covered a similar subject will be investigated for potential willingness to link. (We're probably not going to contact *The New York Times*, for instance, but we'll totally contact Jim's Pirate Coin Blog; it's lower-hanging fruit), and those that seem like they'd be receptive will get personalized emails. Here's what we might write:

> Hey Jim,
>
> Big fan of your blog! None of the other numismatists cover pirate coins with quite the same level of detail and are able to make me laugh at the same time. ;)
>
> I'm currently working with Rare Coin Land and just wrote a fairly in-depth blog entry on the gold doubloons that were just found off the Florida coast. I'm sure you've heard all about the discovery by now. My theory is that they were buried in the sand after the Plate Fleet sank in 1715, and were only discovered because of the recent ground shifts brought on by seismic activity in that area.
>
> Whether you agree with my theory or not, I hope you'll find it interesting enough to share with your readers. We're fairly new and would love to get the word out about our blog.
>
> Thanks either way and keep up the great writing.
>
> Eliza

What you'll notice about this email is that it is succinct, but detailed; warm and friendly, but direct; and has a clear purpose. This is likely to be a successful attempt at attaining a link. If—and this is a big *if*—you can manage to write several of these emails each day, using the content you have created as fodder for your outreach, I have little doubt you will make tremendous strides in attracting new customers.

So now, let's say you follow my advice and start raking in the links. How many is good? This is one of the most common questions I get when I teach workshops. Clearly, the answer is "it depends," but I can't stand when people say that, so I'll give you a real answer. I'm going to say... 50.

It is my belief that having 50 actual, organic, high-quality links would cause any website in a niche industry to rank highly on Google for competitive keywords. Of course, the number of links required to be a top player in an industry varies based on the competitiveness of the industry. So if you're an airline ticket reseller, 50 won't do it. And if you're a purveyor of luxury toenail clippers, 50 would be more than enough. But on average, that number would put your site in quite a good position.

And how long should it take to achieve 50 links? Well, for my company, it would average about 6 months. I may be being conservative there, but it is fairly reasonable to assume that we can procure 2 links per week if we send out at least 25 personalized emails each week. Naturally, certain industries are more or less willing to share the link love. The spirituality industry is much more generous than, say, the semiconductor industry. And one brilliant piece of link bait can attract 50 links in just a few *days*. But for the average marketer who has read this book thoroughly, I'd say that between 6 months and a year is a good time frame within which to build your 50 links.

The Third Pillar of the Nuclear Football: Conversion Optimization

One could make the argument that content and links are all that is necessary for SEO. Technically, this is true. The first two pillars are enough to get your site an up-and-to-the-right traffic graph (see Figure 5.11). But because it is not traffic, but the revenue that results from that traffic, that matters to most websites, conversion optimization is essential enough to call a third pillar.

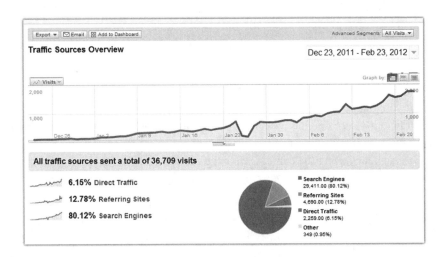

Figure 5.11 *The first 60 days of a well-executed nuclear football. This is a screenshot from one of our clients' Google Analytics account. (In case you're curious, the blip in January occurred because of server difficulties.)*

Conversion optimization is, essentially, the science of getting people to buy things online. In the context of SEO, it's the process of transforming website visitors who are browsing content into customers. To give you a sense of what I mean, the simplest form of conversion optimization is having a button on your home page with a picture of your top-selling product that says "Buy Now." Whatever percentage of your site's visitors clicked on that button and went ahead and made a purchase is your conversion rate. In the e-commerce world, a common conversion rate is 1%, meaning for every 100 visitors to the site, 1 of them buys something.

To me, conversion optimization is fun because it's pure psychology. The fact that, for example, you could sell more t-shirts on your website if the background is white as opposed to red is fascinating. Something is evidently triggered in people's minds when they see a red background that makes them feel overwhelmed and less like buying. And that leaves a world of possibilities to explore about what will convert your visitors best. A big yellow button with blue lettering, imploring a purchase? An emotional video? A picture of the company's staff, all together in a room smiling? Understanding what will put your site's visitors in the mood to purchase is an art unto itself.

Chapter 10, "Converting Your SEO Results into Paying Customers," is dedicated entirely to this art. But for now, I'll leave you with the following idea: For a person to make a purchase on your website, three criteria must be satisfied. They must feel your product fits their needs, is trustworthy, and is priced acceptably.

To accomplish those three criteria, you need an attractive web design relevant to your industry. You also need clear menus and navigation on your site. Finally, you need pictures, videos, and graphics that make people feel motivated to buy. The holy grail of conversion optimization is determining what will trigger the maximum number of purchases from a given group of visitors to your website. While I've never met a company that claims to have accomplished that feat, those who have gotten close have done so through a long process of testing, using both intuition and hard data.

Ultimately, the nuclear football works best as an ongoing strategy. Some prefer to assign people internally to handle each pillar, and others hire companies like mine to take care of it. Whatever you choose, make sure to give the strategy the right amount of time to show you results. You should expect to see promise within 6 months, and a return on investment within a year. Personally, I have found that the nuclear football comes into its full bloom after a year and a half, once Google has fully learned to trust the website. At that point, new content tends to rise to the top of the search results for its target keywords almost immediately.

Avoiding the Panda and Penguin Penalties

I'd like to end this chapter with a warning, as I've seen my share of people who take this concept and try to do it quicker, cheaper, and better. The nuclear football is, essentially, a whole lot of human effort and creativity molded around Google's rules. It can be handled in an intelligent way that minimizes cost and time expenditure; but it cannot be automated. To give you some idea of the kind of pitfalls involved in cutting corners with the nuclear football, a former client of mine once decided that he knew how to execute my strategy better than I did. As soon as our campaign together was finished, he promptly replaced our writer—a thoughtful subject matter expert—with an army of writers from a developing nation, paying them $5 per article. Within a few days of his decision, his website's traffic, which had grown at an excellent clip during his campaign, immediately took a nosedive (see Figure 5.12). Google's reaction to the poor-quality content he was posting is known as the Panda penalty. When a site gets hit with the Panda penalty, Google typically removes the offending web pages from their index, as well as lowers the site's TrustRank score overall, resulting in all pages on the website ranking lower. The combination has a deadly effect on website traffic.

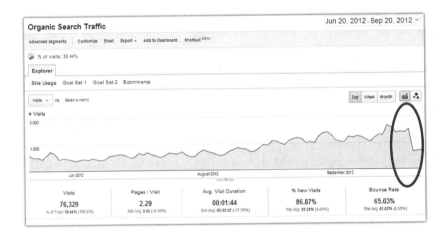

Figure 5.12   *A graph showing a steep traffic drop after high-quality content was replaced by cheap, poor-quality content. This is the Panda penalty in action.*

Another corner people tend to cut when trying to execute the nuclear football is in the realm of links. Google has come a long way since the 2004–2007 heyday of paid links, when many websites reached the top of the search results by purchasing text links from link brokers. Today, Google's spam filters catch that type of behavior very quickly. In fact, not only can they detect paid links, but they are quite good at finding links that have been artificially arranged in any way: via link trades, comment spam, article marketing, paid blog posts... even legitimate channels like social media and advertising. If Google suspects that you have engaged in any link building that is less than organic (that is, anything except the kind of email outreach or link baiting that I advocate in the last two chapters), it may devastate your site's TrustRank via the Penguin penalty (see Figure 5.13).

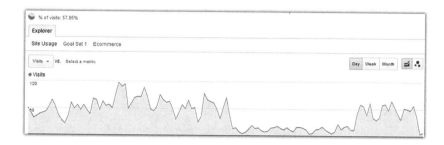

Figure 5.13   *A graph showing a site's traffic before, during, and after the Penguin penalty. Sites that have been hit with the Penguin penalty usually have engaged in low-quality link building.*

I find it puzzling when I see entire chapters in SEO books written about the Panda and Penguin penalties. The only reason you would need to give special attention to either penalty is if you plan on engaging in spammy techniques. If you simply follow the advice in this book, doing things above board, you will never need to worry about either penalty. As a bonus, developing excellent content and reaching out to webmasters authentically to share that content—otherwise known as the nuclear football—won't just help you with your SEO; it will help your entire business to prosper.

6

Tracking Your Progress with Google Analytics and Other Helpful Tools

With a basic knowledge of SEO under your belt, you are now ready to learn how to keep track of your progress. While knowing how you're doing will be interesting, the real objective here is to be able to refine your strategy based on your knowledge of what's working and what isn't. The ability to constantly adjust your strategy in response to data is, in my experience, the difference between mild success and tremendous success in business.

Many analytics tools are available to marketers, but their quality varies wildly. Most of this chapter focuses on the most powerful, comprehensive, and accepted tool out there: Google Analytics. However, I also mention some of the other tools—including Google search itself—that I use regularly to determine how an SEO campaign is going.

None of the tools are, ultimately, intimidating to use, although Google Analytics can feel that way at first.

The Basics of Analytics

There are three metrics that really matter in an SEO campaign: pages indexed, links, and traffic. If a website were a department store, pages indexed would represent the number of entrances to the store, links would represent the reputation of the store that drives people there, and traffic would represent the actual number of people in the store each day. We know, of course, that traffic is the goal of the first two metrics, but the first two are still important because they create the potential for more and better-quality traffic in the future.

Pages Indexed

Pages Indexed is perhaps the least obvious metric of the three. Why is that such a big deal? Well, if I were an oversimplifying kind of guy, I'd say that each page represents a new opportunity for Google to send traffic to your website; so the more pages, the more traffic you're likely to have. The reality, however, is that Google can add a lot of your site's pages to its index but not trust those pages much, resulting in very little additional traffic per opportunity. But as we all know, links = trust, so if you have the focus on link building every reader of this book ought to have, you will see a great deal of benefit from each additional page.

The best way to find out how many pages Google has accepted into its index is to type the following query into the Google search box:

```
site:yourwebsite.com
```

After clicking Search, you will get back a list of all the pages on your website Google has deemed eligible to show up in its results. You can quickly find out the number of pages indexed by looking at the top of the page, where it says "About [152] results." The number that I put in brackets is your number of pages indexed (see Figure 6.1).

In an ideal scenario, this site: search would return a large number of pages, the vast majority being valuable content pages (articles, compendiums, videos) that each focus on one small niche of your business and have well-crafted meta page titles. If you plan to carry out the nuclear football approach described in the preceding chapter, you can expect exactly that.

Figure 6.1 *A "site:" query on Google. By typing* `site:` *followed by your domain name (with no spaces), you can find out how many of your website's pages Google has accepted into its index.*

Links

It's easy to track the links pointing to your website, but tougher to analyze the exact value of each one. I don't think you need to, though. I find that worrying about evaluating the Trustrank of every link is a pointless endeavor, sort of like trying to guess at the value of a new client or customer: You know that they're valuable, but you can never be sure how valuable until some time has passed and you can measure their impact on your business.

At my company, we simply keep a list of all the links pointing to our clients' websites, eliminating any links that are marked with a no-follow tag or are spammy in any way. In other words, we track all the links we feel confident are passing TrustRank to our clients' websites. From that list, we look at organic search traffic patterns and expect certain correlations. For instance, if a client comes to us with 20 good links, and 3 months later they have 50 good links, we expect that their organic search traffic should be 2x to 3x as high. (This assumes that meta pages titles are written optimally and that new content is being added regularly.)

Of course, as the competitiveness of the industry increases, so too does the number of good-quality links needed to make a real presence in organic search (see Figure 6.2).

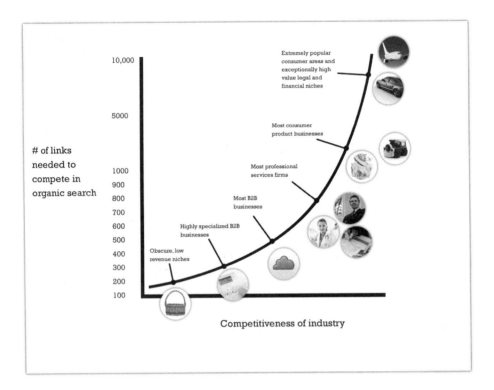

Figure 6.2 *A chart that estimates the number of links needed to compete in organic search for different types of industries, ranging from the least competitive to the most competitive.*

What all of this boils down to is the fact that you should work on getting links consistently—not diverting your focus into an analysis of each link. Yes, a big score like a link on TechCrunch is especially valuable. But your next 10 links combined may matter even more. So, always keep your eye on that next link.

To see all the links pointing to your site, you already know that my favorite tool is ahrefs.com. You can, however, get a rough estimate (for free) from Google Analytics or Google's Webmaster Tools page.

Traffic

Traffic is the most common metric people use to measure the success of an SEO campaign. Of course, the quality of the traffic is much more important than the quantity. To check your traffic, you should install Google Analytics, which involves a basic signup at google.com/analytics, followed by your web person placing a small snippet of code on every page of your website. There are other traffic measurement programs, but they are so shallow compared to Google Analytics that they're not even worth mentioning. Also, Google Analytics is used by nearly every website (except for enterprise-level business sites), and it is useful to be able to speak the same language as other webmasters when discussing analytics.

There are several common terms having to do with the way traffic is measured: *unique visitors*, *visitors*, *hits*, and *pageviews*. I like to look at unique visitors, because that's the number of human beings. (Technically, it's the number of web browser "cookies," but no reason to get technical.) However, I find visitors to be the most valuable metric, because that's the number of browsing *sessions*. So, if someone comes to your website once at 10 a.m., stays for 15 minutes, and then returns later that day at 4 p.m., it counts as two visitors for the day. It would, however, count as only one *unique* visitor.

Hits is something you have no need to understand; it is a common misnomer for the concept of a unique visitor. And a pageview is simply the loading of a web page. So if someone visits your home page, then visits your About page, then refreshes your About page, that's three pageviews. It's a useful metric to look at when you're trying to understand how engaging your website is, but not useful for basic traffic measurement.

All of this boils down to the fact that when you are evaluating the amount of traffic your website received last month, for example, you should look at visitors. Besides the fact that it's a reasonable way to measure the popularity of your website, it's also the most common way that traffic is reported throughout Google Analytics.

Pages indexed, links, and traffic are the three main SEO metrics that most readers of this book need to focus on, but there are other important metrics that I have either already addressed or will be addressing later in this book:

- **Visitor engagement**—This metric essentially tells you how interesting people are finding your site. Does it keep them occupied for just 30 seconds before they jump back to whatever site sent them to you? Or do they hang out on your website for an hour before deciding to move on to something else? Visitor engagement is usually measured in pageviews and time on site.

- **Demographic**—The average age, gender, income, and education of your visitors is usually called its *demographic*. There is no demographic that is quantitatively "better" than another; that all depends on your business. However, certain demographics have more spending power. For example, teenagers have relatively low spending power most of the time, whereas college-educated men and women in their 40s who make over $100K per year have relatively high spending power.

- **Customer conversion**—This metric is not directly related to SEO, but is so important to your overall business strategy that I've dedicated an entirely separate chapter to it, Chapter 10, "Converting Your SEO Results into Paying Customers."

Finally, there are metrics related to site speed and site health, something that some SEO books spend dozens of pages on. Unless your website was coded from scratch or has a significant custom-built component to it, you probably will not need to think about these issues very much. There is no doubt that Google gives preferential treatment to websites that function the way websites are supposed to—namely, quickly and error-free.

 Note

There is one type of error that could significantly impact your traffic: crawl errors. These errors include 404 errors and Not Found errors, something you typically see when a page you're looking for on a website doesn't exist. You can see how many crawl errors Google believes your website has in Google's Webmaster Tools panel under the Crawl section. These errors can be fixed by whoever handles your web development, and must be marked "Fixed" afterward.

With this primer on analytics, you should be able to talk the language of most webmasters. Now it's time to turn our attention to what is possibly the most complicated portion of this book—but the one that separates the men from the boys, so to speak: Google Analytics. I promise to hold true to the title of this book and make it as simple as humanly possible.

How to Use Google Analytics

The reason I say that Google Analytics is a big step in your SEO journey is because it empowers you with data. In most entrepreneurs' and marketers' journeys, they discover intuition well before data. Figuring out how to sell your product begins with a hunch. For many, that hunch, along with informal experience, continues to govern their business for years to come. I am here to tell you today that intuition is not enough. Intuition is good, as is experience, but that experience needs to be formalized, codified into numbers so that it can be looked at in black and white.

Intuition is to data like a monkey is to a man. A monkey is quicker, more capable of surviving, and has overall better instincts than a man. I would not want to fight a monkey with just my fists. However, man has developed systems, tools, and machines to give him an enormous advantage in all the areas that a monkey is naturally superior. Given all of man's modern-day advantages, no monkey would want to fight a man.

In the same way, no entrepreneur who relies on intuition would want to compete against another entrepreneur who has an army of data working for him. Of course, the best situation of all is to have excellent intuition and use data to supplement it. That is the situation that I hope you'll be able to create by using Google Analytics.

Getting Familiar with Your Dashboard

When you first open your Google Analytics dashboard, you see a list of all the sites you are tracking. Maybe you've only got one site you're looking into, maybe more. Click the site you want to analyze. You will then find yourself on the Audience Overview page (see Figure 6.3).

Figure 6.3   *The Audience Overview page on Google Analytics, which is the default landing page as soon as you select the site you want to analyze.*

You are now looking at a page that has a lot of data on it. Before I go further, I want to let you know that this is a book on SEO, not Google Analytics specifically, so you should not rely on this chapter as a full tutorial on the program. Instead, consider it everything you need to know to competently analyze your SEO campaign. If you're interested in using Google Analytics not just for SEO but also to understand your search engine marketing (SEM; pay-per-click) campaign, social media campaigns, conversion, visitor engagement, and demographic, you should watch the official Google Analytics help videos on YouTube. You can find them at http://www.youtube.com/user/googleanalytics.

I usually find the Audience Overview page useful for a quick snapshot of how a site is doing lately. This page shows you the previous 30 days' data on visits, unique visitors, pageviews, pages per visit, average visit duration, bounce rate, and percentage of traffic that is new visits. Ideally, you should become familiar enough with these metrics that you can just glance at them and instantly get a sense of the progress of your marketing efforts. Let's go through them and break down what each metric means and why it does or does not matter.

- **Visits**—As explained earlier in the chapter, a visit is a browsing session. If your website were a doctor's office, a visit would be an appointment. It could be quick, or it could be long, but either way, a single, uninterrupted session counts as one. Once you've left, each time you come back counts as an additional visit. And, just as a doctor might have 100 patients who come in for several appointments during a given year, a website will have a certain number of unique visitors who each visit a certain number of times per month. Most people visit a website only one time per month, though, which is why people usually don't make much of a distinction between visits and unique visitors. Visits are the easiest metric to look at when determining the overall success of your SEO campaign. Every new visit earned organically through great content and link outreach has real value, so the more the merrier.

- **Unique visitors**—Unique visitors are the ultimate determinant of the popularity of your website. The number of discrete individuals who have come to your website each month is a pretty tangible concept. When my kids website first started to become really popular and we were getting 80,000 unique visitors per day, I would exclaim to my brother, "The number of people who come to our site every day could fill up Giants Stadium!" In that way, unique visitors feel very much like real people.

- **Pageviews**—When someone lands on a page of your site, Google Analytics registers that action as a pageview. So, if I find one of your articles on Google and read it; then click over to your home page to learn more about your company; then click your About page to continue the learning process; then leave, I have registered three pageviews on your site. Pageviews are useful insofar as they are one indicator of how engaging your site is: the more pages someone visits, the more interesting your site is to them (at least in theory). Pageviews are also useful for advertising-driven businesses, because online ads are usually sold on the basis of how many total ads can be shown to visitors. (Up to three ads can typically be shown every time a new page is loaded, so pageviews are key.)

- **Pages per visit**—If you were to take the total number of pageviews generated by your site's visitors and divide them by your total number of visitors, you would come up with the average number of pages a visitor to your site hits before leaving. For instance, if in a given month your site receives 1,000 visitors and 2,500 total pageviews, then, on average, each visitor hits 2.5 pages before leaving. Pages per visit is purely an engagement metric, meaning it is used to determine how deep your visitors' experiences are. It stands to reason that if people are visiting, say, 10 pages on your site before leaving, that you have some really awesome content. In reality, the Internet average is somewhere in the neighborhood of 1.5 pages / visit. So where should your website be? Well, it's difficult to find accurate information about websites' engagement metrics, so I have created my own chart, using my clients' Google Analytics data (see Figure 6.4).

Type of Business	Average Pages / Visit (in 2013)
B2B Software	2.4
Web Hosting	2.7
Organic Food	3.2
Business Consulting	3.2
Health & Fitness Advice	3.6
Wedding Planning	3.9
Celebrity Gossip	6.7
Social Gaming	15.5

Figure 6.4 *Average pages per visit for clients of mine in eight different industries. Note that companies that serve other companies have the lowest average pages per visit, followed by consumer-oriented companies, followed by entertainment websites.*

There is some debate about how much it matters to have a high number of pages per visit. Some say that it's a clear indicator of how effective your site is; others say that it's a metric that matters less and less in today's world of infinitesimal attention spans, where decisions are often made quickly. My take is that it's a rough indicator of how you're doing, but unless you're an entertainment property or an advertising-based site, it is merely a distraction from the most important metric, which is conversions.

- **Average visit duration**—Like pages per visit, average visit duration is an engagement metric. Because not all pages are structured the same way—both in terms of coding and layout—I'd say that visit duration is a more accurate measure of how involved your visitors are in your website. In fact, many newer websites use a kind of coding that renders the need to load new pages unnecessary, resulting in visitors effectively staying on one page throughout their entire visit. For those kind of sites especially, average visit duration is a far more relevant metric than pages per visit. That said, the average visit duration for most sites on the Internet is reputed to be about 1 minute. To give you a better sense of how your own site is doing, I have once again picked a few random clients in different industries and shared with you their average visit duration (see Figure 6.5).

- **Bounce rate**—The bounce rate of your site is essentially the percentage of visitors who arrived at your website and then turned around and went back to where they came from. I picture a weary traveler lugging his suitcase into the lobby of a hotel, desperate for a good night's rest; but the moment he enters, he sees that the lobby is filled with drunk college students who have all gathered to celebrate Greek Week. The man looks out at the mob of party animals, blinks in disbelief, and then emits one solid "Hell no!" as he hightails it out of there. That's a bounce.

Not every bounce is as extreme as the example I just gave. Often, the visitor simply failed to find what she was looking for. It may even be the case that she did a poor job searching on Google. That is why bounce rates are seldom less than about 25%. (In fact, if your site had something like a 5% bounce rate, it would probably mean that almost all your visitors are coming from word of mouth and there are very few "cold" visitors from organic search or paid ads.) Personally, I consider a very good bounce rate to be anything between 25% and 55%.

Type of Business	Average Time on Site (in 2013)
Social Media Consulting	1:03
Law	1:58
Fashion Retail	2:05
Accounting	2:15
Medical	2:17
Wedding Invitations	3:26
Green Shopping	4:05
R & B Artist	4:30

Figure 6.5   *Average visit duration for eight clients of mine in different industries. The pattern here is that sites that people visit to quickly look up information—mostly business-to-business sites—have the lowest average visit duration, whereas sites that are meant for e-commerce or leisure—mostly business-to-consumer sites—naturally keep visitors on longer.*

- **Percentage of traffic that is new visits**—The metric % New Visits refers to the number of first-time visitors to your website. Although I probably look at this metric least often, it is instructive; essentially, it tells you how much of your traffic is coming from your marketing efforts versus people that like your site enough to come back another time. You don't want this percentage to be to be too high or too low. If your % New Visits is too high—say, 95%—it means very few people ever come back. Your site is essentially a one-time experience for most people. However, if your % New Visits were too low—10% for example—it means that you are probably not doing enough to drive new people to the site. If your site is anywhere between 30% and 70% new visitors, it's in good shape. Not that lower or higher is necessarily a disaster, but it points to a need for change.

There was never a time when % New Visits mattered more to me than during the time period when I was shopping my kids' website for sale. At one point, our traffic was in a seasonal dip. Desperate to keep our numbers high, I started to make traffic partnerships with other big games websites. Soon, our numbers were higher than ever. I was happy until the head of acquisitions for a large media company was inspecting my traffic one day and called me to ask about my % New Visits. "I'm concerned," he told me to my dread, "that too high a percentage of your traffic comes from first-time visitors, especially referrals from other games sites. What will happen if and when these outside referrals come to an end? We want to know that you have a strong base of loyal users first and foremost." In truth, we did have a loyal user base, but since I had created those traffic partnerships, it just represented a smaller percentage of my site's visitors than it used to. That incident reminded me to always focus on user experience first and foremost; the returning visitors are often the most valuable. (But of course, you need new visitors to make returning visitors.)

Evaluating Your SEO Campaign

Now that you know the basic metrics of Google Analytics, it's time to learn how to measure your SEO efforts. There are five main categories of reports in Google Analytics: Real-Time, Audience, Traffic Sources, Content, and Conversions. Out of all these categories, only two of them, Traffic Sources and Conversions, need to be checked weekly. But let's go through them all—we'll move quicker through the less-important ones—so that you can at least have all the tools at your disposal.

Real-Time

The Real-Time report shows you what is happening on your site at the current moment (see Figure 6.6). While it is super cool and interesting, it is not one I personally spend much time on. In a world of immensely valuable historical data, it is like trying to learn about your business from the five customers currently walking around inside your store. What I do find quite useful about real-time data, however, is occasionally allowing it to remind you what a visitor's live experience is like. Whereas the Content report will give you a picture of what most people do on your site, this report allows you to *feel* that experience better. In watching people browse my wife's theme park design site, for instance, I noticed how certain people come just to research particular live shows at theme parks (something I'd never expect), and others like to read straight through the last 10 to 15 news items. These are two very different types of visitors, and identifying them may influence the way my wife shapes new content sections in the future.

Audience

The report that Google Analytics chooses to show you by default as soon as you log in (previously shown in Figure 6.3) clearly has many uses. Mostly though, it is useful for the Overview. The other categories vary in usefulness. The Behavior category is good for drilling down on how long people stay on your site and how often they return (although you already have a general idea of these metrics from the Overview). The Demographic, Technology, and Mobile sections tell you, respectively, the language and location of your visitors, the web browser they're using, and whether they're accessing your site via a tablet, phone, or a full computer. Although the last three categories are useful, they are mostly things you need to check in on every few months in reference to the way your site functions from a technical or structural standpoint. For instance, if you have a lot of visitors who speak Spanish and that market is valuable to you, you may want to create a Spanish version of your site. Or, if a lot of people visit your site from a mobile device, you should be confident that your site is easy to navigate on a phone or tablet.

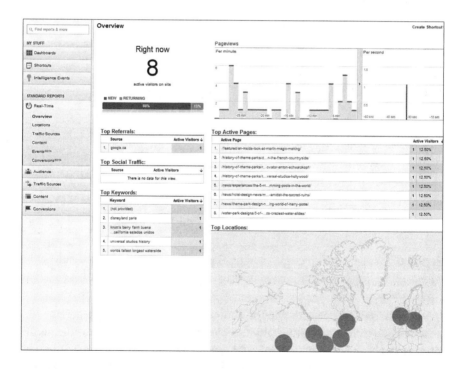

Figure 6.6   *The Real-Time report on Google Analytics. This report tells you how many people are on your site at a given moment, how they arrived at your site, where they live, and what page they're currently viewing.*

Traffic Sources

The Traffic Sources report is easily my most-frequented section of Google Analytics. Essentially, it tells you where all the traffic on your website comes from. You start on an Overview page that shows you the same graph of visits for the last 30 days that you'll find on the Audience Overview. Below that are tastes of things that are truly interesting, like which traffic sources sent the most visitors, which pages most visitors arrived on, and your site's top-performing organic search keywords (see Figure 6.7).

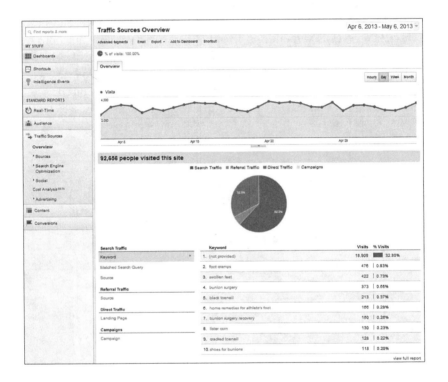

Figure 6.7 *The Traffic Sources report on Google Analytics. This is the Analytics page I use most to evaluate clients' SEO campaigns.*

Apart from the Overview, the Traffic Sources report has five subcategories: Sources, Search Engine Optimization, Social, Cost Analysis, and Advertising. Strangely, I have never found the Search Engine Optimization subcategory to be especially useful. It gives a lot of general data about keywords that could possibly help trigger ideas for new keywords to target, but nothing that you couldn't find by using the Google AdWords Keyword Planner.

I also don't spend much time in the Social, Cost Analysis, or Advertising subcategories when working on an SEO campaign.

The subcategory I find to be most useful is Sources. This report truly gives you a sense of the effectiveness of your SEO campaign, from the sheer volume of organic search traffic your site is receiving to some of the keywords supplying that traffic to the quality of those keywords. When you click in Sources, you are presented with another five options that divide the traffic coming to your website into four main sources:

- **Direct traffic**—Visitors typing your website into their browser or coming from a bookmark on their browser
- **Referral traffic**—Visitors clicking a link on another website to get to your site
- **Search traffic**—Visitors who find your site within organic search (which is the subject of this book)
- **Paid traffic**—Visitors who arrive from advertising campaigns

While I am interested in how a website's traffic is divided between the first three sources (the fourth, paid traffic, is a whole different ballgame), I get a sense of that composition from the Audience Overview page. Where I'm actually spending most of my time is in the Search subcategory.

As crazy as it sounds, there are yet another three subcategories under Search, but you only need to worry about Organic. In fact, this sub-subcategory, which requires you to go through the following click path,

Home Page > Traffic Sources > Sources > Search > Organic

is the hidden gold of Google Analytics. It is the place where you can see all your organic search traffic and glimpse the keywords sending traffic to your website (see Figure 6.8).

When I first arrive on this page, the place my eyes immediately travel to is to the traffic graph. Has there been upward movement in the past few days, or at least since the last time I checked? Any spikes or dips that I need to examine? After that, I take a look at the list of keywords below the graph. Again, this list is just a small sample of the total number of keywords sending traffic to the site—most of which are encrypted by Google—yet it still gives me an idea of what types of keywords the site is ranking for. I then use the search box (the one in the middle of the page with the magnifying glass next to it) to filter out all keywords sending traffic to the site except ones that are particularly valuable to the business that owns the website. I call these kinds of keywords *money keywords*.

Figure 6.8   *The Organic Search subcategory in Google Analytics. I consider this to be the most valuable report of all for an SEO campaign. Although the number of keywords listed in this report is no longer accurate due to Google's encrypting search data, you can still get a sampling of your site's organic search keywords from the 5% or so of searches that aren't encrypted for various reasons.*

In the case of my wife's site, because she is looking to attract people who want to build theme parks and rides, we often type the word `designer` in the search box (see Figure 6.9). We choose that word because people who are searching Google using the word `designer` are often looking to *hire* a designer. If Google returns one of entertainmentdesigner.com's pages, it is likely because the person searched for an `entertainment designer, theme park designer`, or other kind of `designer` within that industry. Because those searches loosely describe what my wife does for a living, all `designer` search terms are valuable to her. Looking through the results of a `designer`-filtered search on her Google Analytics organic traffic report, it is confirming to see that people who land on her site from typing in some form of `designer` spend a disproportionately large amount of time on the site.

ʾrimary Dimension: Keyword Source Landing Page Other

Plot Rows | Secondary dimension | Sort Type: Default | designer

	Keyword	Visits	Pages / Visit	Avg. Visit Duration
1.	entertainment designer	38	6.24	00:10:59
2.	theme park designer	11	4.73	00:03:41
3.	theme park designers	8	14.50	00:33:04
4.	entertainmentdesigner.com	6	6.33	00:06:59
5.	event designer	5	2.40	00:00:36
6.	entertainment designers	4	7.00	00:16:11
7.	roller coaster designer	4	1.25	00:00:28
8.	entertainment designer theme parks london	3	2.67	00:03:26
9.	event designers	3	4.00	00:01:17
10.	amusement park ride designers	2	2.00	00:01:05
11.	designer hammocks	2	1.50	00:00:02
2.	theme park ride designers	2	5.00	00:02:44
13.	walt disney was a entertainment designer	2	3.50	00:02:25
14.	waterslide designer	2	1.00	00:00:00
5.	who are the top theme park designers?	2	5.00	00:03:42
16.	"entertainment designer"	1	5.00	00:02:01
17.	2012 olympic opening ceremony designer	1	1.00	00:00:00
18.	2012 opening ceremony designer	1	1.00	00:00:00

Figure 6.9 *The organic search traffic report on Google Analytics for my wife's theme park design website, filtered by keywords that contain the word* `designer`*.* `Designer` *is one of her business' money keywords, meaning that it directly leads to revenue for her company. As you can see by the highlighted search terms, engagement levels are particularly high when someone finds the site after typing in* `designer`*.*

A site whose organic traffic is substantially made up of money keywords is a site with a strong SEO strategy. The way I look at traffic for most of my clients, the overall traffic to the site is only fairly important (unless the site monetizes through ads). It is the organic search traffic—especially when that traffic is driven by money keywords—that matters the most.

Content

The Content section of Google Analytics tells you what people are doing on your site. I don't find myself here on a weekly basis, but it does have some very interesting features that could shape the way you develop content for your site. The default landing page for this report is the Overview, which shows you a graph of the pageviews on your site in the past 30 days (see Figure 6.10). I usually glance past the graph—I've already gotten plenty of info from the Audience Overview I landed on when I first logged in to Google Analytics—and spend a few seconds looking at the Page list in the middle of the screen. This list tells you the most popular pages on your site, in descending order.

If I'm going to spend more time in this area, I'll usually click the View Full Report link at the bottom of the list of Pages, which brings you to the Site Content report. This report gives you a sense of both the popularity (# of pageviews) and engagement level (time on site) for every page on your site. It is also interesting to browse through the bounce rate of each page—or, the percentage of visitors who landed on the page and then immediately left—because it can quickly clue you in to pages that turn people off in some way. Because most people enter your site through your home page, a high bounce rate on the home page should raise a red flag. It would indicate one of three scenarios:

- You're directing irrelevant traffic to the home page.
- People aren't finding your website trustworthy.
- People are getting the impression that your business doesn't fit their needs.

Figure 6.10 *The Overview report within the Content section of Google Analytics.*

Racing through some of the other reports in the Content section: Site Speed is what it sounds like, Site Search is helpful if you have a Google-powered search engine on your site, Events are useful for tracking on-page elements like downloads and video plays, and AdSense allows you to track data if you participate in the AdSense program (that is, placing ads on your website).

The last two Content reports are quite interesting, even though they are used much less than some of the other reports we've covered. Experiments allows you to run split tests, also known as A/B tests, wherein you try out different ways of communicating with visitors to see which one is the most successful. Experiments in Google Analytics allows you to track several different elements on your website (see Figure 6.11).

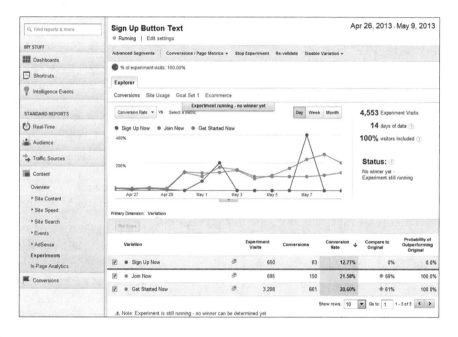

Figure 6.11   *The Experiments report within the Content section of Google Analytics is useful for learning which graphics or calls to action on your pages are most effective.*

Suppose, for example, that you want users to become a subscriber to your online service. You probably have a call to action—a button, most likely—on the home page. What should be written on that button? Let's say your intuition tells you that Sign Up Now is the correct language to use. Well that's great, but what if Join Now has a marginally better effect? And how about Get Started Now? This is where Experiments would come in. It allows you to serve all three options to your visitors in equal proportion. In other words, each of the three buttons would be shown to visitors 33% of the time. From there, it's basically a horse race; at the end of a certain time period, the button that resulted in the most signups wins. You should make that button permanent on your site.

In-Page Analytics is also quite cool. Among other things, it puts notes next to all the links on your site, indicating what percentage of the total clicks on that page each link received. It is likely that important menu items like About Us and Pricing will get clicked on a lot, but you may learn that, for instance, very few people ever click Testimonials and that people are very interested in your Company Story.

Conversions

Possibly the most important Google Analytics report, Conversions allows you to track purchases, registrations, signups, or any other important action on your website. All of these important actions are referred to as *goals*. Although a bit of work is required to set up goals, whoever handles your website should be able to make it happen in just a few hours. First, you need to determine what your goal is. If you've got an e-commerce site, it's completing a checkout. If you are in the professional services industry, it's probably filling out a contact form. If you provide software as a service (SAAS) or generally seek for people to log in to your website, then a signup is your goal. Once you determine your goal, you need to identify a page that visitors would land on *only* if they had completed a goal. That page is almost always a Thank You page—the page visitors see after they have completed a purchase, form fill, or signup, which says something like "Thank you for your order." To activate goals, you need to place a small piece of code on that page. Every time that page is loaded by a visitor, Google registers a goal.

By tracking where each visitor came from who completed a goal, as well as what path they traveled on your website to get there, Google is shining light on one of the most important metrics you can possibly look at. If you know, for instance, that people who complete a goal on your site always visit the About Us page, you'll want to make sure that it is the best it can possibly be (although, clearly it is already working to some degree if people are visiting it en route to completing a goal). Or, even more important, if you see that visitors from a particular traffic source tend to complete goals a high percentage of the time, you definitely want to investigate how you can get your site more exposure on that traffic source. I have a legal client who never used goals until we began working together. He advertised on three small legal sites, but never knew which ones were performing best; he just knew he was getting a bunch of business from advertising on all of them. Once we set up goals for him, we noticed that one of them delivered a good deal of business, especially relative to its modest cost, whereas another, more expensive site, never delivered anything. You can guess what happened next: The nonperforming site got axed, and the high-performing site got a greater investment from my client.

While there is much more to learn about goals, my objective is simply to set you on the right course. As I mentioned earlier, the Google Analytics team puts out some great training videos, and there are also many fine books out there dedicated solely to Google Analytics.

At this point, you should be able to measure the success of your SEO work. (In fact, between Google Analytics, Google Webmaster Tools, and Google search itself, you can measure your SEO results almost exclusively within the Google brand.) And with the close of this chapter, you now have the most important knowledge in this book as it pertains to SEO. The remaining six chapters will clarify and enhance the knowledge you already have, as well as make you think. I've given a lot of thought to every chapter, paragraph, and word in this book, but I advise you to give a particularly thorough read to Chapter 10, "Converting Your SEO Results into Paying Customers," and Chapter 12, "Using SEO to Build a Business."

In the next chapter, we'll squash a few myths.

7

Google Optimization Myths

The purpose of this book is to teach you how to dominate the Google search results and gain lots of new business. However, it is often hard to communicate information if other, conflicting information is present. It would be ideal if everyone reading this book were starting with a blank slate, knowing nothing about SEO. But because most of you have at least some familiarity with the subject, I may have a little battle to wage with commonly held beliefs. There are tons of theories out there, most of them propagated in webmaster forums and free seminars by so-called experts who actually know little about the subject. Here in this chapter, I plan to depose some of the most insidious, widely spread myths about Google optimization.

I can think of two reasons why there is so much conflicting information about SEO out there:

- The first is money. Lots of "gurus" have a financial stake in selling you their own optimization products and services, which means that they need to convince you that whatever they are capable of doing is the right thing to do. A person whose specialty is creating content will tell you that SEO is all about having lots of pages. A link broker will insist that you need to buy links on certain websites to win the first page. A web design firm will be convinced that the way your website is coded determines your rankings.

- The other reason is that this stuff actually is confusing. There are so many factors that might plausibly play a role in SEO, and sorting them all out can make your head spin. Between the onsite factors of website code, structure, layout, and content, and the offsite factors of linking style, type of links, and age of links—not to mention Google's constantly changing rules—it's hard to know what's real. Not helping matters is the fact that Google is a vocal proponent of policies that help them to succeed but aren't necessarily helpful to you, the website owner or marketer.

The truth is that there are only three ways to know for sure what works in SEO:

- Put on a ski mask and creep into Google's headquarters in Mountain View, California, while the engineers are sleeping.
- Isolate every possible ranking factor and conduct experiments for months on end.
- Trust the information in this book.

I recommend a combination of careful research and experimentation with trusting what I'm telling you. And if you do try the cat burglar approach, let me know so that I can interview you during visitor hours at the county jail. But seriously, although it might sound obvious to try different strategies and observe what works, few people actually do so systematically. The average person I've seen trying his or her hand at SEO is fixated on one or two strategies. If those strategies don't perform, he or she will focus on some other aspect of marketing instead. And yet, if this person had only tried out 10 strategies, spending a small amount of money on each, he or she would probably have found the one that works.

I have conducted more than 120 trial-and-error experiments over 9 years. And by this point, you already know what I believe to be true about SEO. But, just to set the record straight, here are the things I am certain are *not* true.

Myth 1: Your Google Ranking Is Based on What's Written on Your Website

This is by far the biggest and most widespread myth. The reason for its staying power is the fact that SEO in the early days was all about your website. It was about the keywords in your website's code and the density of keywords on your pages. Early search engines such as Excite and AltaVista relied heavily on these factors when ranking your website. But then a few people caught on, realizing that if they wrote certain phrases many times at the bottom of their websites, lots more traffic would arrive (see Figure 7.1). And then lots more people caught on—to the point where the search engines were overtaken by these early search engine optimizers. The results were polluted, and instead of changing their systems entirely, most search engines kept putting bandages on the problem by banning the most egregious keyword repeaters and creating filters for keyword density on a page.

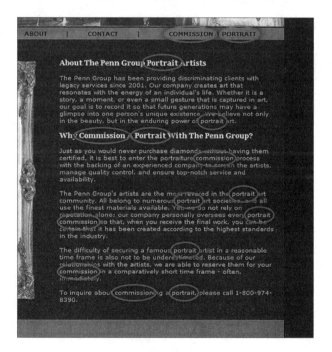

Figure 7.1   *This page was written with keyword density in mind. Clearly optimized for* `commission a portrait`*, it contains the word* `commission` *6 times and the word* `portrait` *11 times. Although cleverly executed to sound natural, this type of optimization is no longer effective for ranking higher in Google.*

Google came along and changed the entire game with its concept of PageRank, which relied mostly on an external factor: links. Links were much more difficult to manipulate, which is why Google's results were famously relevant to your search and mostly spam free. Back then, as well as today, the actual content on your website matters only marginally.

Today, only four on-website elements really matter to Google: keyword-rich meta page titles, SEO-friendly URLs, clean code, and sensible site structure. If you've paid attention to what you've read so far in this book, it is doubtful that any of those elements will be a problem. Just to make sure, let's go through them:

- **Keyword-rich meta page titles**—Chapter 2, "The Five Ingredients of Google Optimization," covered this subject thoroughly, but basically, your meta page title is your only opportunity to tell Google what each page on your website is about. Write the best page in the world on Houston office spaces, but make the meta page title About Our Company, and Google will cause your site to show up in their results when someone searches about our company. Not very useful. But if someone searches Houston office space for rent, Google will probably pass right by your page. Why? You never put your name on the list! Of course, Google *is* capable of knowing what your page is about without you writing it in the meta page title—and technically, it is possible for your page to show up for searches unrelated to what's in your meta page title—but there's no reason to ignore one of Google's clearest preferences.

- **SEO-friendly URLs**—Making sure that your URLs are coded in a way that is easy for search engines to read (which, once again, is a topic I discussed in Chapter 2) is easy nowadays. Most content management systems (CMSs), including my favorite one, WordPress, automatically generate URLs that mirror the title of the page you produce. So, if you write an article called A Beginner's Guide to Russian Roulette, it will automatically publish it as http://www.yoursite.com/a-beginners-guide-to-russian-roulette. (In case you're curious, rule #1 is "Don't play.") What you want to avoid are URLs that are random strings of numbers, letters, and special characters.

- **Clean code**—When I say that your site should have *clean code*, I basically mean that the back-end coding of your website should be neat and organized so that Google's search robots can easily read it. For obvious reasons, if your house is a mess, Google doesn't want to sort through it; they can just as easily skip it. You can usually be assured that your site's coding is clean if you're using WordPress or another popular CMS. If you have a custom-built website, you can have a third-party individual—a reputable programmer would be best—take a look at the back end to evaluate its cleanliness. Of course, you should always check for errors in Google Webmaster Tools, which is the main place where Google communicates with webmasters about the health of their websites.

- **Sensible site structure**—Google's robots are trained to figure out whether your site would be easy for a human being to navigate. All that means for you is that you should put all the pages that you care about Google trusting in the clear light of day. Most business websites have several main sections (for example, Home, About, Services, Contact), possibly some subcategories (perhaps product areas), and, in the case of e-commerce websites, a list of inventory. To receive the best exposure from Google, build your website like you would build a physical building. If you were in charge of building a mall, you'd make sure to put the information booth in plain sight near the entrance, the stores along several main corridors, and clearly mark the bathrooms. You would not hide a bathroom in a secret passageway underneath a clothing store. By the same token, everything on your site should be clearly marked and easy to get to.

  A rule of thumb in website creation is that none of your main pages should be more than two clicks away from the home page. So, let's say you have an important page on your site called About the Founders, which is the page that talks about how the founders started your company. And let's say that to reach this page a person needed to click About the Company on the home page, then Our Team, then About the Founders. That would mean it takes three clicks to get to that page. If that were the case, your page would be too far away from the home page and, therefore, not easily found on Google. Simplicity is the golden rule in on-page SEO as in much of business.

After your website is built, the last three factors won't come into play that often. In your everyday SEO work, the only on-page factor that will come into play regularly is keyword-rich meta page titles.

A final note on on-page SEO: Nowadays, Google's algorithm is much more about what you should not do than what you should do. And so, even if you ace the four factors listed here and do a top-notch job link building, you can still be prevented from ranking because of things you've done wrong. For instance, if you publish low-quality content, mass produce lots of pages that are substantially similar to one another, or link to every other website you own on every page, your site could be penalized. The key is to operate your website as if you're not SEO-ing too hard. If Google perceives that you're trying to beat the system, it will prevent your site from ranking.

In summary, pay attention to your website, mostly by following common-sense practices and avoiding things that Google doesn't like. But if you want to rank high on Google, most of your time should be spent building links.

Myth 2: Doing SEO Requires Technical Knowledge

As explained with regard to the previous myth, it's important to make sure that your back-end website code is clean and organized, but there is nothing technical you need to know beyond that for SEO purposes. The myth that you must embed things into your site's coding to make it rank higher on Google traces its roots back to the early days of the Web. Proponents of this myth argue that the Web was built by engineers, and Google is made up of engineers, so knowing how to code must give you a huge advantage for ranking on Google. Terms such as *XML sitemaps*, *meta keywords*, and *robots.txt* are often thrown around as a way of making the Web more mystical to everyday people. These are real things that appear in your site's code, but in most cases, you don't need to know about them. Only if your site has a complicated back end will you even need someone on hand to handle these kind of technical elements. Unless you have a large e-commerce website, it is probably unnecessary—and even irresponsible on the part of your web developer—to have anything but a simple CMS such as WordPress as your back end.

I think the mystification of SEO continues to be propagated by the technical people who benefit financially from making you feel like SEO is too obscure for you to carry out yourself. As soon as the Web became a place where the average person spent a lot of time (circa 1999), a large rift became evident—the one between the everyday people who use the Web and the software engineers who build it. Because we rely on these all-powerful folks to make our websites work, we also sometimes rely on them for advice about anything to do with the Internet. And that can be a mistake.

In reality, SEO is not a technical skill. Case in point: I majored in English in college and have never written a line of code in my life. And yet, I've attracted tens of millions of visitors to my websites through SEO, learning the art better than any techie I've met. But still, if my programmer were to tell me tomorrow that Google has changed some technical standard that will affect my SEO and he needs to overhaul my website, he would have my attention. There is much power in controlling something that people don't understand.

My point is that some tech folks overemphasize the importance of what they know and underemphasize the importance of what they don't know. And this leads to people paying for unnecessary things.

With all that said, I don't have anything against web developers; I simply believe that, once your website is up and running, they should be needed as little as possible until you wish to add new functionality to your site. At the end of the day, your SEO is still mostly about links and meta page titles.

Myth 3: Website Traffic Affects Google Rankings

This is a particularly tempting myth because it sounds completely plausible. The idea is that the more people who click your website in the organic search results, the higher it will rise. While it is definitely true that Google watches your behavior in the search results—doing so is what makes them so successful at earning ad revenue—they do not equate a click with a stamp of approval. Google knows that people click on things and then bounce right back to the search results all the time.

A more interesting question is whether they collect data on which sites typically get bounced off of by people for a given search, and demote those in the rankings. Officially, Google claims that they don't "learn" about results this way, as it could be too easily manipulated by cunning crowdsourcers. (For example, you could pay people small sums of money to type in a certain search, click on your website, and then stay there for 5 minutes.) It would also create a system where the high-quality sites at the top of the rankings would continue to gain credibility, while high-quality sites on the second or third page for a given search would fail to get recognized simply because fewer people are testing them. My guess is that even if Google does use this data, it's only in a limited way.

Google's actual method for ordering the search results—relying heavily on inbound links—is much more reliable because links tend to be earned by people with real knowledge of what is on the other end of them. Most of us wouldn't post a link to another website without vetting it. And because links are built upon a deeper level of knowledge, they have proved over time to be a much more consistent gauge of value.

Myth 4: Pay-per-Click Campaigns Affect Organic Rankings

Many people have asked me whether spending money with Google AdWords will improve their search results. Google is clear about the fact that no correlation exists between the paid results and the organic results, and for good reason: It would undermine consumers' trust of the search results, making its system more overtly capitalistic than it already is.

Some people refuse to believe that, though, insisting that Google uses its advertising program as a sort of backdoor bribe that gives you extra consideration in the rankings. It's like greasing the palm of a maître d'—a quick exchange, a nod toward the man in the back, and suddenly you hear, "Right this way, sir."

Of course, any kind of "pay for play" system would be patently corrupt, especially for a public company leading the world of technology. If Google sold its results, it would lose its reputation as a trusted search engine in a matter of weeks. After all, there is a reason *Consumer Reports* doesn't accept advertising of any kind: The first whiff of any kind of conflict of interest can destroy a reputation. And besides, Google already uses AdWords to get people to pay for first page placement and is making a few billion dollars a quarter from it. So it doesn't need to meddle with its most sensitive asset—the organic results.

Myth 5: Submitting a New Site to Google Is an Essential Way to Get It Recognized

This myth, like all the ones before it, has been around since the early days of search engines. It used to be that search engines asked webmasters to submit their websites so that there was a better chance the search engines would index those websites. Today, technology is much better than it used to be, and submission is no longer important. Getting a single link from another website typically gets your site indexed by Google in less than a week. The only time when submitting your site is a good idea is if you don't plan to get any links for your website, in which case Google might not know about your site until you make such a submission. But I have seen sites get indexed with no links countless times, so even in this situation, it's not a must to submit your site.

 Note

A related myth is that you must pay to get your site admitted to Google's index. This is hooey. I can't even imagine why people would think this myth is true unless they have been confused by the charlatans who charge for "submission to hundreds of search engines!" Putting aside the fact that there aren't hundreds of search engines that people actually go to, there certainly is no need to submit your site to them. Search engines follow links—that is how they discover the Web. And Google will find your site, whether you like it or not.

Myth 6: PageRank Matters

I started off this book with a discussion of the myth of PageRank. However, let me put it more succinctly here. Many people believe that PageRank is Google's rating of the importance of your website on a 0 to 10 scale. In reality, PageRank is a slippery, correlative measurement. It is a distraction from TrustRank, which is the real measure of a site's importance to Google. The fact that a PageRank bar is available for the Google toolbar is misleading—and somewhat mean—because it keeps people thinking about the wrong system.

One thing PageRank does indicate is the frequency with which your site is visited by Google to be indexed. But you can also learn that by monitoring when Google tends to cache (take a picture of) your site. You can find out your latest cache date by doing a Google search for your site. Next to the URL, you will see a little arrow indicating a drop-down menu. Click that and then on the word *cached*. The resulting page, a recent snapshot of your website, displays a date at the top (see Figure 7.2).

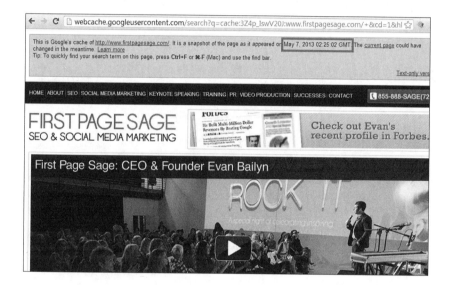

Figure 7.2   *A search result on Google almost always has a small link to the right of the domain name that says "cached." Clicking it tells you the last time Google visited your site. Sites with a high PageRank tend to get cached more frequently.*

While PageRank does not tell you the importance of your site in Google's eyes, nor whether it ranks for any competitive keywords, it does tell you something. In truth, no matter how much I denounce PageRank, I still find myself looking at it from time to time, especially if I'm on a call with someone who tells me about his or her website and I want to get a quick picture of the site's credibility. If I see a PageRank of 3 or higher, it indicates to me that the site has been around a while and has links coming to it. In short, PageRank shows whether a site is established.

But in the same way that a person can have had a long career in a given industry but not be trusted by her peers, a site can have a high PageRank but a low TrustRank. Any site in this situation has only superficial value.

Myth 7: Commenting on Blogs and Forums Is an Effective Link-Building Strategy

In 2004, it was a fabulous idea to comment often on high-TrustRank blogs and forums, discretely leaving your link at the end of your comment. As long as you wrote something intelligent, people figured that the link was just your usual way of signing off, left the comment up, and the links passed TrustRank. All was good. But then the spammers came in. From 2005 to this very day, there has been such a plethora of linking being done in the comment section of blogs and forums that a new category has been invented to describe it: comment spam (see Figure 7.3).

Figure 7.3 *A view of the moderation panel for one of my blogs. This page is 100% comment spam. All comments are meant to look real but are just a thinly veiled disguise for the spam they truly are.*

I will end any speculation that putting links in your comments works. Not only do most blogs mark all comments with a no-follow tag, which, as you may recall, blocks the passing of TrustRank, but Google very likely de-emphasizes comment links anyway because the system has been so abused. After all, put yourself in Google's shoes: Links are supposed to be editorial votes of confidence from one site to another. But comments are not within the editorial domain of the owner of a website; they are written by the very people hoping to receive the benefit of those links. So there is no reason, in Google's eyes, to consider those links a vessel of trust. In fact, they are not.

Myth 8: Google Changes Their Algorithm So Frequently That There Is No Way to Keep Up with It

The #1 most common question I get when I give seminars is "How do you keep up with Google when their algorithms are always changing?" This is a very reasonable question, and the answer may surprise you: Google's algorithms *aren't* always changing. In fact, a company that ranked well in their industry in 2004 could use the same strategy today and rank just as well if that strategy were simply to put out great content, create custom page titles for each page of content, and earn links based on the strength of that content. References to "all those changes" in Google's algorithm are mostly to Google's spam-prevention efforts, which have made it so that you can't do SEO the quick and easy way anymore. This brings us back to the Panda and Penguin penalties, which, once again, punish sites for poor-quality content and links, respectively. These algorithm updates are not changes to Google's search algorithm any more than cameras in a casino are changes to the rules of blackjack: They're simply a way to prevent cheating.

There is, however, one exception to this rule, one thing that *has* changed about Google's algorithm in 2012 and 2013: the inclusion of social data. Google has assiduously dedicated itself to the task of gathering enough information about your relationships with the people in your network (both business and personal) that it can alter your search results based on those people's recommendations. I go into depth on this topic in Chapter 11, "Social Search: The Intersection of Social Media and SEO," but bear in mind that, as of late 2013, Google had not gathered enough collective social data to significantly change its search results based on your relationships. Sure, your search results are influenced by what the people in your Google network (which mostly includes Gmail, Google+, and YouTube) "plus," as well as websites' and bloggers' popularity on Google+, but the changes aren't impactful enough to worry about quite yet. Besides, I believe that the current link-based algorithm will continue to be dominant well into the future, as we often search for things our friends and colleagues don't know about, or about which we don't want their opinions.

Separating Truth from Myth

So what is the larger lesson here? I think a lot of SEO myths rely on a rule-centric view of Google. If you hit a certain keyword density, you're golden. If you use precisely the right kind of markup code and XML sitemaps, your work is done.

Engineers love rules such as these because rules govern the entire field of software design and because rules reduce the world to a set of comprehensible laws. Rules are comforting, easily explained, and easily achieved.

But rules are a pretty poor snapshot of reality. The real world simply doesn't abide by them, and the Web is a reflection of the real world. It isn't possible that all the most useful websites about sharks use the word sharks exactly 15% of the time, nor is it possible that the most useful websites about dental veneers are linked through images 20% of the time. In fact, very few things about great websites can be said to be universally true.

Google is well aware of the limitations of rules. That's why the company is always on the lookout for anything that appears suspiciously programmatic, homogenous, or precise. The actual Web is a messy and chaotic place, and sites that are truly valuable tend to have widely varying on-page factors and backlinks. There is no one "magic formula" for high rankings. The most popular sites are all coded differently, written differently, and saddled with thousands of links beyond their control. Actual popularity doesn't look like a formula.

Your job as an optimizer is to stimulate true organic behavior. This is why the nuclear football is all about creating content that people genuinely want to share. When a website magically acquires 100 links that are all phrased the same way, a bell goes off in Google headquarters that says "fake." When a keyword appears in precisely the same proportions on every page of your website, the bell rings again: "formula." Google's mission in life is to separate real value from artificial manipulation.

But now that we know that randomness is the only true reflection of reality, it's worth asking what randomness really looks like. Human beings are notoriously bad at identifying true randomness because of our tendency to find patterns in everything we see. If you flip a coin 1,000 times, the chances are that you will get a string of 10 heads in a row somewhere. Most people would view such a coincidence as exceedingly rare. But that string of heads is no more or less likely than any other combination of flips.

The same idea applies to the Web. Sometimes a good site will have a dozen links in a row that use the same exact words. Other times, they will have none. Sometimes a stellar article will use a keyword in every other sentence. Other times an author saves it for one big bang at the end. Statisticians describe such randomness using terms like clumping and standard deviation, but they are all just fancy ways of saying that anything is possible.

So what is the upshot for SEO? Just keep making your site as great as it can be, keeping close tabs on your progress. Go easy on the formulas. Accept that you don't have full control over the outcome of your SEO efforts. There is no one optimal set of conditions for achieving a top rank in Google. The only real commonality in all high-ranking sites is that they have links from many different websites and do not violate any of Google's rules. Everything I recommend in this book is meant to create that situation.

8

White Hat Versus Black Hat SEO

It is tempting to tell the story of white hat and black hat SEO in the same way one would tell a fairytale, with a good side and an evil side. White hat SEO would be the pure-hearted hero and black hat SEO would be the dark villain. But because this is a business book, it's important to stay realistic. White hat SEO is, simply, the SEO tactics that will cause Google to send more traffic to your website, and black hat SEO is the tactics that will cause Google to limit the traffic it sends to your website. There are no ethical or legal considerations in this discussion because we're speaking in the context of Google's made-up rules. However, being that Google is probably the biggest single driver of commerce in the United States, we all care a lot about its perception of good and bad. For a professional search engine optimizer, engaging in black hat tactics is one of the worst things you can do because it puts your client's website at risk for getting penalized or banned from Google's search results. Most clients would gladly banish you to Siberia for doing that.

In point of fact, it is rare that you meet an optimizer—especially someone within the United States—who participates in straight-up *black hat* SEO. Most optimizer's tactics fall under the definition of gray hat: stuff Google doesn't particularly like, but won't cause permanent damage to your website's reputation. Of course, gray hat tactics span the spectrum; however, most of the time they result in holdbacks from Google that create frustration and extra work for a company. That is why this chapter is so important: You've got to know what's okay and what's not.

And so, in this chapter we're going to cross the spectrum of SEO together, beginning with the briniest black, and going all the way to the most angelic white, the kind of behavior that would make Google beam with pride and buy you an ice cream sundae.

Black Hat SEO

The furthest end of the spectrum, the worst of the worst you can do in Google's eyes, has to do with malicious trickery. Much like the way a court would judge the perpetrator of a crime, your punishment is in line with your intentions. A black hat optimizer uses hacker-like techniques to deceive search engines into believing that a site is more worthy of a high ranking than it actually is or to show human visitors different things than what is shown to the search engines. These methods are in direct violation of the search engines' rules. Black hat SEO includes the creation of dummy sites and doorway pages, performing tricks such as cloaking and using hidden text—all described in this section. It is about short-term gain; in fact, the expectation of getting banned from the results and needing to start over with a different identity is inherent in the black hat philosophy.

So why do people become black hat SEOs? There are probably a few psychological reasons—a need to rebel, a desire to get attention by breaking rules, a thrill in outwitting The Man—but the most common reason is to make money quickly. Black hat SEOs are typically less financially successful than white hat SEOs because their vision is so shortsighted. In business, playing just within the boundaries makes you more money. Play like a complete boy scout and you'll probably fail; break all the rules, and you'll also fail; but aggressive play within the rules is the real recipe for success.

Although it is getting increasingly difficult to pull off a really clever black hat trick, if you do succeed, you can get tons of traffic from Google for a few days or weeks of work. But the second Google's spam team notices what you're doing—and they will—your site will be permanently banned from Google. While black hat SEO tactics can deliver lots of traffic before they are stymied, they sacrifice long-term profitability, growth, respectability, and brand awareness.

Following are a few of the most common black hat tricks. I think it is important that you be aware of them so that if you do run into a company that engages in any of these practices, you know to stay away.

Link Farms

Link farming is probably the most well-publicized black hat tactic, mostly because it has an intriguing name but also because it used to be very effective. Optimizers have been aware for years that links are the key to rankings, and it's easy enough to register a site, throw a design template up, and add links to it. So why not do that 100 times over, interlinking all 100 sites and creating a network of websites that all have 99 links pointing to them? Sure, the links on these brand new sites will not have much TrustRank, but surely they must have enough to earn a site some ranking power. It's a logical thought, and one that many people have had. The only tiny problem with it is that Google specifically prohibits this behavior and, if discovered, they will cripple your websites' ability to pass TrustRank and de-index them.

Even the situation I just described is small scale for most link farms, though. Typically, there will be thousands of sites linking to each other in a link farm, with 100+ links on each page (see Figure 8.1.) If you unknowingly pay an offshore "SEO company" for links and receive this service, you will probably have to end up submitting your site for re-inclusion in Google's index.

Doorway Pages

Doorway pages are web pages that send visitors to websites they didn't click: "I won a free teddy bear? Cool! Wait, how did I end up on this page that's trying to sell me a credit report?" Doorway pages are often optimized for a high-traffic keyword phrase and, when clicked, show the relevant page for a second and then hastily redirect the visitor to a page that has nothing to do with that keyword. You may or may not have ever come across one, as Google has gotten very good with algorithmically decimating sites that contain doorway pages. The practice of setting up doorways was so common years ago that Google specifically warns against them in its *Webmaster Guidelines*.

Cloaking

Cloaking is another black hat trick that involves using pages that nobody is ever intended to see. But unlike doorway pages, cloaked pages don't even appear for an instant. They are designed specifically to be visible to search engines and completely hidden from human beings. Thus the name: That cloak is of the invisible variety.

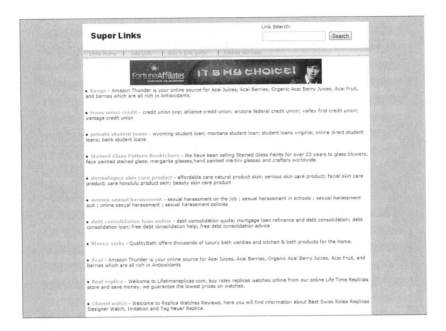

Figure 8.1 *A typical link farm website. Posing as a page of "super links," the page is covered with text links that have no purpose other than to attempt to manipulate Google's ranking algorithm.*

The advantage of showing one page to the search engines and another to human beings is that you can draw people in based on a particular subject and then change their experience shortly thereafter. For example, one common cloaking scam goes like this: You're looking up some popular news topic, maybe the discovery of a comet or asteroid, and suddenly the site you're on tells you that your computer is infected with a virus and you need to buy a special antivirus program for $70 (see Figure 8.2). Most people realize this is a scam, but some of the less-Internet-savvy among us might truly believe they have a virus and need the $70 program.

Google despises cloaking for the same reason it despises doorway pages: These tricks break its users' trust in the search results. Relevance and trustworthiness are the two greatest assets Google possesses. If you use any tricks that could undermine either one, your site is doomed to incur the wrath of the search behemoth—and, in many cases, the law.

Hidden Content

So now we have discussed pages that disappear in an instant and pages that never really appear at all. Other black hatters employ a different trick: disguising the content on their pages.

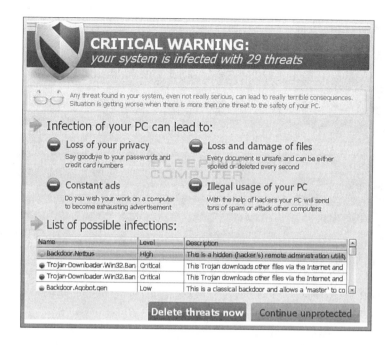

Figure 8.2   *A common scam of the late 2000s, the "fake virus" works by cloaking an innocent-looking page—the kind of page you might stumble upon while doing research—and then flashes a window like this one, warning you that your computer has been infected and offering to sell you a "solution."*

Hidden text in its simplest form is making text on the page the same color as the page's background (see Figure 8.3). To human beings, the text is completely camouflaged unless they know where to look for it. But to search engines, the content is readable and apparent. Some more advanced versions of this trick involve hiding text behind images and other media, or covering it with a foreground effect that renders it invisible without changing the background at all.

Hidden text is an amateur's trick and sites that use this tactic never last long. All of the known ways to hide text are easy marks for Google's spam team.

Spam

The oldest and most common black hat practice is spam. Spam in the world of SEO refers to the creation of pages that have no value other than to attract search engine traffic and make money from scams or ads (see Figure 8.4). These pages are not hidden, cloaked, or specifically designed to redirect the user somewhere else. Spam pages are, quite simply, useless pages littered with ads and links.

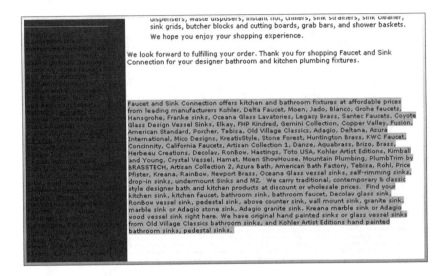

dispensers, waste disposers, instant hot, chillers, sink strainers, sink cleaner, sink grids, butcher blocks and cutting boards, grab bars, and shower baskets. We hope you enjoy your shopping experience.

We look forward to fulfilling your order. Thank you for shopping Faucet and Sink Connection for your designer bathroom and kitchen plumbing fixtures.

Faucet and Sink Connection offers kitchen and bathroom fixtures at affordable prices from leading manufacturers Kohler, Delta Faucet, Moen, Jado, Blanco, Grohe faucets, Hansgrohe, Franke sinks, Oceana Glass Lavatories, Legacy Brass, Santec Faucets, Coyote Glass Design Vessel Sinks, Elkay, FHP Kindred, Gemini Collection, Copper Valley, Fusion, American Standard, Porcher, Tebisa, Old Village Classics, Adagio, Deltana, Azura International, Mico Designs, KreativStyle, Stone Forest, Huntington Brass, KWC Faucet, Concinnity, California Faucets, Artisan Collection 1, Danze, Aquabrass, Brizo, Brass, Herbeau Creations, Decolav, RonBow, Hastings, Toto USA, Kohler Artist Editions, Kimball and Young, Crystal Vessel, Hamat, Moen ShowHouse, Mountain Plumbing, PlumbTrim by BRASSTECH, Artisan Collection 2, Azura Bath, American Bath Factory, Tebisa, Rohl, Price Pfister, Kreana, RainBow, Newport Brass, Oceana Glass vessel sinks, self-rimming sinks, drop-in sinks, undermount Sinks and MZ. We carry traditional, contemporary & classic style designer bath and kitchen products at discount or wholesale prices. Find your kitchen sink, kitchen faucet, bathroom sink, bathroom faucet, Decolav glass sink, RonBow vessel sink, pedestal sink, above counter sink, wall mount sink, granite sink, marble sink or Adagio stone sink, Adagio granite sink, Kreana marble sink or Adagio wood vessel sink right here. We have original hand painted sinks or glass vessel sinks from Old Village Classics bathroom sinks, and Kohler Artist Editions hand painted bathroom sinks, pedestal sinks.

Figure 8.3   *Believe it or not, this page of spam is actually the "thank you" page of a sink website that customers see after placing an order. This site is attempting to attract search engine traffic by writing keywords all over the page. Below the gray paragraph are more keywords, but they are almost the same color as the background. Google banned this site for hidden text and keyword stuffing.*

Figure 8.4   *A typical spam page. This type of spam is known as a splog, or spam blog. The Penguin updates of 2012 and 2013 have eliminated most of these useless pages.*

Why does spam persist at all? Because, sadly, there is money to be made. Spam pages might attract only a sliver of traffic, but many are created in huge numbers by scripts without any human intervention, and they can throw off thousands of dollars or more for their unethical purveyors.

Google detests spam pages and can see them coming a mile away. So if you are thinking of creating lots of websites automatically and monetizing search engine traffic with ads, know that many people have tried before you, and your odds of succeeding today are nearly zero.

Page Hijacks

The final black hat trick, page hijacking, is fairly sophisticated. A page hijack involves reproducing a popular website in an attempt to get Google to show some of the copycat site's pages in its search results rather than the original site's pages. When searchers click the links inside the copycat site, they are brought to a competitor's website or a spam page.

You won't find many page hijacks on Google nowadays, but they were common up until about 2006. They are a particularly clever trick, one that has cost certain popular websites a substantial amount of money in lost business because their customers were deceived. It can also cause reputational damage to the original website if the copycat website directs its visitors to a spam page.

As you might suspect, page hijacks are punished by instant banishment. Just like with every other black hat trick in this chapter, hijacking is the sort of gimmick that works for a short time and then quickly stops working: a bad trade-off for anyone looking to grow his or her business over the long term.

If you do run into an SEO company that appears to be engaging in any of these tactics, run far, far away. You can usually tell a black hat SEO company from a white hat or gray hat one by its website. If the website looks spammy, with a long page that keeps going on about "#1 rankings" and "thousands of links," it's probably best to steer clear. Also, if there is no phone number, take a pass. If there is a phone number, call and ask them to show you some examples of sites they caused to link to their clients. If what you see is a page that smacks of any of these techniques, you'll know to avoid that company.

Dark Gray Hat SEO

"Dark gray hat" tactics are not going to get your site banned, but they will cause Google to lose trust in your website, resulting in a cap on the amount of traffic Google will send your way. I strongly discourage your use of them. However, many SEO companies still employ dark gray hat practices, so you should be aware of what they are.

Comment Spam

Although comment spam straddles the line between black hat and dark gray hat SEO, its perpetrators do not conduct it on their own sites, and therefore it's less likely to trigger a penalty than something like cloaking or hidden content. Comment spam is something we've all seen: the act of placing a comment on a blog or discussion site for the sole purpose of getting a link back to your website (See Figure 8.5). It amazes me how much comment spam still takes place (if you own a blog, you know that dozens of spam comments can come in within a single day) when they are almost completely ineffective. Nearly every CMS nowadays automatically places a nofollow tag on comments, and besides that, most people delete spam comments rather than allowing them to stay up. If you do let spam comments through, Google might penalize your site and send you a message through your Webmaster Tools page, but they will almost never count the comments' links toward the TrustRank score of the spammer who put them there.

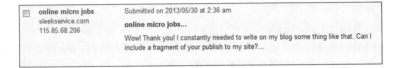

Figure 8.5 *A typical spam comment on a blog. Comment spam is highly ineffective, yet all too common.*

Paid Links

The greatest thorn in Google's side between 2006 and 2011 was paid links. While Google's army of Stanford-educated engineers wiped the floor of almost every black hat tactic, paid links remained an effective way of cheating the system for far too long. However, the paid-link party all but ended with Google's Penguin update in 2012 (although, Google struck its first major blow to paid links a year prior), and was finished off for good in late 2013. Today, even though Google is easily able to verify the worst paid-link offenders, they are unable to ban sites for utilizing paid links because of how common paid links have become and how difficult they are to identify in small numbers. Most SEO companies prior to 2012 relied on paid links, and thus they are pretty well mixed into the web ecosystem. Google also struggles with the idea that many paid links are honest forms of advertising. If you, for instance, pay a blogger to place a link to your site in their blogroll for the purposes of advertising, is that a reason to get penalized? Google has attempted to solve that problem by stating that all websites that accept text-based advertising place a no-follow tag on links to their advertisers' sites. That tag removes any

TrustRank that would pass to the advertiser, and thus avoids the possibility of Google's algorithm getting artificially influenced. Still, Google knows this system is not perfect, so they will nearly always give sites that incur paid linking penalties a second chance.

Duplicate Content

Duplicate content is one of the most common ways to get on Google's bad side, and almost always comes about by accident. Simply put, duplicate content is when a substantial number of pages from your website are copied—verbatim or almost verbatim—onto another website or on other pages within your website. When people come to me because they have experienced a traffic drop on their site, one of the first things I do is check to see whether they have inadvertently gotten involved in one of two scenarios:

- **Syndicating content**—If you own multiple sites in the same industry and regularly produce content for one of them, it may be tempting to publish that content on your other sites as well. Google doesn't mind if you copy content for the purposes of people enjoying it, but can only give credit to one site for creating it. Knowing the original publisher of content allows them to give the proper site a place in the search results if that content is relevant to somebody's search. Google can usually determine the original content producer based on who published it first, but when content is syndicated, it occasionally goes live on multiple sites before Google's robots have had a chance to make that determination. Occasionally, this can lead to the original publisher's content getting ignored or, in some cases, triggering a penalty. If you do syndicate content on multiple websites, it is best to leave the content up a few days on the original site before publishing on other websites. Another option is to place a `rel=canonical` tag on the source of the content's URLs. You can Google that term and read Google's official help page on the topic for more information.

- **Improperly forwarding URLs after a site relaunch**—When you are changing the URLs of your website—say, for instance, your URLs were long and filled with special characters and you learned from this book that they should be short and filled with keywords—a common mistake is to leave the old URLs sitting on your server without any special instructions for Google. Doing so leaves you with two copies of every page on your servers, which Google interprets as duplicate content. The proper procedure is to place a special instruction called a 301 redirect on each old page, causing it to automatically redirect to its equivalent newer page. Your web developer would usually handle this for you. Keep in mind that there are several types of redirects, but the correct one when changing URLs is the 301.

Although it might seem like a stretch to call a behavior that is usually accidental a dark gray hat technique, there have been plenty of scenarios in which people have duplicated content in an effort to game Google. The most common scheme employed by SEO companies (and some innocent business owners) is where a national business creates a landing page for every city in the country, copying the same content to every page except for the name of the city. This tactic was considered clever in 2006, but by 2009 was triggering penalties from Google. As of 2013, very few sites that had groups of nearly identical landing pages for different geographic regions were in Google's good graces, though I continue to see websites that seem to have been grandfathered in.

Light Gray Hat SEO

Light gray hat tactics are still used by most SEO firms today. To some small degree, they still work, but not enough to make an investment in them worth it; in fact, they may even result in a penalty.

High Keyword Density Content

For some reason, it is still part of the average SEO copywriter's cannon to keep a certain "density" of keywords on each website page. According to this theory—which was only partially true many years ago and today is not even remotely true—search engines will cause a web page to show up higher for a given keyword if that keyword is written the right number of times on each page. Adherents to this theory believe that if, say, 4% of the words on your page are your coveted keywords, your page will get maximum attractiveness for those keywords without tripping a filter and getting your page penalized. Although it can't hurt to write an important keyword once or twice on your page, Google mainly makes its decision about which keywords your page is attractive for based on its meta page title. If you do attempt a certain level of keyword density, your efforts will be ignored at best, and rewarded with the Panda penalty at worst.

Link Trading

Link trading is treated similarly to link buying in Google's eyes, but with slightly less stigma. I remember the day that Google announced that link trades were no longer kosher. It came at a time when paid links were still the SEO industry's secret lover and traded links were its less-coveted cousin. Google's distaste for traded links quickly became an outrage, as many webmasters claimed that exchanging links was a common way to mutually promote businesses among friends. Google never gave a lot of details about just how bad a traded link was in their eyes, but after observing the practices of hundreds of clients, I think I have a pretty good idea. Google is smart, and they know that sometimes two sites that work together will link to each other within the same time period. However, they also know that systematic link exchanges are a clear way of manipulating their algorithm. Therefore, the rule with link trades is to keep them to a minimum; do them only when they feel natural, rather than as part of your everyday optimization work. For example, if you're a blogger and another blog frequently links to your site in their articles, it would be perfectly reasonable to link to them in one of your articles. However, you would never want to go into a forum and announce "I've got a PageRank 3 blog. Who wants to trade links on our blogrolls?" As we've seen many times in this book, Google looks for natural behavior—marketing in moderation. In link trading, as in all other on-the-fence tactics, it is best not to think too much about it. If you happen to trade links by accident, you'll probably be fine. Just don't make a habit of it.

Link Networks

Link networks, as opposed to link farms, are a practice that is rampant in certain professional industries like law. When I refer to a link network, I basically mean a group of ostensibly high-quality sites that all exist for the sole purpose of linking to one main website. Staying in the legal field, a criminal lawyer might have one main site with a home page, an About page, a Contact page, and a list of practice areas. Nothing unusual. However, if we were to look at its links and engage in a bit of sleuthing, we might learn that this site belongs to a family of 20 other websites that all appear to be professional blogs and yet are owned and controlled by that very same criminal lawyer. Within the content of these 20 satellite websites, links to the criminal lawyer's main website abound. Perhaps there are links out to other sites as well—mainly big sites like Wikipedia and the *New York Times*—but it's clear that those satellite websites live to support that main website. Putting together a network like this is expensive, and for many years skirted Google's guidelines in the prettiest of ways: The satellite sites were self-sustaining, with decent quality content, and most people who stumbled upon one of them would think nothing of them. But their underlying purpose is to trick Google into believing that the main website is more popular than it really is. And thus, the network fails my favorite sniff test: "If a Google engineer were sitting next to you, would they be okay with what you're doing right now?"

Today, many link networks still exist and a few remain effective. But with a set of algorithm updates that Google released in late 2013 ("Penguin 2"), their days are numbered.

White Hat SEO

White hat SEO is everything you are reading in this book. It is the world of optimization tactics that fall within Google's terms of service and that do not attempt to dupe Google in any way. White hat SEO helps websites to rank at the top of the results using every advantage available except breaking Google's rules. Essentially, it involves building genuinely compelling content, formatting your site's meta page titles in an SEO-friendly fashion, and building links organically by earning the attention of other webmasters.

It's obvious that I don't recommend any black hat tactics. But now that you know what the most common ones look like, you can keep yourself safe from them. I also believe they can be instructive as a contrast to what actually creates successful companies. The thinking behind black hat SEO endeavors is defeatist. Short-term gain followed by needing to start from scratch is a cowardly approach to business. I advise entering the business world with a view toward long-term value for your customers, because doing so allows you to work backward and figure out how your company should be run. If your customers are to get the most value, you will need good relationships with the tools of your trade, including Google. You'll also need good relationships with your employees, partners, and vendors. Apart from the financial implications of doing your whole business "white hat," let's not forget that you only get one reputation in life, and in today's age that reputation is bound to stick around a long time. Remember to play smart.

9

Optimizing for Yahoo! and Bing

Google commands a 67% share of the U.S. search market and doesn't seem to be slipping. That means that the rest of the pie is divided up by Bing, Yahoo!, and a smattering of smaller search engines. Although I don't know many people who use Yahoo! and Bing regularly, combined they apparently do make up about 28% of the search market, and so it is worth spending a bit of time understanding what makes them happy. My general rule has been "Optimize for Google first, and throw a few things in place for the other search engines."

Yahoo! Introduction

Say what you will about Yahoo!; it's a survivor. As of this printing, the brand represents one of the only remaining companies from the Internet's early portal days, when dialup access usually came with a customized "front door," or portal, to the Internet (see Figure 9.1). Yahoo! has evolved considerably over time, outlasting other creaky contemporaries such as Excite and Netscape that were slow to adapt. Yahoo! still tries to guide its users through the Web, giving people a home page to find news and content in which they are interested. But the company now also focuses on its search business because that is where they make a good slice of their money, via advertising.

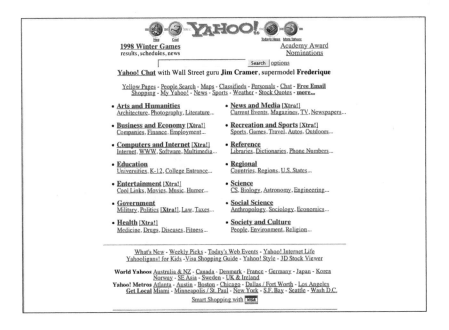

Figure 9.1   *The Yahoo! home page in 1998 during Yahoo!'s heyday.*

The history of search earned a new milestone in the summer of 2009 when Yahoo! announced that, after years of tweaking and refining its algorithm, it had decided to scrap it altogether and use Microsoft's Bing search engine to power its searches instead. The deal effectively combined the second- and third-place search engines into one, creating a potentially formidable foe to battle against Google. In reality, it has simply increased Bing's market share and not threatened Google in any significant way.

Yahoo!'s search market share has been in decline for some time now. However, Yahoo! search will not go away for a while because so many users, especially older users, still associate the brand name with a place to start their Internet searches.

The Advent of Bing

Where did Bing come from, anyway? For most people, the rise of Bing occurred pretty quickly. First you saw an advertisement for it on one of your favorite websites. Then you read a news story about the $100 million that paid for the aforementioned advertisement campaign. Then you began to see it popping up in random places such as toolbars, maps, and travel sites. This was Microsoft's big attempt to grab a piece of the search pie. And Microsoft definitely got its share of publicity.

Bing grew out of Microsoft's long-held frustration with its stagnant share of online search. After more than 10 years of failing to compete with Google with products such as MSN Search and Windows Live Search, Microsoft announced a massive code and interface overhaul, and a new name, in June 2009.

Bing was the result of that effort: a so-called decision engine that boasts interesting new tools, cutting-edge integration with travel information providers, and lots of other goodies. By most standards, Bing has been a success for Microsoft, capturing an additional 2% of search share in its first year, mostly at Yahoo!'s expense. It has also gotten plenty of attention in the media for its eye-catching photo-rich home page and innovative features. Even Google appears to have recognized that Bing has gotten a few things right, "borrowing" from its interface and design, and rather obviously adopting some of its features. Google fans remember the day in June 2010 when Google allowed users to upload their own Bing-like backgrounds to its famously simple home page.

Bing's taking over Yahoo! search was good news for the world of SEO because it meant less confusion and fewer conflicting instructions. After all, it wasn't long ago that thorough webmasters had to optimize for three search engines in addition to, perhaps, Ask.com. Today, you're wasting your time if you optimize for any search engine besides Google and Bing.

How Optimizing for Bing Differs from Optimizing for Google

If Google's great innovation was organizing the Web around editorial votes, or links, Yahoo! went in the opposite direction for many years: analyzing the websites themselves and returning search results based around on-page factors. Today, Yahoo! is powered by Bing, and so it puts much more faith in links than it used to. However, Bing's technology holds onto this page-based legacy in some important ways. Most optimizers appreciate the fact that on-page factors matter to Bing because it makes optimization easier. Google's system of needing to attract other websites' votes is much more difficult than just following best practices when building your site. Exactly what those best practices are is a subject of ongoing debate, but a few basics are beyond controversy. Figure 9.2 shows a side-by-side comparison of Google and Bing.

Figure 9.2 *A side-by-side comparison of Google and Bing. The two search engines have traded features in the past few years, with Google borrowing from Bing's more image-focused interface and Bing borrowing Google's expanded results. Notably, Bing offers social results from Facebook and Google does not.*

Keywords in Your Content

The biggest difference between Bing and Google is their respective emphasis on keywords within the content of the site. I have already discussed the main ways that keywords matter to Google—namely when they appear in the text of an inbound link, or in a website's meta page title or URL. But Google does not care very much about keywords in the content of your site. That's why, when optimizing for Google, most people just include their keywords whenever they come up naturally in the site's content. As mentioned in Chapter 8, "White Hat Versus Black Hat SEO," aiming for a particular "density" of keywords on your page is a relic of the past and can actually have negative effects on your Google ranking.

Bing is much more receptive to keywords written within the text of your pages. Many webmasters report great strides in their Yahoo!/Bing rankings just by using keywords more often (see Figure 9.3). This isn't to say that you want to sacrifice syntax or intelligibility, of course; spam is spam, and every search engine knows it when it sees it. But you might see a bump in your ranking just by leaning a bit more heavily on the keywords you are optimizing for. Playing around with these keywords for maximum effect in this area is a must, especially because Bing is constantly refining its keyword detector. Someday, keywords inside content may matter less than they do. But for now, pay attention to them if you want your website to rank on Bing.

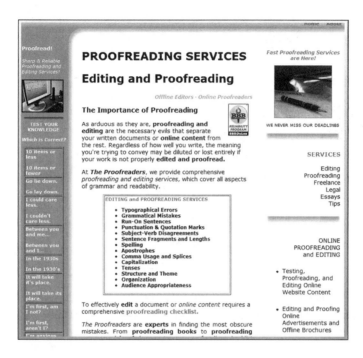

Figure 9.3 *A page that has keywords sprinkled throughout its content. This page ranks excellently on Bing for its main keywords.*

Meta Page Titles

Another area that Bing seems to care a lot about is the meta page title. You already understand the importance of this bit of code to Google, and it matters at least as much to Bing. Run a search for any popular term on Yahoo! or Bing, and you will notice that most of the first page results will use that exact term in their meta page titles. Google, in contrast, tries to return results whose meta page titles have the same words that the user searched for but not necessarily in the same order. So if you search for best brownie recipe, Google doesn't differentiate too much between web pages whose meta page titles are "The Best Darn Brownie Recipe" and "Mom's Recipe for the Best Brownie Ever" even though neither of those titles contains the exact phrase *best brownie recipe*. Bing, however, is more likely to rank a web page at the top if it has that exact phrase in its meta page title (see Figure 9.4).

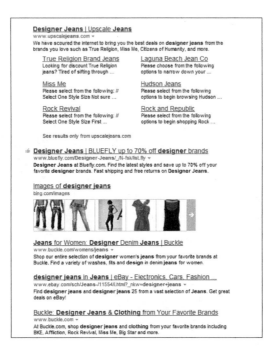

Figure 9.4 *Bing attempts to find sites whose meta page titles match what the user is searching for as closely as possible. All of the top five results have the inputted search* designer jeans, *in that word order, in their meta page titles.*

Meta Description Tags

Meta description tags are a factor that Bing cares a lot more about than Google. Meta descriptions are—like meta page titles—text that is written into the code of every web page. They then become the two lines of text that show up underneath the blue underlined heading of every search result (see Figure 9.5). Unlike meta page titles, though, they usually don't show up anywhere on the web page or browser after you've clicked the search result. They exist merely to improve the experience of using the search engine.

For Parents - The **Dream Mining** Company
The **Dream Mining** Company is a safe and creative virtual world for girls to play. Our mission is to provide girls with characters, stories and games to ...
www.dreammining.com/abouts/parents - Cached

Figure 9.5 *The meta description tag, a part of every web page's coding, appears in search engines as the line or two of text underneath the blue heading of each search result.*

Google cares about meta descriptions a small amount. Bing cares about them a good amount more, specifically looking for keywords in the meta description that also appear in the meta page title and on the page itself. That trio of keyword placements is a killer combo in Bing's eyes.

So when you are optimizing for Bing, make sure that your page's meta description includes your keyword at least once and that the same keyword appears in your meta page title. For instance, if your site sells scuba gear and your keyword is `caribbean scuba gear`, a good meta page title and meta description is this:

> **Meta page title:** Top Caribbean Scuba Gear | Snorkels, Masks, Tanks & Cameras
>
> **Meta description:** Elite scuba gear for Caribbean divers at any level

Headings

Another important on-page factor to Bing is headings. Headings are the text at the top of a page, usually in larger letters, announcing the title or subject of the page. They're sort of like a meta page title except they're in the actual content of the page, front and center to visitors. Headings used to provide one of the bases of the early search engines' algorithms, but as soon as people started manipulating headings so that more traffic would come to their websites from search engines, headings became de-emphasized. Google, for instance, gives headings very little weight in its algorithm. Bing must not have gotten that memo, though, because it still factors headings into its algorithm quite a bit.

Because most webmasters understand the importance of writing headings with real people in mind, optimizing your headings for Bing is a sensitive issue. You have to be one of those people who excelled at high school English assignments where you had to use vocabulary words in a sentence. I walked to school `surreptitiously` today. Remember that? Those are the types of skills needed for sewing keywords into headings naturally (well, better ones than that).

For example, if my keyword were eco-friendly cleaning and I were looking to write a page that is well optimized for Bing, I'd make a page with the following heading:

```
How Eco-Friendly Cleaning Can Tidy Up Your Home and Your
Planet
```

My keyword sounds natural in that heading, making it good for both human beings and the Bing search engine. When Bing's spiders see that you have used the same term in both the heading of your page and the text of your page, it might conclude that your site specializes in whatever that keyword is. If this sounds simplistic, it is; so enjoy it. Bing will probably eliminate easy-to-manipulate on-page factors like this one in time.

Alt Tags

Alt tags are nothing more than little text descriptions associated with the images on your site. They are an important part of the code because as smart as the search engines are, they are not yet smart enough to look at a picture and identify precisely what it is. If you have ever seen a web page load slowly, you might have noticed a descriptive phrase sitting in the empty box that the picture soon occupies. That's an alt tag.

Bing shows images in its regular search results as well as, of course, its image search, and relies heavily on the alt tag in its algorithm. Google does the same and also puts a strong emphasis on alt tags. For that reason, I highly recommend that you properly describe all of your images. Searchers click pictures way more than most people realize, and having lots of properly labeled images can bring a ton of traffic to your site.

Although I encourage you to use keywords in your alt tags, do not go overboard or describe a picture totally inaccurately to attract more traffic. Indeed, it is tough for search engines to know whether your label is accurate—there is nothing to stop you from posting a picture of a scientific calculator and labeling it as "Jessica Alba"—but manipulating the system only annoys users and will be identifiable soon anyway, as image-recognition software is already pretty advanced.

Outbound Links

Outbound links are the opposite of inbound links, or backlinks. Instead of pointing toward your own site, outbound links point out of your site toward other websites. The philosophy behind using outbound linking as a tool for SEO is simple: Acknowledging other authoritative sites is considered good Internet behavior and is the sign of a quality site. Whereas this philosophy is only lightly espoused by Google, Bing closely abides by it.

The practice of liberally linking to other websites is not exactly a crowd favorite among webmasters, who generally want to hold on to visitors at all costs. But many of the same webmasters have found that a few well-targeted links to other sources can help demonstrate mastery of a subject. Also, the Web is very much an open place to explore, and so being too protective of visitors is not a winning strategy. Linking to authoritative sources will not cause a visitor to be lost for life if your site is providing something of genuine value.

Speaking of authoritative sites, outbound linking comports best with Bing's algorithm only if you direct your visitors to established and trusted sites such as news organizations and universities. And if you place one of your keywords in or around the anchor text for that link, Bing likes that, too; it further binds the keyword with your perceived area of expertise. In other words, this is another chance to use your keywords to improve your rank: Link out to well-known sites, and some of that reflected starlight should improve your site's rankings.

Site Structure

The final on-page factor that matters to Bing is site structure, or the layout of your pages and the way they are interlinked. This principle is common to all search engines, including Google, and if you think about it, how could it not be? A site that is easily crawlable by search engines is usually easily navigated by people as well, and is therefore a good website to present to users in a search. Both Bing and Google favor clean, easy-to-navigate architecture, fast-loading pages and easy-to-follow links.

What makes for clean site architecture? Think of it the same way you would when teaching a child how the natural world is organized. You start with the highest-level categories: the plant and animal kingdoms. Then you get more specific, going down to phylum, classes, and so on. (I'll stop the taxonomy lesson now because I don't really remember anything past that.) This kind of hierarchical structure is the same thing that web designers make when they create product pages. Bing likes sites that get increasingly specific as you link further into the website. Walking your visitors from category to subcategory to item is also a great way to ensure that all your product pages are focused on one thing at a time, which is a natural form of optimization that search engines love.

Links

If I were to summarize the entire chapter up until this point, I would simply say that Bing cares a lot more about what's on your site than Google does. But that doesn't mean it ignores what the rest of the Web thinks about your website. Bing actually uses an equation that works like Google's TrustRank system to determine which sites have earned the credibility of other webmasters. In fact, links are the most important factor in Bing's algorithm, too, although by not nearly as wide a margin as in Google's.

With that in mind, all the advice that you have read about linking throughout this book applies just as well to Bing. Whether your goal is to optimize for both search algorithms or just for Google's, you have to focus on collecting highly trusted links from good sources—blogs, news outlets, resource pages, and other popular websites. The many ways to acquire links are covered in Chapter 3, "How to Reel In Links."

Domain Age

A final element of SEO that is important to Bing is age. We know by now that age is important to Google, but Bing feels even more strongly about it. Of all the factors that affect a site's ranking, only links and age cannot be easily controlled by the webmaster, which is why they are so essential to the algorithm.

As with Google, there is no substitute for an established website with aged links, and the only way to acquire that kind of credibility is to buy one.

A Word About Demographics

One of the biggest differences among Google, Yahoo!, and Bing has nothing to do with search at all. It is the crowd of people that frequents each search engine, which has a big impact on the type of visitors your site receives from appearing high in the search results. The people who use Bing are different from the people who use Google, and those people are different from Yahoo! users. Each group has unique habits and tendencies, and getting 100 visitors from Yahoo! is not identical to getting 100 visitors from Google.

Yahoo! is by far the oldest search engine of the big three, and as you might expect, its users tend to skew older as well. Many Yahoo! users have Yahoo.com set as their default home page, and have had for many years. These are not your typical web-savvy surfers. They navigate the Web from their favorite portal and aren't the type to try and find the latest, coolest web trends.

That is a demographic if I have ever seen one. Yahoo! users can be highly valuable to business owners. Because they are not as skeptical about online sales tactics, they are more likely to "bite" on a sales pitch or online ad. Also, Yahoo! users tend to spend more money on average than Google users—a byproduct of their more established place in life and the fact that younger searchers typically demand cutthroat comparison shopping and free services.

Bing is similar to Yahoo! in one respect and completely opposite in another. As with Yahoo!, the vast majority of Bing users run their searches from an old, established portal: MSN.com. MSN is typically the default home page on Microsoft's Internet Explorer, which still commands abour 20% of all browser usage. Most people who use Bing through their MSN home pages might not be aware of what is powering their searches or how to find other options. In this sense, they are similar to Yahoo! users in their online habits and are valuable visitors for the same reasons.

But Bing is unique in that it has attracted a completely different population, as well. The search engine was launched to great acclaim on tech blogs and media outlets, and as a result it has attracted a high number of unusually savvy surfers.

Bing's innovations to Google's sparse search interface appeals to Internet sophis-
ticates and the general population alike, and its status as an upstart challenger
attracts people who root for the (ironically, because it's Microsoft) underdog.
Bing also gets a shot of youthful users because it powers Facebook's "web search"
results.

As a result, Bing is in the peculiar position of being represented among the very
old and very young. And both of these populations are worth optimizing for: Older
people tend to bring purchase power and trust, and younger people tend to bring
advertising cachet and viral attention.

Bing even has the potential to challenge Google in the arena of brand name coolness, although it's certainly got a way to go. There is something satisfying about
saying "Bing!" when getting something done. But it's not quite as much fun as saying "just Google it."

Pay per Click: Where Bing Shines

The demographic differences among Google, Yahoo!, and Bing are a big deal
because they can lead to vastly different sales figures depending on which search
engine your site's visitors are using. Google users tend to be more skeptical,
whereas Yahoo! and Bing users tend to be more trusting. These are, no doubt,
products of the different generations that the search engines represent.

These differences become especially interesting when we talk about pay-per-click
(PPC) advertising. Most people tend to ignore Google AdWords links unless they
are so targeted as to be almost irresistible. So who is making Google their billions?
Studies show that the people who click these ads tend to be disproportionately
older and less current in the ways of the Web. Sound familiar? This is precisely the
same population that is more likely to use whatever search portal came autoloaded
into their browsers: MSN and Yahoo! And so if you're going to take anything from
this chapter, take this: Yahoo! and Bing boast a much higher click-through rate for
search advertisements than Google. If you have a limited budget for a PPC campaign and your customers tend to be middle-aged or older, make your investment
in these smaller, higher-producing search engines.

Bing's Advantages

It's tough for me to honestly say that Bing has many advantages over Google as
a resource for marketers. However, it does have a few nifty features that can help
you with your SEO. In the final part of this chapter, I will highlight two of these
features.

Search Operators

Both Google and Bing have features called search operators, which allow you to input a command into the search box and get information back about a website. For example, Google has a search operator called `site:`, which allows you to see how many pages of a website Google includes in its index. I use this operator all the time to see how many different opportunities for organic traffic a client's site contains. To use a search operator, simply type the operator into the search box followed by the URL of the website or web page you're seeking information about. For example: `site:evanbailyn.com` will show you all the pages that Google knows about on my professional website.

Bing's most talked-about search operator is probably `linkfromdomain:`, which generates a list of every site that a particular website links out to. It's basically an outbound link viewer. This is useful as a way of seeing the kind of sites that certain websites link to. For instance, I am always curious as to whether certain .edu sites—the websites of universities—link to regular sites that are not part of the academic world. If I can find a particular page on an .edu that gives out links for any reason at all, I want to jump on that opportunity. And Bing is the only search engine that lets me inspect all of a given website's outbound links. More generally, `linkfromdomain:` is a great way to analyze a website's linking philosophy. Remember how I told you at the beginning of this book to look for sites that usually do not sell links because they are more likely to be trusted by Google? `Linkfromdomain:` is a great way to analyze those potential candidates in your quest for links.

Bing also lets you search for sites that contain a certain type of file, such as a Word document or a PDF. This operator is called `contains:`, and you just pair it with the file suffix you're looking for (see Figure 9.6).

The `contains:` operator is handy for finding specific documents, of course, but it's also a good way to see what your competitors are doing media-wise. After all, SEO in its full bloom is about more than just gaining visitors. It's about improving your visitors' experience so that they eventually convert into paying customers. Using this search operator can help you see how many sites in your niche are posting videos, for example, or publishing e-books. The `contains:` operator also lets you find and download material quickly, which can be a good way to perform research quickly.

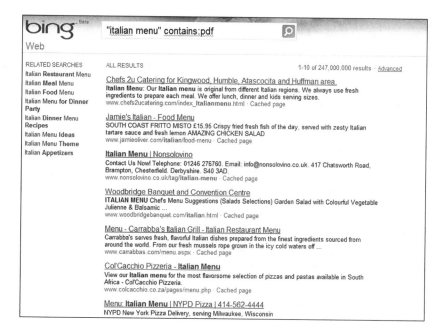

Figure 9.6 *Bing's* `contains:` *search operator is a great way to discover documents and media embedded inside websites.*

Bing Webmaster Tools

Bing also offers a set of webmaster tools that are similar to Google's. If you are serious about optimizing for Bing, it is essential that you sign up for these tools. Just like Google, Bing Webmaster Tools let you dig deeply into the metrics of your site, analyzing your traffic in several ways and monitoring the success of your optimization efforts. You can even customize how you want your site indexed and which pages, if any, you want Bing not to acknowledge.

For more advanced management tools, Bing encourages the use of a basic download for these tools called Microsoft Silverlight—its answer to Adobe's Flash plug-in. Through Bing's Silverlight interface, you can analyze data that stretches back 6 months, giving you access to a trove of research and data on everything from visitor behavior to backlinks. Although not more interesting than Google Webmaster Tools, Bing's way of organizing information is worth looking at, if only for comparison.

Bing's Social Search

A final differentiator between Bing and Google is Bing's emphasis on social results. Not only is Bing the only search engine with access to Facebook's fire hose of social data (it helps that Bing's parent company invested in Facebook and that Bing is less threatening to Facebook than Google), but it is also the first to prominently feature search results from other social media sites such as LinkedIn and Quora. Social results are displayed on Bing through a sidebar to the right of the search results. For example, if you search "Tom Hanks" on Bing, it will display a rich sidebar containing the actor's picture from IMDB, a bio from Wikipedia, and links to his Twitter, Facebook, and Klout pages.

Bing hasn't enhanced the search experience in any important ways with its social sidebar, nor has it used social data to influence organic search results in a meaningful way. The company seems to be confused about what to do with all the data it possesses. It will be far more interesting to see what Google does with social data when Google+ gathers enough data to be a threat or Facebook finally shares its social data with them. I delve into this topic more deeply in Chapter 11, "Social Search: The Intersection of Social Media and SEO."

In the long run, Bing and Google's algorithms will probably grow together. Both are interested in the quality of user experience and relevance. More importantly, both are watching each other closely to see the other's newest innovations and user reactions to it. Google is undoubtedly the king of search—that's why I recommend focusing the vast majority of your efforts on it. However, there is something to the mild threat that Google perceives in Bing. Ultimately, it is good for we consumers that Bing and Google compete because we are the beneficiaries of their battle to help find information more easily on the Internet.

10

Converting Your SEO Results into Paying Customers

By this point, you know how SEO works. If you were to stop reading right now, you would see significant improvements in your rankings and website traffic. But there is still one itty-bitty thing missing. (Don't you hate that?)

That itty-bitty thing is getting your visitors to buy your product or service. Without this last step, optimizing your website is but a pretty distraction.

At first glance, the concept of customer conversion might seem as if it falls outside the purview of SEO. When you think about it, however, all the same factors we use in SEO—building trust, using good site structure, employing careful language to make a point—apply just as well to conversion. In fact, I like to think of conversion as another kind of optimization: human being optimization.

Optimizing for human beings is not nearly as mysterious as it sounds. In fact, I have found that four simple elements can get you to a healthy place. Conveniently, they all start with the letter *D*:

- Design
- Differentiation
- Data
- Deals

Design

Every day, it seems, a new study comes out analyzing people's behavior on the Web. Companies underwrite these studies because they are constantly trying to answer a simple question: What makes people trust one site and flee another? What exactly goes through our minds when we arrive at a site?

The first answer is, undoubtedly, design. Most people do not consciously notice web design, but there is no question that it plays an enormous role in gaining or losing a visitor's trust. Websites are like commercial buildings: If you walk into one and feel surrounded by symmetry, calm, and beauty, you feel comfortable transacting with the business. If you walk into a building and there's a sign for the business written on an oak tag with magic markers scotch-taped to the wall, you feel a lot less comfortable spending money there. Websites that look spammy or amateurish simply turn visitors off. People turn away from them not just because they aren't pretty, but because poorly designed sites imply that the business behind them is inexperienced or unprofessional.

Aesthetic design is less important than functional design for giants such as Amazon and Netflix, mostly because their reputations precede them. Most people know that they can safely use these sites, and so their design teams are free to focus more on conversion. But smaller companies and new businesses do not enjoy this kind of built-in trust, and as a result, they often suffer from a high bounce rate, meaning many visitors leave their websites within a few seconds of arriving.

As far as we have come from the days of being afraid to make a purchase on the Internet, there is still a leap of faith involved in buying something without guidance from a human being.

Put yourself in the shoes of a customer for a second. No matter how many adjectives a website uses to describe its credibility, when you send your 16-digit credit card number, you are placing your trust in the hands of a stranger. If that stranger is a celebrity like Apple.com, you probably have confidence enough. But if that stranger is a newcomer, you might want to seek a second opinion first. The great fear is not just that your money will vanish into the void; it's that you could lose your identity along with it.

Aesthetic

The aesthetic, or look, of a site is the first thing visitors notice. Their reaction to it is an important factor in whether they remain on the site or flee. It's sort of like going on a blind date. If that initial impression is positive, you might just stay for a while. But if your date is a bomb, you're out of there as soon as the first opportunity arises.

Consider the two home pages shown in Figures 10.1 and 10.2. Both are from websites in the same industry, and both sell essentially the same service: restoration of your home after a flood or fire. Which site inspires greater confidence?

Figure 10.1 *The home page for RestorationSOS, a disaster restoration business.*

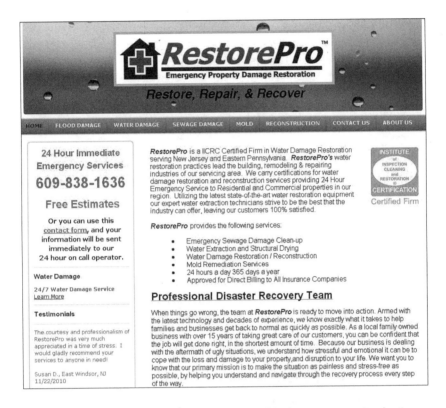

Figure 10.2   *The home page for RestorePro, another disaster restoration business.*

Now, I admit that there is an economic advantage acting here: RestorationSOS is a major corporation with offices nationwide, and RestorePro is a small, New Jersey company serving Princeton and Trenton. But what better way to underscore the power of design? You probably found the RestorationSOS page cleaner and easier to navigate, and the RestorePro site a bit confusing and homegrown looking. (In reality, RestorePro is a professional company, but its design doesn't communicate that.) I believe that the majority of visitors to both sites would choose RestorationSOS over RestorePro, regardless of name recognition, solely on the basis of design.

This chapter is not a primer on web design (I'll leave that to the experts), but it is worth noting a few things that stand out:

- The RestorationSOS site makes it easy to understand exactly what the company does and how to find it. The RestorePro site makes it more challenging to figure this out.

- The RestorationSOS site uses a confident picture of a professional seemingly preparing for the task at hand. The RestorePro site has no photographs other than the use of water drops as a background on its top banner.

- The RestorationSOS site has a cogent design aesthetic with clear edges and defined layout. The RestorePro site's color choices are all over the place, with blue, white, gray, fire engine red, and burgundy fonts.

Overall, RestorePro website's design elements are disconnected:

- The menu bar floats out beyond the edges of the header and the body of the page.
- The phone number gets lost in a sea of red.
- There is a misuse and overuse of formatting, including bolding and italics for the company name and paragraphs that are completely bolded.
- The website could use a good copywriter.

These little details, when looked at as a whole, undermine RestorePro's credibility. It's remarkable to think that if the company simply had a well-designed website, its client list might be twice as large. And an aesthetically pleasing website doesn't have to cost a lot more than a poorly designed website. But if it does, trust me when I say that the money is well spent. The simple fact is that when you look like a big player in an industry, people treat you like one. And that means sales.

Layout

Before we go any further with these examples, I want you to consider the design of fast food advertisements. Picture a billboard that features a giant juicy hamburger. Could you imagine what it's like to eat that hamburger? You could! The science of food photography has become so sophisticated that advertisements are specifically designed to invite this kind of unconscious action in our minds. Our brain says, "If I had that burger, I would lift it here and bite it there." Without fail, the place on the burger where you could best picture your mouth chomping down is the main focus of the advertisement.

Web design works the exact same way: You want to invite an immediate action with your layout. Let's look again at those same two disaster restoration sites, previously shown in Figures 10.1 and 10.2. Beyond the different appearances, you might have noticed there is an organizational difference, as well:

- The RestorationSOS site has a neat little form at the top, just begging to be filled out. The RestorePro site seems confused about where you should click or why.

- RestorationSOS walks its customers through their choices with clear tabular categories. RestorePro leaves users wondering what to do next: Do you call for a free estimate, fill out the contact form, or learn more about water damage?

Put another way, you know what to do when you get to RestorationSOS. You don't with RestorePro.

Structure

That brings me to structure. Just like layout, structure is a way of organizing information. If layout is way of describing just one page, structure is a way of describing how your entire site works. Websites are a little bit like machines: You press a button, and something happens. Most websites by now use a familiar layout; there are big sections across the top and, if needed, smaller categories below or down one side. Some clever designers have strayed from this formula to great success, but most people do not want to tinker with a formula that already works fine.

A good site structure can make a big difference. Web users are fickle and impatient people, and the last thing they want is to navigate a dizzying set of links within links before they can locate what they're looking for. A simple hierarchy, moving from vague to specific, will speed your visitors along toward that all-important inquiry or purchase without any friction.

Differentiation

After you have achieved a clean and organized design, there still remains the question of what you should put inside that design. What do you need to say to convince people to take that leap of faith with your company instead of another one?

Differentiation refers to all the things that make your business special, unique, and worthwhile. The Web has completely eliminated the old adage "location, location, location." Today, your site is exactly the same distance away as all your competitors': one click. As a result, your visitors are probably checking out the competition in another window while they are browsing your site. That means your site needs to quickly answer the question "Why choose us?"

Us Versus Them

Differentiation comes in many forms, but the classic version is the "us versus them" comparison. You do a little research on your competitors, and then think about what you offer. Are your products or services unique? Do you approach your business in a different way from the other guys?

Suppose you run a cleaning company. Questions to ask include the following:

- Do you only use organic, nontoxic cleaners?
- Does your staff speak perfect English?
- Do they wear booties or take off their shoes?
- Will they use the customer's own special cleaning supplies if asked?
- Do you provide post-holiday party cleanup?
- Are you fully bonded and insured?

In an online age where barriers to entry are often low, your point of differentiation can't simply be "because we're the best." You need reasons. And making those reasons easy to find on your website is essential. Consider the proofreading company's website shown in Figure 10.3.

Figure 10.3   *A proofreading site that states its case confidently.*

Although this site's design is a bit basic, the differentiation factor is there. Look at what's stated in the top right:

WE NEVER MISS OUR DEADLINES

The word *never* implies a comparison, and the copy further emphasizes that the company's proofreaders are professionally trained, work in the United States, and speak English as their first language. The owners of the site probably made that statement to highlight their own strengths and cause visitors to distrust the competition. They probably found themselves repeating certain points on sales calls and decided to emphasize them. Placing these points right on the home page is a smart way to capture visitors who may be comparing multiple websites.

Awards and Press

Of course, differentiation comes in many forms. One of the other big tricks in customer conversion is to mention awards you have won and press mentions you have received. The reasoning behind this method is the same as why people prefer organic SEO: We trust information when it comes from an outside and impartial source.

Awards come in many forms, and most can be beneficial to your business. Your company might have gotten recognized by some outlet or organization. Or it might have been cited as a favorite business or service provider in your local area. Better yet, it could have earned a spot on someone's "Best Of" list. Even if the most prestigious acknowledgment your company has received is becoming one of Bob and Jean-Anne's Favorite Websites (I made that up), you should consider putting it on your home page until something better comes along. Every little bit helps.

And what if you haven't received any awards yet? Well, then it's time to start lobbying. Look for bloggers in your industry, media outlets, critics, and columnists who compile award lists. Maybe they don't know about your business yet, or perhaps they will be flattered enough by the attention that they'll give your company a second look. Again, don't overlook the little guys. Any award is a good opportunity to show your customers that people prefer your company.

Press mentions are similarly useful but have the added advantage of binding your company to a well-known media outlet. Because of their value, a great deal of thought and strategy can go into earning them. You can try to get your own press using a site like HARO (helpareporter.com) and networking with bloggers and journalists on Twitter, or you can hire a publicist. If you don't have a publicist yet and can afford one, I highly recommend it.

After your company has found its way into newspapers, magazines, radio, blogs, or TV shows, you'll want to create a special section on your website to display your press. Of course, you should still display the best press on your home page. Customers who see the logos of local and national media outlets on a home page automatically assume that site has been vetted and approved by established arbiters of taste (see Figure 10.4).

Figure 10.4   *My company is not shy about the press it has received, and yours shouldn't be either.*

Client Testimonials

Of course, not every endorsement comes with a famous name attached. You don't have to make the cover of *Time* to show that you are loved. Every message of support from someone outside your company is a vote of confidence in what you are selling, and, in fact, quoting an ordinary customer can be more powerful than a press mention. With client testimonials, the key is getting potential customers to relate to the person who is quoted. If, for instance, I were thinking about hiring a web design firm, and I saw a testimonial on the firm's home page from the CEO of a technology company the same size as First Page Sage, it would make more of an impact on me than seeing the logo of a local newspaper.

Testimonials are especially important if your company is new. To go about getting them, start by contacting your most satisfied customers and asking their permission to quote them on your site. Some people might blush at the publicity, but others will appreciate it. A lot has to do with your delivery when asking. Saying "I would be honored to have you write a few words about your experience with our company" is a confident but humble way of proposing the idea. Remember to ask for testimonials from past or current customers who best represent the future customers you want to attract. Also, doing the testimonials by video—or at least including a picture of the person who is being quoted—helps to humanize the endorsement.

Social Media

A lot of these differentiating factors fall under the category of credibility. When you demonstrate that people like and respect your business, people view it as proof of legitimacy. Coming across as established is a self-fulfilling prophecy on the Web. Everybody loves a firmly rooted member of the community.

Which brings me to the final way you can show that you are loved by others: social media. This is a topic big enough for its own book (See my last book, *Outsmarting Social Media*), which is why I reserve most of the discussion for the next chapter. But I do want to point out a couple of simple ways you can use social networking sites to help differentiate your company:

- **Facebook**—While the sheer popularity of Facebook is well established, it's important to look at the way that people use it. Facebook is, essentially, a tool for socializing with friends past and present. If your business might be part of a social conversation, then it will probably benefit from having a page on Facebook. Industries that people speak about socially include restaurants, nightlife, travel, fitness, health, news, and technology. However, if you have a specialized B2B business such as semiconductor manufacturing or even commercial real estate, you probably won't get as much value out of Facebook. Most of the time, Facebook is better at getting existing customers to make more purchases than it is at getting new customers in the door, because people prefer to use Facebook to interact with people and pages they already know.

  If you do believe that Facebook is a good place to establish a presence for your company, the best way to tap into its audience is to create a Facebook business page. By gaining at least a few hundred "likes," you will demonstrate that people are fond of your company and that you encourage an open dialogue with your customers. Once your community of "likers" is sizable, affix a link to your Facebook page to the home page of your website (see Figure 10.5). Doing so has become a standard practice for businesses nowadays.

- **Google+**—While having a business page on Google+ still has a ways to go in terms of being recognized by the average consumer as a mark of credibility, it is a very smart idea for SEO purposes. Google+ and YouTube are the only substantial social networks that Google owns and controls, and Google+ certainly aims to be a place where all businesses hang a shingle. By getting Google+ users to add your business to their "circles," you will be making it more likely that your business page appears in search results in the future.

- **Twitter**—Twitter is a somewhat different animal than Facebook and Google+, but we can simplify it by saying that it's a community of people who like to see what other people, organizations, and businesses are doing. People express this interest by "following" your company's Twitter username, and you can send out short messages anytime telling people what your company is doing. This practice can lead to new connections. And just like with Facebook, you should link to your Twitter account from your home page once you have a few hundred followers.

Figure 10.5 *A New Jersey doctor, Joel Fuhrman, M.D., links to his Facebook and Twitter pages from the home page of his website (top right).*

Data

We have now covered design and differentiation: building a clean, professional site that highlights your company's advantages. After you've accomplished these two goals, and visitors are regularly impressed by your company's aesthetic and credibility, they will now look for more information. This means providing your visitors with answers to the many questions streaming through their minds. What do you sell? How does it work? What does it cost? And who are the members of your team?

Simply put, give your customers everything they need to commit. Too many websites hide information behind unnecessary walls, such as making people request a quote. Unless your product is so customized that general information cannot reasonably be given, be up front with your potential customers. Doing so will help to filter out customers who aren't a good fit for your business and make it more likely that those who are a good fit will actually contact you.

Price

Price is by far the greatest area of sensitivity for business owners. So many websites are chock full of information but shy about listing prices. At some point in the past, it must have become common practice to withhold your prices so that you could collect more information or do the sale over the phone. That is the only way I can explain the trend of asking for a potential customer's contact info for them to ascertain your business's prices. In an age where competitors are just a click away, it just doesn't make sense to withhold the answer to a question everyone is asking. Rather than risk turning off a potential customer, give at least some idea of your company's prices.

When you announce your rates publicly, you send the message that your company stands by its products, believes in what it's worth, and is unafraid to compete in the open marketplace. You project confidence, transparency, and convenience, which are three things new customers love. And, once again, you prevent yourself from having to take calls from people who can't afford your services.

Products

Clarity is also important when showcasing your products. Many e-commerce sites boast extensive inventories but have no photographs or copy to support those claims. Others might include pictures, but they are grainy, small, and lacking explanation.

Consider this: When you walk into Sears to check out a new electric drill, you can weigh it in your hands, hold it up against other models, pantomime a home repair, and load multiple drill bits. The Web is a visual medium, so you must make up for all that physical contact with pictures, diagrams, and words. Customers are much more comfortable buying something on the Web if they believe they have seen it from every angle. Good photography and videos can dramatically increase your conversion rate.

And don't forget the words. There is a reason the J. Peterman catalog was an American institution for so long despite the fact that it contained only watercolor illustrations of its products. Words can paint a picture, evoke the emotions you want, and answer countless technical questions about what you're selling. Words also demonstrate that you are paying attention to detail and that you care about the shopping experience on your site. Words can also help define your site for indexing and ranking. The moral: Don't think of your site as a computerized inventory machine. Think of it as a catalog, complete with glossy photos and plenty of professional copy. Your customers will reward you for it.

One final note about product information: There is one way the Web actually outshines physical stores, and that is comparison. Effective sites often have side-by-side tables that line up the features on electronics, spa packages, and what have you. Customers who like comparison shopping—that is, most people—tend to return time and again to the one resource that puts everything in front of them in a clear format. And from there it is a short trip to the Order Now button.

Process

If you have a service business, all the same rules apply, but they must be catered toward process rather than products. It is equally important to explain exactly what you do, how it works, why it works, and how long it takes. It doesn't matter if you are a dentist or a dry cleaner; people want to know what they're getting into.

One of the simplest ways to explain your process is to walk customers through everything step by step. Tell them a story. You could create pages for each step or simply show the process visually with a flowchart. If you do plastic surgery or web design, show before and after pictures. If you're a lawyer, describe every step of the process from initial consultation to conclusion. If you're a massage therapist, talk about what happens from the moment your customers walk through the door to the time they leave totally zonked out, water in hand.

Resources

Another good way to increase conversion rates on your site is by creating a Resources section. This section is devoted entirely to educating customers about topics related to your business. If you sell cars, consider writing some articles about how to buy a car. If you sell ant farms, write an article about the communal behavior of ants or how to extend the life of an ant community. (As you know, articles like these will also help with SEO.)

Sites that contain lots of useful information tend to be "stickier" than sites that do not, which means that people keep coming back. Adding expert-level information also enhances your site's prestige and respectability, showing your customers that you know your industry inside and out. Implicitly, you are saying, "I'm an expert, and I would never offer anything but the best products." Good resources are also an effective form of link bait, drawing attention from bloggers and other companies who want to share useful information with their audiences.

People

One final way to fill out your site's data is to create a page about your team. Let's go back to the Sears example for a second. In the physical world, you know exactly who is trying to sell you something. You can look that salesman in the eye, shake his hand, and decide whether you trust him. The Web is an anonymous place, however, and often it is not clear who is on the other end of that sale (if anyone).

Business owners are sometimes reluctant to add detailed bios to their sites if they are not eager to be in the spotlight. But everybody wants to attach a face to a purchase, especially online. My advice is to hire a photographer to take a professional headshot. Then, underneath that beautiful photo, tell the story of your business simply, emphasizing your passions. Often when purchases are made, it is not just the product or service being sold; it is the people behind it.

Deals

And so we come to the final *D*: deals. By now, you should have a pretty good idea what goes through your visitors' heads when they arrive somewhere new. There is an initial snap judgment based on the look of the site (design), followed by a quick decision about whether to stay or go (differentiation), followed a bunch of questions that require answers (data). At this point, your visitors are actively looking for a reason to buy. Give them one.

Deals are a good way to make your products more competitive, attractive, and affordable. An intelligently crafted deal can also give your visitors a sense of urgency, encouraging them to buy now instead of later. Promotions are some of the oldest tricks in all of marketing, but they have been around so long precisely because they work. There is something about the notion of a "special offer" that just taps into our natural instincts.

Sales and Promotions

The simplest kind of sale is a discount. If you charge $10 for a widget, you will sell more of them when you tell people it's marked down from $15. Everybody loves a bargain, and one of the surest ways to inspire immediate action is to create a special value, then put a ticking clock on that value. One-week deals, weekend deals, holiday deals—these "bargains" are everywhere online because they are so effective.

Bundling items is another time-tested way to get your customers to buy more than they otherwise might have. If you sell baby onesies, throw in a free one for every four they buy. If you run a book-of-the-month club, create an annual rate that is much cheaper than the month-to-month rate. Bundling products lets your customers buy more and save more simultaneously. Everybody wins.

Another promotion that works well on the Web is the "first time" offer, in which new customers have a limited-time opportunity to save substantially on their first purchase. Also in the "new customer deals" family is the concept of a referral program, in which you reward your customers for spreading the word to their friends.

Because the Web works in such a viral way, you can greatly increase your reach and brand awareness just by giving customers an incentive to market your site for you.

Finally, you can invite guests to submit their email addresses for future correspondence with the company by offering something with that signup information. A lot of people offer guides, white papers, or other types of resources that will give potential customers useful information within your area of expertise. You can also make a coupon or a discount code available with signup.

The goal of all promotions is to make your customers feel as if they are getting something, not giving something; so think carefully about what you would genuinely want if you were in their shoes.

An important point about sales and promotions is that different types are appropriate for different businesses. If you offer too many discounts on a medical website, for instance, you will seem desperate for business. But for a mobile phone site, all the discounts in the world will be appreciated. Professional services businesses and other companies selling more expensive products might feature free consultations, high-end handbooks, and other similarly fitting fare.

With certain service businesses or creators of custom products, it can make sense to go against all the advice in this section. If what you are selling is precious or high quality enough, sometimes customers will want to know that the company providing it is being well compensated. For instance, would you want your therapist to be paid through a "10 sessions for the price of 5" deal? Chances are you'd worry that the quality of your treatment would suffer if the person providing it didn't pay herself adequately. Higher prices can be perceived as the sign of a company that does excellent work and has the integrity to pay its staff fairly. But keep in mind, this is the case only with higher-end businesses.

Point of Purchase

My final thought on conversion may be self-evident, but it's worth repeating: Nobody will buy anything if he or she can't figure out how to get it. For commerce sites, this means you want to create a big Order Now or Add to Cart button on every product page. For services, it means offering an extremely simple way for people to book your services. If you take appointments, have your webmaster create a simple appointment form, possibly with a calendar, that people can understand instantly (see Figure 10.6).

Figure 10.6   *The Midas front page appointment invite. Figuring out how to make an appointment couldn't be easier.*

A big part of moving customers closer to purchase is the so-called call to action, which is industry lingo for encouraging people to take an action (usually, completing a purchase) right now. Some of the most effective conversion tricks involve nothing more complicated than putting a call to action on every page. Nobody should ever have to click more than once to become a customer. So put a call to action on every page. It doesn't have to be big and gaudy, and you never know when your customers are ready to check out.

SEO is worth little without a website that is optimized for conversions. Put thought into your customers' psychology when they arrive on your website and make sure that your site addresses their anxieties, questions, and expectations. Then, simply stand out of the way of them making a purchase.

Conversion optimization is work, but it's time and money well spent. Doubling your conversion rate is much more profitable than doubling your traffic because only conversion translates directly into revenue. Give your site the consideration it needs to thrive, and it will give you the economic reward you're seeking.

11

Social Search: The Intersection of Social Media and SEO

If marketing were a family, SEO would be the smart, hardworking daughter. Her parents would be very proud of her, and nobody would have any doubt of her growing up to be an independent, productive member of society. But she would have a hotter sister who always gets more attention than SEO for no reason other than her good looks. That sister's name would be social media.

As people interested in growing website traffic, it is important that we understand these two sisters for who they are. SEO is the one that, through time and understanding, will bring you the most valuable traffic, most consistently. She is ultimately the better investment of time. But social media can do some surprising things for your business. SEO may work hard for you during the day, but social media can take you out at night, wink at the bouncer, and dance the night away with you. And happily, there is a way for SEO and social media to complement each other.

The areas in which SEO and social media intersect are still developing. All the big social media sites would like Google to incorporate them more seamlessly into its search results, but few of them want to hand the search behemoth the valuable social data they've spent years collecting from their users. So, Google had to invent its own social network, Google+, for the purpose of collecting data about its users to be used in future search results. For example, if you discuss and share Hugo Boss clothing on Google+, you may discover that the Hugo Boss website shows up higher when you search `mens suits` on Google at some point down the road. Another way Google will probably use social data is promoting certain websites based on your friends' interests. So, if many of your friends recommend a Hawaiian touring company called Tiki Tours, you will probably see that company's website pop up in the search results when you search `best hawaii tours` on Google in the future.

A related function of Google+ is the +1 button. Similar to a Like button on Facebook, it is an expression of approval for a piece of content on the web. The value of a +1 seems to have increased over time. Today, it is nearly as valuable to get your content +1ed as it is to build links to it.

To make your content eligible to receive +1s, you just need to add the Google+ button to a page on your site. The button appears on your site in the same way that other social buttons do (see Figure 11.1). Your web developer can acquire the source code for the button at https://developers.google.com/+/web/+1button/.

Figure 11.1   *The Google +1 button.*

The Google +1 button is a social plug-in like the other popular plug-ins placed around articles, videos, games, and other content all over the Web. However, what makes it unique is its special influence on a piece of content's ability to rank in Google search results. The more +1s a piece of content has, the more likely it is to show up in relevant search results.

An even more SEO-applicable way that search and social media intersect is in the area of links. Social media sites like Facebook, Twitter, LinkedIn, Pinterest, and Instagram have huge audiences, and when your content is shared on them, it can lead to high-TrustRank links on news sites, social bookmarking sites, and popular blogs. In this way, social media is an indirect way to get webmasters to notice your content and link to it.

Social media as link bait basically works like this: Big websites like Nytimes.com, CNN.com, and Huffingtonpost.com are the ones that everyone seeks attention from but are largely controlled by an elite group of journalists. Social networks like Facebook, YouTube, and Twitter represent the masses. And although a link or status update on one of these social networks does not transfer any TrustRank to your website, there is significant SEO potential for posts that get a lot of attention. If you post a link to a video you took of your dog doing a back flip, and it strikes a chord in the average person, she will share it with her friends, who will share it with their friends, and so on. The reach of a single output of content that is adopted by the social hoi polloi can be much greater than the reach of a mainstream media outlet. And if that content is popular enough with the common man, it will reach the elites as well. It's all about "going viral."

If you are the creator of a piece of content that goes viral, your website can get links rained upon it. While it bears repeating that most links that appear on social media sites are tagged no-follow, crippling them from passing TrustRank, popularity on social media is often what causes *other* websites, which can pass TrustRank, to link out your content.

In the next section, you learn how you can use social media sites to boost your website's ranking on Google.

Social Media Sites and the Flow of Information

As a business owner, you already know that exposure is the key to success. Traditionally, the most powerful ways of getting exposure have been advertisements, press, and word of mouth. Although these tools have always been the backbone of marketing, the rise of social media websites has opened up a whole new world of possibilities for online marketers. Comparing the type of exposure available to online businesses nowadays versus what used to be available to traditional brick-and-mortar stores is eye-opening (see Figures 11.2 and 11.3).

The main thing the Internet has changed—other than vastly expanding the number of outlets for communication—is the flow of communication in our world. While opening it up and speeding it up, it has also made communication occur more on our own terms. Today, we have far more control in our interactions with people. For example, instead of having to experience the social pressures of an in-person encounter or even a phone call, we can now write an email or text message, which we respond to at our own will. (The merits of this "advantage" are, of course, debatable.)

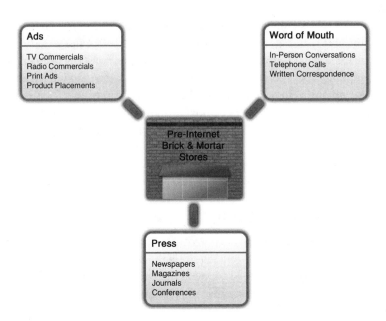

Figure 11.2 *Exposure available pre-Internet.*

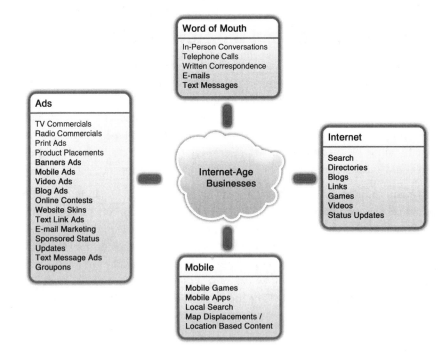

Figure 11.3 *Exposure available today.*

I remember experiencing the benefits of Internet-era communication back in 1998, when AOL chat was extremely popular. If a girl I liked was online, I could chat with her, saving myself the awkwardness of having to call her or ask her to meet up. Obviously, I wanted to do those other things, but I needed a bridge, an intermediary, before gaining the courage to do so. Chat was perfect. I would write something, she would write back 30 seconds later, and I would write back in another 30 seconds or minute. If I needed to think of something witty to say or consult a friend, there was always the built-in excuse that I was involved in other chats or had a phone call come in. I have AOL chat to thank for many interactions I might never have had due to shyness.

The convenience I just described is a huge reason why the Internet—particularly social media—has so profoundly influenced our culture. And it extends into the world of marketing as well. Let's take ads as an example. In the past, I might see an ad in a magazine, stare at it for a few seconds, and then either remember it or forget about it. If the advertiser were persistent (and deep pocketed), I might hear ads for that company on radio or see them on TV.

Now the same company might place an ad on Facebook. Recognizing the company, I might click Like underneath the ad, indicating my acceptance of the brand. The next day, because of that like, I might get a status update showing me a humorous YouTube video that company made as part of a campaign for a new product. Finding the video funny, I might then post it on my friend's profile page. His 1,000 friends might then see it, and 3 of them might post it on their friends' profile pages. An additional 2 of my friend's friends might tweet about it, exposing it to their 800 combined followers. One of those peoples' followers might then submit it to a social bookmarking site like Reddit, where the best content of the day gets posted on the home page. If enough people voted for this video, it would hit the front page of Reddit, get 150,000 additional views and 2,000 comments, and even more sharing would occur. Because of the Reddit exposure, 15 blogs might repost the video, including a major outlet that gets millions of visitors per month. And on goes the sharing. That entire journey started with just one click.

Forgive me if I seem to have lost the thread of where SEO plays into this concept. The significant event, SEO-wise, in that story was the part where the blogs reposted the video to their sites. If 15 blogs repost a video, that's 15 links to a single web page. In this case, the web page hosting the content was on YouTube, but it could easily have been hosted on your website. As you know from earlier chapters, acquiring a link can be pretty tough in an age when most webmasters understand the value of linking. So, 15 links in a single day is quite a payload. Social media regularly delivers that kind of link jackpot; you just have to make a piece of content that is creative enough to earn it.

Chapter 3, "How to Reel In Links," covered some of the best ways to create viral content to tempt webmasters into linking to your site. Straight link baiting is important, but social media can be a great way for content to find its way to webmasters in a less pushy way. It's one thing to write to the owners of blogs and tell them you created this awesome infographic. It's another thing for them to come across it in their stream of status updates one morning and think it's really cool. The feeling of discovering something is much more powerful than having that something pushed on you.

Marketers understand that social networking sites such as Facebook and Twitter are the breeding grounds for virality. But most go about their social marketing strategy incorrectly, simply posting links to their latest blog articles every day. In fact, as I think about it, almost every company I know that has a Facebook page does exactly that, so let me be clear about how effective it is: not at all. If you want to attract links to your content via social media, you will want to follow these rules:

- **Build a rapport with your audience**—If your social media page is nothing but an automaton of content with no humanity emanating from it, it is sure to be ignored. This idea slips under the radar for many in-house marketers because they think it's a social media page's job to deliver regular content from the company. But in reality, it's the page's job to build a rapport between the company and its audience. And that is done by acting like a real, thinking, breathing person. So let's say you're a sport shoe store in Newark, New Jersey. The content of your posts should not be purely about the specials and promotions your store is having or about the new inventory it gets in. Instead, post about what a fine day it is today in Newark. Post about a local guy who built an airplane using spare parts from his garage. Post about how crazy the potholes are on the main avenue near the store. People can relate to those things. Yes, a post about a sale is certainly more targeted, but you need to keep your followers interested as well.

- **Only promote the content that's genuinely good**—Imagine if a comedian got onstage and made 10 bad jokes in a row followed by 1 good joke, then repeated that pattern for 30 minutes. He wouldn't be working much longer. Now imagine if that same comedian used only his good jokes and stayed onstage for only 5 minutes. The guy would be a hit. That's what you need to do with social media. The less-than-awesome content can still have a home; put it somewhere on your site, and the people who really want to see it will find it. But reserve social media status updates for really good content. Everyone misses more than they hit; but you have a choice not to publicize your misses.

Tip

There is a more technical reason to only post your best content, as well. Facebook, Twitter, and YouTube look at the percentage of people who interact with your posts. If everyone ignores your content, it might be algorithmically demoted and shown to smaller audiences in the future.

- **Respect that social networking sites are their own community**—As much as marketers would like all social networking sites to be a traffic funnel to outside websites, they simply aren't. Most people who are on Facebook, YouTube, Twitter, Tumblr, or any other big social network want to be there. To get people to see content that is on your website, you do need to direct them outside of the walled garden, but the key is to do so sparingly. For instance, suppose that your viral content is a simple game. Allow visitors to your social media pages to play that game on the social media sites themselves for a while but offer a better version of the game, or more games, if they come over to your site. The same would be the case with a great video. Keep users on YouTube for the video, but then tell them if they want to see other, exclusive videos, they must go to your website. Lure them over.

The overall concept to keep in mind if you want to understand the social networking environment is that everyone is there to socialize and share fun content. There is no major social networking site that is built to send traffic off the site for the purpose of making sales. All of them allow it, but it is not the main activity. So just be conscious of that, and if your content is exciting enough, the masses will visit your website in droves. It is that kind of mass adoption that will lead to more links.

Creating Great Content

For all I talk about the importance of posting great content, a refresher is in order about what that really means. Sure, different people find different things entertaining. But certain categories of content are interesting to most of the population. Through studying the popular content on major social media sites, I have come up with a guide to the types of content that the masses love:

- **Amazing or dramatic stories**—True or half true, wacky or amazing things happen every day that most people don't know about. I remember a story about a guy who set out to trade a red paper clip for a new house. By trading the paper clip many times for increasingly more valuable items, he eventually got his house. This incredible chain of events occurred back in 2006, but I never forgot it. Believe it or not, there are plenty more out there like that one.

- **Scandal**—For better or worse, people love to share scandalous stories on the Internet. No matter how distasteful the situation may be, never underestimate the power of the "Can you believe she did that?" factor.

- **Exclusivity**—People love to read a story directly from its source. If you are the first to get the scoop, you will get linked by every other blog that finds your content interesting enough. And if you don't have an exclusive for a story, you can still take an exclusive angle on the story and use the *E* word nonetheless. Just make sure that you have made the story your own by filling in missing background info, adding new facts and opinions, and overall looking at the story differently than other outlets did.

- **Pictures**—Which would you be more likely to click: a link that says "Gorilla Saves Injured Boy from Lion" or that same headline above a picture of a massive primate shaking his fist at a lion with a scared boy cowering beneath him? Words can be more vivid than images some-times—as when a book is better than a movie—but for quick Internet consumption, a picture will win every time. And by the way, videos are even better than pictures.

Promoting Your Content Through Social Media

Let me back up a bit. To promote your content on the various social media sites to which you belong, you need to have friends, fans, followers, or subscribers. Whatever the "audience" is called on each site, you need a solid base of them to promote your article, image, or video.

Building your audience is a pretty straightforward process: You just start by adding all the people you already know, and then send friend requests (or the equivalent) to friends of theirs. For every friend you add, you gain the potential for members of that new friend's network to become future connections of yours. Not everyone will accept your invitations, but a lot of people will, and you don't need that many people to start anyway. New connections naturally sprout just from being active on a social network. Also as a general rule, do not send more than 10 requests in one day; otherwise, you might run afoul of the rules.

After you establish your presence on the various social networks you've joined, the steps for sharing your content are pretty straightforward. The following sections show how to do so on a couple of the big sites.

Facebook

After you've established a personal profile, you can create a business page. Business pages want to attract likes the same way that personal pages want to attract friends. To gain likes, send a page suggestion to all your friends. Hopefully, at least one-third will like it. When people like a page on Facebook, the action is sometimes announced on their News Feed, the page that lists all their friends' status updates. Here is an example of a typical News Feed item:

> Mary Jo likes Donuts Galore.

In this case, many of Mary Jo's friends will see the announcement about her liking Donuts Galore in their News Feeds and, if they click the hyperlinked `Donuts Galore`, it will take them to Donut Galore's fan page, where they can click Like, too, which will then show up in their friends' News Feeds, and so on. Of course, Donuts Galore's Facebook fan page will want to have a link to the actual Donuts Galore website so that the Facebook exposure can help sell donuts.

YouTube

After creating an account, which will establish your own channel, start uploading videos. Until you have friends or subscribers on your channel, you will have nobody to share the video with. While you can send friend requests to other YouTube users, subscribers are more valuable because they will probably see every new video you post. However, people usually subscribe to your channel only if they find your videos genuinely enjoyable.

The best way to get initial traction on your YouTube account is to post your videos on Facebook so that your friends who are also on YouTube can become your friend or subscriber there as well. Twitter is another good channel on which to post your videos. Ultimately, if your video is so good that thousands of people watch it, it has a chance of showing up in more places on YouTube (such as the all-valuable Related Videos area on the side of every video page) and getting embedded on other websites.

Social Bookmarking Sites

The main social bookmarking website at the time of this printing is Reddit, with StumbleUpon a distant second in terms of traffic volume. Creating an account on these sites is simple. Then all you have to do is submit content to the community for consideration. The community will view the content you submitted on a new page, discuss it, and determine whether it's worthy of promoting. If people like it, they can give it an upvote. With enough upvotes, the content will appear on the front page of the site and get a huge burst of traffic and potentially many new links.

Twitter

Starting a Twitter account couldn't be easier: Just fill out your name and a line or two about you, and begin talking about the random things you think about or find on the Internet (beginning with your own content). The main way to gain followers on Twitter is to ask your friends to follow you and then tweet interesting status updates to them. Twitter also has an algorithm that encourages people who are similar to you to follow you, so you might see followers appearing like magic. If your status updates are scintillating enough, they will get retweeted, meaning echoed by other people in their own status updates. If your updates include a link to your website, retweets can be especially valuable because they can lead to new people discovering your website.

As your website gains exposure and links from social media virality, you should look to sustain that success by adding engaging content on a regular basis. Remember to always sprinkle in personal, down-to-earth status updates alongside your links to your own website.

A Final Word

As search engines become more sophisticated, the intersection of SEO and social media will not just be about links. SEO and social media will be mixed together as social preferences, location, friends' interests, and other "social" factors influence what we encounter in our search results. We have already seen these changes beginning to take root on Google and, to a lesser extent, on Bing. As we look forward to the future, no matter what changes occur, the rule of thumb for social media will always be to contribute quality content to the community and engage in thoughtful conversations with customers, critics, and the general public. Do so, and you might find your site showered in traffic and TrustRank.

12

Using SEO to Build a Business

When you've mastered SEO, you have a skill that enables you to start nearly any business. No matter how much Google's algorithm changes, the core abilities of creating engaging content, authentically sharing it with people, and carefully measuring the results are timeless. Before the Internet existed, those skills led to success in business. Today they've been codified into a formula that allows you to achieve high rankings on the world's largest search engine. And tomorrow they'll be useful in many other ways we can't yet predict.

So now, in this final chapter, let's turn our attention to how you can translate all the skills you've learned thus far into a fully operational, successful entrepreneurial pursuit. This chapter covers the major steps required to create a business, but the reality is that a smoothly operating company works like a symphony. All of its parts function well on their own, but as a whole they create something entirely unique, the interrelation of which is too complex and well integrated to ever break down and explain.

Of course, it all starts with an idea.

The Power of an Idea

People have business ideas all the time. How many times has your dad, or your aunt, or your friend said something like "I've got a business idea that could be worth a million bucks!"? Although it might seem like a pipe dream, I encourage such thinking. The key, however, is to actually do something about it afterward. Most of us are not cut out for entrepreneurship. It's lonely, frustrating, laced with failure, and the gratification is severely delayed. But for the very few who have what it takes to do it, it can lead to a better life.

The fact that few people take ideas and run with them is actually the reason I can write this book. If everyone who read *SEO Made Easy* digested it fully and then went out and applied all its principles, the online marketing landscape would change. My SEO company would have trouble servicing its clients because so many mini-Evans would be running around dominating every business niche. But I know that that won't happen. Although I expect everyone who reads this book to benefit from it, very few people have the inclination and natural drive to become the next SEO guru. So I'm safe for now.

For those who *are* ready to become an entrepreneur—or who already are one and are looking for their next venture—keep reading.

Differentiating a Good Idea from a Bad Idea

There are three ways to test whether that idea that popped into your head while you were in the shower is a good one:

1. The first is intuition. Do you and the people you know think it's a good idea? More importantly, would they actually use it if it were produced? This is the lowest barrier to entry. If you can't even get your friends to like your idea, you may not go very far with it.

2. The second test is informal market research. With some simple Googling, can you find references to people who are lamenting the fact that a particular idea doesn't exist? For instance, before a backpack that dispenses water through a tube to runners became well known, you could see grumbling about the subject on runners' forums. Some runners prefer to carry a water bottle in their hands while they train, others have a wrist strap, and others a soft pouch they tuck into their shorts. Still others pre-hydrate as much as possible so that they don't have to deal with the hassle of transporting water. Even today, if you search `how do runners carry water`, you will see long discussion threads about the subject. By finding common problems among

communities of people (runners, stay-at-home parents, doctors, photographers, building operators, or what have you), you can confirm whether demand exists for a new business.

3. The third, and most important, way to test the viability of an idea is to actually sell it. My friend Lisa used to make wallets and purses from old drink pouches (see Figure 12.1). Although she wasn't sure whether people would buy them, the idea was validated when a small boutique in SoHo New York ordered a few dozen as a test. She also had more requests for her handmade items than she could fulfill at any given time. Lisa's concept was a good idea. It was intuitively appealing to those who had seen her creations; it solved a problem of people wanting unique, environmentally sustainable fashion accessories; and she was able to sell dozens of them. But none of that made it a business. Not yet, at least.

Figure 12.1   *Handmade purses from drink pouches—a clever fashion accessory my friend used to make.*

Going from Idea to Business

Lisa was still in college at the time we talked about her handmade purses and wallets. She had pressure from her parents to get a respectable job when her schooling ended. This left her in a position where she needed to prove that her purses and wallets were more than just a fun hobby and could support her financially. There's no better way to find out whether an entrepreneur is serious about a venture than to tell her that it will be responsible for paying her rent. So, was Lisa's idea a business?

Yes, one boutique had ordered Lisa's products, but it wasn't interested in ordering more. Even though her purses eventually sold out, they seemed more like a limited edition item than a long-term seller to the boutique owner. Thus ended the relationship. And Lisa, with all the other things she had going on in her life, didn't feel like approaching every boutique in Manhattan. Thus ended the journey of the drink pouch purses and wallets. Conclusion: Not a business.

Lisa's story is like hundreds of others I've heard where exciting ideas don't ultimately come to fruition. So what was lacking? Let's go through some of the factors that prevented the business from getting off the ground.

Motivation from the Founder

Although it's undeniable that Lisa worked hard, spending untold hours sewing her products and promoting them, she lacked both the experience and the support system to keep going. Without those two factors, it was nearly impossible to succeed.

Experience is, as they say, the best teacher. Many entrepreneurs have role models who have started companies before and know what it feels like to take a huge risk. If you've seen that model—or better yet, experienced it—you can often tough it out when failure occurs. If Lisa were a seasoned entrepreneur rather than a college student, she might not have thought twice when that first boutique owner discontinued her products. Perhaps the next boutique owner would have ordered 100 of them. Perhaps several boutique owners in a row would have rejected them and then she'd bump into a buyer at Wal-Mart who thought they were perfect for back-to-school season. (Hey, you never know.) The point is, viewing failure as part of the process, rather than the *end* of it, is something all entrepreneurs learn. It's a sign of experience. Lisa never learned that.

Support is the other factor here. If you have plenty of support—say, entrepreneurial parents who encourage you to start your own business—you might feel particularly motivated to press on with your idea. But if you grow up in a more "normal" home with nonentrepreneurial parents, it will probably be hard to navigate the perils of starting your own company. Lisa came from parents who are a teacher and an electrical engineer, and who probably wanted to see her take a safer path. Without an atmosphere of encouragement for this type of venture, Lisa had little chance of surviving the inevitable first few failures.

Market Testing

Lisa began to test the viability of her product in the marketplace by approaching a boutique. In fact, the boutique accepted her product. But when it didn't place any additional orders, she took it as a sign that the entire market had rejected her. If she had shopped it to, say, 50 specialty boutiques in Manhattan, she might have gotten a more accurate picture of the demand. That said, physical boutiques are not the first place I would look to sell a funky fashion accessory in the 2010s. With targeted social media ad buys, submission to social bookmarking sites like Reddit and StumbleUpon, and outreach to Cool Thing of the Day-type websites such as coolthings.com and thisiswhyimbroke.com, the product could have found its home on the Internet.

Focus on Business Model

When a first-time entrepreneur comes up with an idea, typically it is passion, rather than profit, that leads his or her charge. In Lisa's case, this was indeed the scenario. She charged $45 for a handmade purse, and it took her about 3 hours to make. She had no partners in the business. While she did plan to get others to make the purses if they ever became popular, she had no concrete plan for scalability. An example of a more sustainable business model would be Lisa hiring an outside company to create the purses for a flat rate of $30 each while she handled the marketing and outreach to boutiques. If demand for the purses increased, it would also be crucial for her to understand how low the price of making a purse could become. If, for instance, she ordered 1,000 purses from her manufacturing team, could she get the price down to $15 per purse? If so, she'd have a healthier profit margin.

She also needed to understand the mechanics of wholesale and retail. If she made the product for $30, she might want to sell it to a boutique for a wholesale price of $45, giving her a $15 profit margin. But if the boutique were to buy the purses for $45, they would likely have to mark them up to a retail price of $60 or more. Unfortunately, that's probably more than people are willing to pay for a purse made of drink pouches. The problem then becomes, how low can she go? Should she sell the purses to the retailer at the same price she pays for them, hoping that the boutique eventually orders a lot more, allowing her to get a bulk discount from her manufacturer and finally squeeze out a profit? Or should she seek out a cheaper manufacturer and possibly sacrifice quality? These are some of the basic business model issues that Lisa would have needed to understand to succeed.

Online Presence

As mentioned in the market testing section earlier, the real place for a specialty product like Lisa's purses and wallets is the Internet. Therefore, a thorough exploration of the online landscape for such a product is needed. Being a search engine optimizer, my mind always starts with *search*. Do people search for this kind of thing? As much as I hate to say it, I don't think they do. These products fall under the category of Things People Don't Know They Want Yet, and in that case we must turn to two other marketing channels: discovery and branding.

Online discovery, as opposed to online search, is the act of finding a product on the Web through casually browsing around as opposed to actively seeking it out. Coming across a product in a "People who bought this item also liked these items" box on Amazon.com is a well-known form of discovery. So is online word of mouth, as in seeing a picture on Instagram of a friend wearing a pair of jeans you like, then messaging her to ask where she got those jeans. Another form of discovery is social ads. Facebook has been hard at work for years figuring out the best way to include personalized ads in your News Feed so that you naturally stumble upon products and services that you want to buy. To utilize discovery, Lisa could have used Facebook's current advertising offering, which allows advertisers to place highly targeted ads. She might have targeted cities that are known for individuality and style, such as New York and Los Angeles. Within those cities, she could have advertised to women ages 13–30 who like edgy brands like Urban Outfitters.

Another avenue for building awareness of a unique product is branding. Although it is probably the most expensive way to get your product out there, branding can make a serious impact. When I say *branding*, I mean getting people to notice your company slowly and over time through display ads, billboards, TV, sponsorships, or anything else that gets your product seen. However, if you're not a big company, as in Lisa's case, you could start by creating inexpensive videos with viral potential, sending free samples to popular bloggers, and assembling a grass-roots team to showcase your product in major cities.

All told, Lisa didn't have the right knowledge, experience, or strategy to succeed in her first business. Perhaps she also didn't have the right idea: I see lots of similar products for sale on Etsy and eBay, and they seem to sell slowly, mostly as one-off novelty items. My hope is that by reading this section you can recognize some of the threads of Lisa's journey in your own entrepreneurial attempts and know what to watch out for.

Using SEO to Start a Business

Once you have found the right idea and believe it can become a business, it's incumbent on you to consider how SEO can help you start that business. The first question to ask yourself is this: What would potential customers of my new company type into Google if they wanted to buy what I sell? We'll get back to that question in a moment. But let's create some context first.

Let's say you love fine wine but can rarely afford to buy it. You're out walking your dog one day when the idea hits you: What if a group of people all went in to buy a wine collection? By purchasing bottles as a group, we could afford to try wines none of us could afford individually. If we chose to drink the wine together as a group, it would also be a great way to get wine lovers together in a social atmosphere. Plus, we could collect a small admission fee at each event and use the proceeds to buy more wine! Thus was born The Wine Commune.

Now, let's think about how to turn this idea into a business. Before getting too excited, you would want to market test the viability of the idea. Start by telling friends and family about it and asking if they would pay the membership fee to join. (Because these are, presumably, your supporters, take what they say with a grain of salt.) Then search Google for discussions about wanting to drink fine wine but not being able to because of its expense. I might search `inexpensive ways to drink fine wine`. Then see what other solutions exist and how popular they seem to be. If all the signs of a business opportunity seem to be there, it's time to do a real-world experiment: email people you know and see if you can organize an informal gathering to try out the idea. If people are willing to show up, and especially if they are willing to part with any money, you might be on to something.

After you've successfully soft-tested the market, it's almost time to get started on formalizing the business. The last thing to do is to take a moment and honestly ask yourself: Am I in this for the long haul? If the idea appeals to people and the business begins to take off, will I be excited to get out of bed every day to work on it? Am I comfortable with this business being a central part of my identity? If the answer to all of those questions is yes, you've reached the starting line.

Establishing Your Website

To make your business official, you need a domain name (see Figure 12.2). In the example we're using, winecommune.com would be the perfect domain name. If your ideal domain name is taken—and nearly every domain name on earth is taken by spammers and squatters—continue looking until you find a name that is as memorable and short as possible. Keep in mind that if you register wine-commune.com, you will have to say "wine dash commune dot com" to everyone who asks for years to come. And if you register thewinecommune.com, nearly everyone will go to winecommune.com anyway. A better alternative domain to register would be mywinecommune.com because it feels personal and therefore is more memorable. Even if all the domains you like are taken, you can always make an offer to buy the domain (see Figure 12.3). Many decent domains are available for less than $1,000.

Figure 12.2   *Registering a domain can be as simple as going to a domain registrar such as Register.com, GoDaddy.com, or Moniker.com (pictured) and typing the domain you want into the search box. A few steps later, you'll be the owner of a new home on the Web.*

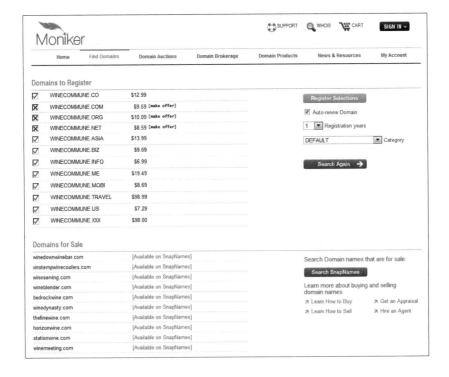

Figure 12.3   *If the domain you want is taken, your registrar will probably offer you the same domain with a different extension (.org, .net, .com) at the end. It may also offer you similar domains that are for sale at a premium price from private bidders.*

Now that you've got a domain, you need to create the website. As far as the logo and design goes, if you're looking to save money, try to find a talented younger person rather than an established company. A recent grad, for instance, will not need to charge you for the overhead that a web design company would have and probably values his time far less. The other element of the website is the copy, and for that, I do not advise hiring someone. It's best to write the content on the website yourself, because doing so often helps a founder define his business better and form the initial messaging for his brand. For instance, is The Wine Commune "The premier network for lovers of fine wine"? Or is it simply "A place for people that love good wine"? By the time you've finished writing the website, you will have a firm grasp of your brand, including its voice, look, and feel. Now it's time to start marketing.

Choosing Keywords

And now, we're back to the all-important question posed at the beginning of this section: What would potential customers of my new company type into Google if they wanted to buy what I sell? To find the answer, try three things. The first is the commonsense approach of asking friends and family. In the case of The Wine Commune, you might ask them what they would type into Google if they were looking for a way to enjoy fine wine on a budget. However, just as in opinion polls, the way you pose the question will influence the answers you get. If you posed it exactly as I just wrote it, many people would answer "fine wine on a budget" or something else that they would not actually search. If you ask it in a more anecdotal way, however, you might get a more honest answer: "Let's say you're a person who lives on a budget, but you absolutely love expensive wine. You're determined to find a way to get your hands on some of that wine, so you go to Google and start browsing around. What would be the first thing you would type into the search box?" My guess is that you'd get answers like "affordable fine wine," "how to buy good wine for cheap," or perhaps just "fine wine." That is a good starting point.

The next thing to do is check out what competitors are doing. After a few hours of Googling, you might come to the conclusion that your closest competitors are wine clubs that mail members wines from exclusive vineyards at discounted prices. With The Wine Commune being a fairly unique concept, wine clubs seem like their closest analogue. Also, some people might type in wine club in search of an in-person experience rather than the mail-order experience that most wine clubs actually are. Therefore, it appears that marketing to people looking for a wine club seems like a good idea. Looking at the top-ranked wine clubs on Google for a search of wine club, it seems that the only other keyword phrases included in these websites' meta page titles are of the month (as in wine of the month club) and the location of the club (in this case, San Francisco). Finally, it may occur to you that your business is a kind of social club, and therefore the word *social* would be a great addition to your keyword list. At this point, we're starting to build a pretty solid meta page title for the home page of your website:

> The Wine Commune | Social Club in San Francisco (SF), Bay Area | Fine & Rare Wine Of The Month

This meta page title, weighing in at 95 characters including spaces (safely under the 100-character limit I recommended in Chapter 2, "The Five Ingredients of Google Optimization"), uses its real estate maximally. Here's why I like it:

- For branding purposes, the actual name of the business must be the first thing people see when they search for it in Google. We've achieved that by making the first three words The Wine Commune. In addition, we used our most important keyword, wine, in there.

- We put Social Club next, which gets two important keywords in but is also helpful for humans browsing search results who are actually seeking an in-person experience. Their eyes will read "wine commune social club" as one even though there is a separator in the middle of the phrase.

- We've gleaned from competitors that people seem to search for the physical location of the wine club. That also makes intuitive sense, and once again appeals to the folks who are actually looking for a way to socialize with other wine appreciators. Therefore, including San Francisco was a good idea. Plus, it also makes grammatical sense with Social Club coming right before it. But we also included the common abbreviation for the city (SF) afterward in parentheses. Most Google searchers won't notice this inclusion, and yet it ensures that Google recognizes the site for searches like wine club SF and social club SF. Finally, we included Bay Area, as well, because it is a third way that people refer to this geographic location.

- The last segment of the meta page title is dedicated to all the other key-words that might attract searches. The Of The Month phrase appeals to people who have the phrase "wine of the month" stuck in their heads and go searching for that. And Fine and Rare are two adjectives that people often use when describing the types of wines that The Wine Commune will offer. Although Fine & Rare Wine Of The Month is not a description you would ever use when describing the actual business, it is the most sensible and human-friendly phrase I could think of that included these important keywords (and it is not unreasonably far off from the real description).

The final way to figure out your business's main keywords is to use the Google AdWords Keyword Planner. You should already be familiar with this tool from Chapter 2. Once again, it comes in handy by being the definitive list of keywords that people actually type into Google. Notice that we've already formed a potential meta page title for the home page of your new website *before* consulting the Keyword Planner. The reason I suggest this is the same reason that SAT courses suggest coming up with the answer to a question in your head before looking at the answer choices: It allows you to make a proactive, thoughtful decision rather than passively selecting from four choices. If you use the Keyword Planner first, you might miss out on less obvious choices that could potentially be lucrative for your business. For example, if you went to the Keyword Planner first and typed in how to buy good cheap wine, you might not trigger a suggestion about wine clubs, which ultimately appears to be the smartest search term to focus on. However, in this case, the Keyword Planner is quite perceptive and does suggest wine clubs as well as several other interesting keywords (see Figure 12.4).

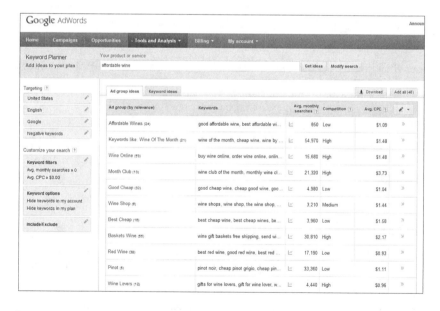

Figure 12.4   *The Google AdWords Keyword Planner is a valuable resource for giving you keyword ideas for your new website. I advise coming up with keywords first from your own research and common sense before checking the Keyword Planner.*

From the Keyword Planner, you now have some other ideas for keywords, including best, cheap, affordable, and red. Given that we already have a 95-character home page meta page title, the only relevant keywords we could fit in now are red or best. But before discarding all the other keywords, let's see if we can eliminate anything from our previous meta page title. Here it is once more:

The Wine Commune | Social Club in San Francisco (SF), Bay Area | Fine & Rare Wine Of The Month

Now that we have the equivalent of the answer key to the SAT at our disposal—I'm referring of course to the Keyword Planner—we should use it to verify that all the keywords we included in our meta page title were good choices. I spent some time doing this and came to the conclusion that all the keywords made sense to include except the word fine, which apparently is not used much in the context of wine clubs. Also, it seems that the keyword red is very heavily searched, so it must be included. That leaves only five characters to spare. Do we include best, cheap, or affordable? Since affordable is longer and less searched than its synonym cheap, it can be eliminated right away. Between cheap and best, I prefer best because I'd rather attract the perfectionist than the cheapskate. So best it is. Even though we have eliminated both economics-related keywords from the meta page title, we will just have to live with it, all things considered. After all, this meta page title is just for the home page; other pages on the site can address affordability.

Your final home page meta page title, weighing in at 99 characters, is as follows:

The Wine Commune | Social Club in San Francisco (SF) Bay Area | Best Rare Reds | Wine Of The Month

With your main keywords chosen and your home page main meta page title created, you now understand how to market your business on Google much better than before.

Creating Content

Now that we have a business idea, a potential market, a completed website, and a list of SEO keywords, our venture is real. It's time to market the business and organize our first event. Let's begin with the marketing.

For me, marketing a new business always begins with giving Google everything it wants. To figure out what that is, let's step back and think about what Google's job is. As the world's largest search engine, it is responsible with providing searchers with the best possible response to their query in the shortest amount of time. It is in the business of satisfying its users' curiosities so well, and so often, that it becomes indispensable: a natural extension of every person's mind. You, as a website owner, can further its mission—and therefore get lots of traffic from it—by creating content that fully satisfies its users' curiosities about whatever it is that you do. For example, if a user types japanese dinosaur movies and you provide it with a page that summarizes all the Japanese movies that involve dinosaurs, linking off to subpages that summarize and analyze each of the films, you are doing everything you can to help Google do its job for this user. In exchange, Google will send traffic to your website whenever users search for Japanese dinosaur movies and related terms. If other websites provide equally relevant content, it will decide which of the websites to recommend highest based on each website's trustworthiness (that is, its number and quality of links).

For our wine business, we want to help Google by providing people who want to join wine clubs with the best information possible, breaking up the concept into sub-niches such as `best wine clubs` and `wine of the month clubs,` and even delving into related long-tail searches such as `wine tasting parties san francisco` and `ways to drink rare wines affordably.` Keep in mind that Google conducts search behavior tests with real people constantly so that they can learn what kind of content people find valuable. So, if you have a page that addresses the long-tail search `pinot noir tasting bay area` and you simply offer the user a chance to join a wine club, you may be hitting the dart board, but you're not hitting the bull's-eye. In Google's eyes, the ideal page for this search term will tell the user how to find a Pinot Noir tasting in the San Francisco Bay Area, not a Cabernet Sauvignon tasting, not a Pinot Noir store, and not a Pinot Noir tasting in Sacramento; but rather, exactly what the user was looking for.

The way to manifest this mass satisfaction of Google's needs, and more importantly this mass attraction of relevant traffic to your website, is to create a web page for every search query that a potential customer of your business would input. Doing so could take forever in most businesses, so just do the best you can within the limitations of your time and interest. A good idea for The Wine Commune would be to create a section on the main menu of the home page called Our Wines, with a submenu that links to pages named after all the most popular wines people search for. Each of these pages is effectively a landing page (that is, a page meant to welcome people looking for specific search terms). So, the Cabernet Franc landing page would talk about how The Wine Commune throws in-person tasting events in San Francisco that focus on Cabernet Franc. It would probably also describe what the experience of attending a Cabernet Franc tasting event is like, remaining as focused on that type of wine as can be, since any visitors to this page probably included the phrase `Cabernet Franc` in their search.

Another idea to generate more keyword-targeted content is to create a detailed FAQ page explaining how the wine-tasting events work, dedicating a different page to each question (although you would also probably want to have a single-page FAQ with a shorter answer to each question to provide a better user experience). Some questions might be "Are all your wine tasting events in San Francisco?" and "Is this a social club or a wine of the month club?" Notice that both questions contain important search phrases within them. In this way, they play the dual role of educating your site's visitors and attracting new users who are typing things like `San Francisco tasting events` and `wine of the month club.`

In addition to creating landing pages, it would probably also be wise to establish a blog in the spirit of the nuclear football. By doing so, you could cover all kinds of other keywords that potential members might type into Google. Equally important, a high-quality blog that discusses interesting topics of value to the San Francisco wine community would provide the link bait necessary to attract many high-quality links back to your website.

Once you've got great keyword-targeted content and high-quality links, you're flying. Over the course of several months, traffic will come pouring into your site; and if you've created something people want to participate in, your business has a real opportunity to succeed.

Before ending this section, I want to cover the things that I took for granted but that must be accomplished to get the outcome you're looking for. Your website has to have the on-page factors right: SEO and human-friendly meta page titles, URLs with keywords in them, and a clean site structure. It is helpful to have a content management system like WordPress installed to make the on-page factors easier to handle. Also, before investing so much time on content creation and link building, I might do some market testing via highly targetable and easy-to-operate ad platforms like Facebook and LinkedIn.

Running a Business

When you've gotten a business off the ground, you've accomplished something incredibly difficult. But running the business is another matter entirely, which requires great dexterity and skill. I wouldn't presume to explain how to run a business in one section of one chapter, but I can tell you what I, a product-focused CEO, champion most. Whereas other CEOs might focus more strictly on financials or operations, I have always believed that it is a CEO's job to provide a solid product, an exemplary work ethic, and a vision that inspires his organization. If that is the type of leader you wish to be, here are a few of the areas you need to cover.

Perfecting Your Product

It would be wise to do everything you can to make your first event at The Wine Commune a success. After all, a failure on your initial foray into the community will strike a big blow to your morale and call into question the viability of the idea. It's easier to get over the inevitable difficulties of a new business if you have at least one early success under your belt. Plus, it will create momentum for future events. The reason I recommended supplementing SEO with paid ads is to quickly build a list of members to give your event the best chance of having good attendance. And in general, I recommend spending a bit more than usual on making sure that the first event comes off as seamlessly as possible.

The Wine Commune is an event business. But, like with any business, it has a product. That product is the experience people have when they come to the event. And it is your job to make sure that people's expectations about the product are met: that they get to taste fine wines, feel they're getting a good value for their money, and most importantly, have a good time.

In all businesses, the concept is the same. Your product has a set of expectations associated with it. Your customers will want the product to function as advertised, feel like a good value, and meet their expectations as far as the experience of working with your company.

In my own business, I have spent a long time shaping the product—which is, essentially, daily content creation, email outreach, conversion optimization, and analytics—through careful observation and, let's face it, trial and error. I've noticed certain rules that I've found to be fairly universal:

- **Be great at customer service**—I was surprised to learn early on that my company's product is *not* just the four services I just mentioned. It is those services plus customer service. That means, of course, that delivering outstanding results is not enough. Delivering outstanding results while walking our clients through them, discussing the trajectory of the campaign, brainstorming new ideas, and sometimes simply spending time together—*that* is the product we sell. Whatever your business, think of how you can improve it through customer service alone. We've all thought about this in obvious contexts like the restaurant and transportation industries. If our server or taxi driver treats us well, we have a better experience. Sometimes the way we're treated matters more than the core product. If a flight takes off an hour late and there is a lot of turbulence, but an especially sweet flight attendant sympathizes with how frustrating a delay can be and moves you to an empty row, for instance, you might walk off that flight happier than you got on. Sure, the core product disappointed in two important areas, but you felt understood and cared about—a priceless commodity. All people can appreciate good customer service.

- **Continuously "plus" your product**—The term *plussing* was invented by Walt Disney. It refers to incrementally improving your product. When Walt had his imagineers plussed a new ride, for instance, the process seemed to go on forever. A ride could be great, but was it the best it could be? It may have thrilled the audience, but did it also transport them to another world? And if it did all that, did it leave them fully satisfied afterward? If not, should they get a picture to take home to remind them of the experience? And might their favorite character from the ride come home with them in the form of a stuffed animal? As you can see, the possibilities are endless. It was this philosophy that made Walt's studio and theme parks infinitely better than his competition's during his lifetime. If you can always see a way to make your product better, and you have the resources to continuously implement those changes, you will eventually have the best product in the marketplace. Finding the resources is the tough part, I know; but if you work within your limits, even pushing them sometimes, you will still get a great deal of value from this philosophy.

- **Do good**—No matter what your product is, how is it making the world a better place? You might not have an obvious answer to this question, but you should. Far from being a trend, doing good is an aspect of your brand that consumers remember. In fact, there is a growing base of consumers that will always choose the more socially conscious product or service over the one is indifferent to the need for positive change.

- **Act like you don't have competitors**—I have always believed that a business's goal should be to make its product the best it can possibly be, not to make its product better than the competition's. Companies that focus on one-upmanship have their eyes on each other, but companies that focus on their product have their eyes on their customers. Some exceptions to this rule apply, though, like when you sell mass-produced unspecialized products such as chemicals or memory chips where your price relative to competitors' is a major factor; but by and large, those with a pure focus on product come out ahead. After all, the people who buy from you are not concerned about your rivalries. If you take great care of them, they will stick with you. It's kind of like jealousy in a romantic relationship: Every moment spent worrying about other people's interest in your mate is a moment you could have spent concentrating on your own relationship.

Selling Like a Champion

We are now at the point in the process where you have a great idea, a website, an online marketing plan, and a clear focus on product. To move your business forward, you must now turn your attention to sales.

I have learned everything I know about sales from not being a salesman. Far from subscribing to the typical corny sales tactics, I've found that conducting myself as a confident leader filled with passion and purpose has been my best asset. Sales take care of themselves when you radiate the value of your product in the way you carry yourself each day.

But let's get a little more down to earth. When you really break it down, three things make you want to buy from someone

- First, their knowledge of what they sell should be stellar. You should be able to hit them with any question and get an immediate, competent answer.

- Second, they need to be excited about what they're selling. Try to sell me a BlackBerry when you're carrying around an iPhone and I'm not sure I want your BlackBerry. Not from you, anyway. Enthusiasm is contagious. If I can plainly see that you believe in your product with all your heart, I'm ready to invest my own money in it.

- The third thing that makes you want to buy from someone may sound silly, but it's true: You have to like the salesperson. Sometimes that connection can be what tips the scales toward a sale. The first car I ever bought, a pre-owned BMW 5 series, was an emotional purchase, and I mostly made it because the salesperson was a nice guy who reminded me of my dad. I'd wager that billions of dollars have shifted hands for reasons no better than that one.

A salesperson's job is to at once be an expert in his field, a lover of his product, and a people person. The first two should be givens, but not everyone is a people person. If you aren't, it would be wise to partner with, or hire, someone who is.

In your time as a founder-salesperson, whether it's for a few months or a few years, you'll meet all sorts of characters. Some will be pleasant, some less pleasant. To help you know what to expect, I've outlined a few of the prospects that you are guaranteed to run into:

- **The Negotiator**—It's all about the deal for this prospect. Find a way to give him a deal and he's likely to move forward. Sometimes negotiators are less concerned about the money than the psychological idea that they've gotten a bargain. It is often useful to have ways of satisfying negotiators that don't involve lowering your profit margin too much, including offering free items that you don't mind giving away, or incentives that can be redeemed later, once they're already a customer.

- **The Action Guy**—This type of potential customer, usually male, knows what he wants and how to get it. He likes what he hears, and as long as you are willing to sell him your product in the way he expects, he's ready to buy. For many salespeople, this prospect is a dream. But the flip side is that the Action Guy will often take action in the other direction as well. If you tell him something that goes against the way he is used to doing business, he may disappear on you in a hurry. And when Action Guys do become customers, they need intuitive customer service to avoid rubbing them the wrong way.

- **The Results Guy**—You can't really blame the Results Guy: He just wants results! However, these are often tough customers to convert because they ask for a lot of promises. As any seasoned salesperson knows, promises are easy to make but not always easy to follow through with, so they should be made sparingly. When selling to the Results Guy, be armed with specific benchmarks and outcomes that you are very confident about.

- **The Time Waster**—When doing sales, it is imperative for you to be able to identify this prospect type because, as the name implies, dealing with them can drain your time and lead to disappointment. The hallmark signs of the Time Waster are long phone calls with little talk about price or next steps; reference to a high-up decision maker who will need to buy in to the idea; mention the fact that he is speaking to several of your competitors at the same time; and, of course, multiple meetings without clear forward momentum. Thankfully, you can use a litmus test that is near-guaranteed to tell you whether a prospect is a Time Waster: Ask for money. For example, if you are a consultant and you think that you might have a Time Waster on your hands due to multiple conversations with little forward momentum, try telling him that you will need to be paid a retainer for further conversations at this point. If he is a Time Waster, he'll be gone in a jiffy. Although it can be tough for some people to make such a blunt request, keep in mind that the price of having your time wasted in a new business is far greater than the discomfort of alienating a potential customer.

- **The Sweetheart**—The rarest of sales prospects is the Sweetheart, a person who gets what she wants through kindness. While she is a fantastic customer to acquire, do not mistake her kindness for weakness. If she doesn't get the product she is looking for, she will quietly go away, and you'll have lost a true asset to your customer base.

One of the most important overall principles in sales is also one of the simplest to understand: Trust your first impression. If someone is difficult, distrustful, or rude on the first phone call, that person will rarely improve after becoming a customer. But if someone is respectful and friendly on the first call, there is a shot that he or she will turn into a great, long-term customer. If possible, choose your customers carefully. As much as it may feel counterintuitive to choose your customers rather than be chosen by them—especially in a new business—it will make a big difference in the long term. A happy, energized customer will aid in your business's financial success and reputation as well as your own quality of life. So think before you sell!

Conquering Customer Service

I've already told you that customer service is an inextricable part of the product you sell. But telling you to have good customer service is not going to make you embrace it. Customer service is the type of thing whose value you either need to understand intuitively or learn through experience. Some businesses need to start without a focus on customer service to truly recognize its importance. In the first year of my SEO business, I thought it was good enough to get my clients to the top of the search results. I used to justify my company's weak customer service with the idea that "if I'm getting good results for my clients, then there's nothing more to say." And for some clients, that was true. But for those for which it wasn't, I paid the price of my ignorance in unnecessary cancellations.

What I learned from that first year changed the way I do business completely. Before long, even the clients who seemed to occupy a permanent spot at the top of the search results were receiving weekly emails and calls from our account managers. I was shocked to learn that many of our clients didn't realize that we were responsible for their excellent search results. The fact that these clients weren't ranking well before we began working together but now were wasn't in itself enough to prove my company's value. Some thought that it had happened naturally or that a web designer or intern was responsible. Mostly, they were busy focusing on their own businesses and not thinking too much about it. And who could blame them: We weren't in the picture to tell them otherwise. Something as simple as sending them progress reports each week was enough for clients to begin giving us credit for our hard work. And with that credit came renewals, larger investments, and a deeper sense of loyalty to my company.

But the lesson didn't end there. We had increased our average lifetime of a client and our average revenue per client. But I sensed that there was room for more growth. At that point, our customer service team was in touch with clients once per week, mostly to send reports. Our clients clearly realized we were responsible for their top rankings. But then one week, seemingly out of the blue, we lost two great clients. Distraught, I did a thorough investigation of their accounts. I found that both of their websites were ranking exceptionally well at the time of cancellation, and that our reports clearly showed that we were responsible for the results. I was perplexed. But after a lot of thinking, I came to a hard conclusion: Good results are not enough—not even when they're combined with competent customer service.

I'll skip the agonizing research and sleepless nights that helped me understand what was happening and bring you straight to the epiphany: Our clients' true goals for the SEO campaign were not always high Google rankings. Not only that, but our clients often didn't even know what their goals were. Sometimes they just signed up because a friend of theirs had told them "SEO is a good idea. You should work with these guys." For clients like these, who did not have clear goals, we needed to determine their goals for them.

Today, a piece of internal data we keep front and center for each client is their true motivation for the SEO campaign. When we know that a client, say, wants to exhibit thought leadership within his industry, we can do specific outreach to industry publications and discussion forums, preparing targeted content for each outlet. And when we report on our progress to this client, we don't just talk about rankings and traffic; we show them comments that members of their industry have made about them on the websites we've pitched, and we talk about the press hits we've gotten on publications that matter in their field. As a result, there is now a palpable feeling of satisfaction among our clients that didn't exist in earlier years.

In addition to focusing on our clients' goals, we also keep a watchful eye on what we believe *ought to be* their goals. Experience has taught me that sometimes clients start out looking for one thing and then arrive at something completely different later on because of pressure from advisors or investors. (Hint: It is almost always bottom-line revenue.) So, even if the client's goal is seeing buzz about their company in their industry, we're always working on converting more visitors into paying customers. We've found that this technique leads to maximum client satisfaction, and subsequently the highest engagement with, and loyalty to, our company. The relationship truly becomes a win-win.

So that's the first half of customer service: keeping the customer happy. The other half, the one people talk about a lot less, is choosing the right clients so that it's actually possible to keep your customers happy. As soon as my business was generating enough revenue to support me and my employees, I gained a certain luxury, which I've come to believe is less of a luxury and more of the hallmark of a successful business: cultivating a customer base that matches the culture of your company. If you are a serious, practical group that sells ball bearings, you can have any customer that just wants their ball bearings to function like ball bearings do. But if you have a service business like, for example, interior decorating, you probably want clients who trust your style and give clear direction from the start. Perhaps you like to get lots of client feedback, perhaps you like busier people that just want to get it done. You have to decide that. But not accepting clients unless they are a good fit for your business will keep your company's integrity intact and put minimal strain on your customer service team.

Personally, I am an optimistic and upbeat person with a strong interest in making the world a better place. So I love clients who are one or more of the following: friendly, passionate about their work, and socially conscious. I find that I don't mix well with folks who are curt, solely focused on profit, and not concerned about people. Not that I deny these folks' right to be how they are, but I just think they'd be a better fit with another SEO company. It feels good to say that and to make it a part of my mindset when I show up to work every day.

When you genuinely care about your customers—partly because you chose the right group of companies and individuals—your business has the best possible shot at thriving. Although it can take some time to get customer service right, mastering it will create a business that is sustainable for the long term.

Hiring Top Employees

So much of a founder's time is spent focusing on what her company provides for the world, yet the issue of *who* provides it is among the most important she will ever make. The right employee can do five times what the wrong employee can do, and can teach you things that you never would have otherwise known. It may seem that good employees come along by chance, but in truth you attract them with the way you describe your company in job ads and the overall brand your company puts forth.

When I first started my business, my requirements for a new employee were intelligence, knowledge about SEO, and likability. Today, that description misses the mark. It is much more valuable for me to find an employee with the right attitude than it is to find someone who is an SEO expert. Although recruiting someone with a particular skill can be very important for some businesses, I would rather invest my time training the right type of person than waste my time training the wrong type of person. An employee who doesn't care, makes a lot of mistakes, or quits early can be damaging to a company in many ways. Hiring a new employee is like planting a seed in your garden. Plant the right one, and your garden will prosper. Plant the wrong one, and your best-case scenario is having to do a lot of extra work; your worst case scenario is suffering a blight that kills your garden.

Earlier in the chapter, I talked about how writing your website's copy can help you solidify its brand. By the time you've been working on a company long enough to hire your first employee, you should have a fully developed idea of your company's culture. Let's return to The Wine Commune for a moment. You've had your first few events and they've gone well. You feel like you're ready to bring someone on to help coordinate the events while you focus on building membership. What are your requirements?

Again, it would be a mistake to post an ad that essentially says "Wine club looking for someone to coordinate monthly events. Candidate must have event management experience, interest in wine, and be personable and detail oriented." This type of ad will attract someone with the right resumé, but not necessarily the right disposition to be a long-term member of your team. To clarify who you're really looking for, you must sketch out the character of your ideal candidate in advance. Writing down what you want will help you to attract the right person.

Here is how your sketch might look:

> *Bill is my new event coordinator. He's one of those people who just has a contagious enthusiasm that makes you want to be around him. He loves wine, but if you look hard, you'll find that wine is merely a medium for his larger love of life. He knows a lot of the venues in San Francisco, having done events for a big beverage brand here in the city, and is still friendly with most of the owners of those venues. What I love about Bill is that he treats The Wine Commune like it's his baby, just like I do. When we had our last event and it looked like we were going to be short on a particular Bordeaux that the members were requesting, he located a wine store that had it in stock all the way in Palo Alto and convinced them to stay open late so that we could pick up a few bottles. That's just the type of guy Bill is; he didn't get paid a penny more to drive an hour to Palo Alto after work hours, but it mattered to him that our members should get every wine they requested.*

As silly as it may seem to create such an emotionally rich character sketch of your desired employee—down to making up a name for him—there is something very powerful about knowing exactly what you want. Reading it over, you may even learn some new things about your brand. After I wrote this sketch, putting myself in the place of the founder of The Wine Commune, I found it peculiar that I had cited Bill's love of wine as a vessel for a greater love of life itself. It indicated to me that The Wine Commune's brand, which should be clear to me but merely implied in the minds of my members, is in fact a passion for the enjoyment of life.

Now that we know the type of person we want for this position, our job ad will look very different from the last one. It might start out as follows: "Wine event business looking for a passionate wine enthusiast to coordinate our events. Are you the type of person who would drive an hour out of your way to get an '09 Chateau Clinet when an '11 is right in front of you? Do you not only love wine yourself but also take pleasure in others' enjoyment of it? Are you willing to dedicate yourself to the difficult task of making a room full of demanding people happy? Then this may be the right job for you."

This ad would attract far fewer applicants, but those who apply would be much more likely to fit your Bill. In my own company, we have sketches of every job. Although our PR outreach folks have very different descriptions than, say, our web designers, there is one ideal that all of our employees must embody: the passionate overachiever. That phrase, in a nutshell, describes what I want from every member of my team. I invite you to come up with your own phrase that perfectly encapsulates who you want to have at your company.

Aside from determining the type of person you want in your new business, you will have other decisions to make about staff, including how much to pay, whether to hire full-time employees or independent contractors, and whether employees will congregate in a physical place or work virtually. While these subjects are on the outskirts of my expertise, I will leave you with a word of advice about each:

- Overall, money plays a large factor in every decision you make regarding your staff. Employees are a major expense, and should only be brought on when the value of their work is greater than the cost of their salary.

- It's often a good idea to bring on your first staff members as independent contractors until it's clear that you'll be working together for the long term (if feasible and legal in your circumstance).

- You should pay an amount that feels fair to the individual person given the cost of living in his or her area; however, ultimately it comes down to what each person feels satisfied with. If you put a person in a position where he or she is making barely enough to cover personal standards, you are hiring a temp, not a permanent team member. That said, you'll find that different people have wildly different salary expectations for the same positions, and often those with lower salary expectations end up contributing more to your company than people with higher salary expectations.

- As far as where your staff should be located, it is a personal decision that has to do with your company's needs and your style of management. I am a big fan of virtual employees because I've found that they are more productive than office employees given the greater number of social distractions. However, you'll get more creativity out of a room of people sitting around a table brainstorming.

Succeeding in the Shark Tank That Is Business

Starting a new business can be overwhelming. But if you have the discipline to succeed at SEO, you'll be well prepared for it. What I've realized from 10 years of search engine optimization is that its skill set is widely applicable. The genius of the

Google search algorithm is that it is modeled on how all of business, and indeed all of life, works. Content, links, and conversion: That's what it's about. In business, you need to invent a product that is useful or interesting, get people to trust you through votes of confidence from other customers, and finally, sell your product.

All of this is easier said than done, of course. And as you set forth to make your mark on the world, I implore you to enter a field that you are genuinely interested in. Enough challenges in the business world exist already, without putting yourself into a daily routine that bores you. You should also do something you're naturally good at. There is usually a lot of overlap between the things one likes and the things one is good at, so you should be able to work this part out.

Once you've found your calling, your success will come down to your abilities in three main areas: hard work, smart work, and natural talent. If you work harder than others in your field, you'll have an immediate advantage. And although natural talent is not nearly as valuable as hard work, when you combine the two, you get an unbeatable combination. Professional sports are a great example of hard work mixing with natural talent to create the ultimate competitors. Michael Jordan may or may not have been the greatest natural talent to ever play in the NBA, but he was definitely one of the hardest working. With both factors in play, he was far and away the best player of his time. I share this so that you don't work yourself to exhaustion only to find yourself outcompeted by people with a greater penchant for your profession. It goes without saying that you must put in the sweat; but when you do, make sure that you're competing on a playing field that complements your strengths and that you enjoy coming to each day.

Then there's smart work—otherwise known as scrappiness. In business, if you can manage to innovate on a product that already exists, or even just become more organized or financially clever than the market leader—you might just do even better than the naturally talented hard workers. So scrappiness is a skill to aspire to as well.

Another important point about succeeding in business is that you will never learn everything you need from a book. You have to go out there and do it, and more than anything, you've got to make mistakes. Every good businessperson tries a lot of things, quickly discarding the strategies that fail and diving deeper into the ones that work. Eventually, your intuition will be sharp enough to tell you what to try next, and your experience will make sure that you implement it properly; but trial and error will always play a role in leading you to your best business ideas, marketing methods, and revenue sources.

And when you do find something that works, there will be ups and downs. Nobody is immune to them. In fact, I've realized that if you do everything right in business, most of your long-term key metrics will look something like what you see in Figure 12.5.

Figure 12.5 *The trend that seems to represent the long-term growth of all success-ful businesses: generally moving in a positive direction, but with lots of ups and downs along the way.*

Notice how there are plenty of valleys even though the long-term trajectory is upward. These are times when most people in the company are probably feeling like things aren't going well at all. The reality is that business is a messy art. There will be many times when you will be confused, frustrated, and lost. And yes, there will be times of glory as well. But the glory isn't what makes starting your own company worth it. The reason I, and maybe you, and all entrepreneurs, do what we do is because it gives us a measure of control over our lives.

The freedom that entrepreneurship—and truly, SEO—has given me is vast. I am able to work from anywhere, alongside a team of bright, passionate people, on companies owned by brilliant individuals. I am constantly challenged, and there is never a dull moment. This is, to me, a blessing. And so, as much as Google has confounded me over the years, I have to be grateful to it for teaching me how to be an entrepreneur.

As you go forth on your chosen path, remember that SEO is more than a game to be beaten. It is a microcosm of a much larger lesson: the idea that bringing value to people and earning their trust will get you ahead in life.

Content. Links. Conversion. That's what it's about.

A Final Word

Now that you are finished with the content of this book, I'd like to talk briefly about what happens next. More than anything, I want you to know that I am available to you should you have any questions or wish to share your ideas. Simply email me at evanmbailyn@gmail.com.

I'd also love your feedback. Whatever you thought of this book, I welcome you to review it on Amazon. Not only will it build a public dialogue about the book, but it will also allow others to see what you thought and make their own decision about buying it.

Finally, I wish you luck. In 2014, 2015, and 2016, thousands of people will establish websites, and countless more will rely on Google to jump-start their businesses. SEO is one of the most vital skills a marketer can possess, and it's only becoming more important. Now that you are armed with the knowledge from this book, I hope that you go out there and make a difference.

Index

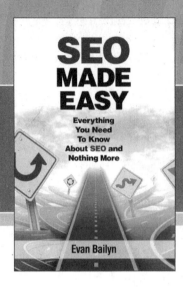

SEO MADE EASY
Everything You Need To Know About SEO and Nothing More
Evan Bailyn

FREE
Online Edition

Safari··›
Books Online

Your purchase of **SEO Made Easy** includes access to a free online edition for 45 days through the **Safari Books Online** subscription service. Nearly every Que book is available online through **Safari Books Online**, along with thousands of books and videos from publishers such as Addison-Wesley Professional, Cisco Press, Exam Cram, IBM Press, O'Reilly Media, Prentice Hall, and Sams.

Safari Books Online is a digital library providing searchable, on-demand access to thousands of technology, digital media, and professional development books and videos from leading publishers. With one monthly or yearly subscription price, you get unlimited access to learning tools and information on topics including mobile app and software development, tips and tricks on using your favorite gadgets, networking, project management, graphic design, and much more.